# THE PHOTOSHOP GRAYSCALE BOOK

## 1ST EDITION

JIM RICH

Rich & Associates, LLC

# CREDITS

**Editing:** Karren Alenier

**Book Design/Illustration:** Sandy Bozek, Jim Rich

**Cover Design:** Studio IX, c/o Randy Morgan

**Special thanks to:**
Karren Alenier
Bruce Ashley of Bruce Ashley Photography
Sandy Bozek
Howard Ehrenfeld of Studio H
Paula Gaerlan
Julianne Kost of Adobe Systems Inc.
Randy Morgan of Studio IX
Victoria Porter
Miles Southworth
Karen Zigorsky of Pilot Marketing

**Photos:**
  NASA image collection

**Scanning and Digital Cameras:**
  AGFA Arcus Plus, Sharp JX600, Microtek 600ZS, Umax Powerlook II, Kodak DC 210, Nikon CoolPix 950

**Computers:**
  Apple Macintosh G4, Dell Dimensions XPS 166

**Page Layout:**
  QuarkXpress v. 4.04

**Drawing Programs:**
  Adobe Illustrator v. 8.01

**Color Management:**
  Colorblind Pro, Prove IT!, Color Synergy, Xrite DTP 92, Xrite DTP 41

**Imagesetting:**
  Heidelberg Hercules

**Printing:**
  Bladen Lithographics, Inc.

---

**THE PHOTOSHOP GRAYSCALE BOOK** 1ST EDITION
Jim Rich

Copyright © 2000 Jim Rich. All rights reserved.
(Parts of this book referencing earlier versions of Photoshop were previously published under the title *Adobe Photoshop In Black and White* by Bozek Desktop Inc. and *Adobe Photoshop In Black and White* by Peach Pit Press).

**RICH & ASSOCIATES, LLC**
P.O. Box 70882
Chevy Chase, MD., 20813-9998
(301) 652-7266 voice
(301)-652-8665 fax

All rights reserved. No part of this publication may be reproduced, stored in a retrieval system, or transmitted in any form or by any means, electronic, mechanical, photocopying, recording, or otherwise without the prior written permission of Jim Rich.

**NOTICE OF LIABILITY:**
The information in this book is distributed on an "as is" basis without warranty. While every precaution has been taken in the preparation of this book, neither the author nor Rich & Associates, LLC., shall have any liability to any person or entity with respect to liability, loss, or damage caused or alleged to be caused directly or indirectly by the instructions contained in this book or by the computer software or hardware products described or contained herein.

**TRADEMARKS:**
The software described in this book is furnished under license and may only be used or copied in accordance with the terms of such license. PostScript™ is a trademark of Adobe Systems, Incorporated ("Adobe"), registered in the United States and elsewhere. PostScript can refer both to the PostScript language as specified by Adobe and to Adobe's implementation of its PostScript language interpreter. Adobe, Adobe Photoshop, Adobe InDesign, Adobe Type Manager, Adobe Garamond Type, and PostScript are trademarks of Adobe Systems Incorporated, which may be registered in certain jurisdictions. AGFA, Arcus Plus, and Agfa-Gevaert AG are trademarks of the Agfa Corporation. Cromalin is a registered trademark of DuPont. Color Key and MatchPrint are registered trademarks of 3M. Macintosh is a registered trademark of Apple Computer, Inc. QuarkXpress is a trademark of Quark Inc. Umax Powerlook is trademark of Umax Data Systems. All other brand or product names are trademarks or registered trademarks of their respective holders.

ISBN: 0-9647627-3-0

Printed in the United States of America.

# PREFACE

Photoshop is not just for color image retouching. It has dozens of tools that enable you to correct and enhance photos of any type. The feedback we get from our clients and and students is that once the topics of this book are mastered, the end-user has a solid foundation to work successfully with color. We also want you to know this book is not about special effects, design, or page assembly.

Previously, parts of this book were published as the book *Photoshop in Black and White*. Since then, over ninety pages about our favorite image editing program has been added to that material. While this book has only one author listed, that's me Jim Rich, there are references to *we* throughout this book. This refers to the former co-author of *Photoshop in Black and White* Sandy Bozek and colleagues that are listed on the credit page.

**The goals of this book are to explain:**

- How to efficiently use the tools in Adobe Photoshop.

- How to make working with and navigating through Photoshop easier.

- How to recover from imaging mistakes.

- How to work with Selections and create masks.

- How to adjust the tones of black-and-white images for reproduction purposes.

- Critical imaging techniques. We relate the tools to conventional methods for producing quality images and we establish a method for the user to achieve consistent quality results.

- How to use Photoshop for many types of output. We use print as the metaphor for reproducing images but the reproduction concepts of the book easily apply to output for digital photography, multimedia, and the World Wide Web.

- Retouching methods and strategies.

- Tips about how to calibrate your imaging system.

The differences between Adobe Photoshop for the Macintosh and Adobe Photoshop for Windows are minimal, and we point out most of them right up front on page 2. We used a Macintosh computer to create this book, so the screen shots of dialog boxes and menu options are slightly different than on a Windows operating system. While the user interface might be slightly different, the tools work identically.

We realize that no one (including us) likes to read a lot of technical stuff, but after you have used the techniques outlined in each section of this book, and have gained more experience in using them, you might like to read some of the more detailed information about the imaging process. At the end of the book, you will find five appendices. Four of these appendices go into further technical detail about (1) image resolution, (2) desktop scanning, (3) calibration, and (4) how to calibrate a desktop scanner with Photoshop. The fifth appendix is the *At-A-Glance Index*.

Now go into that closet at the back of your office or reach deep into that desk drawer, find the good photos and the bad ones that you could not bear to throw away and learn to work a little magic!

Jim Rich<br>Chevy Chase, Maryland

P.S.

While Sandy Bozek has moved on, she will be missed and will definitely not be forgotten.

# TABLE OF CONTENTS

**Getting Started** .......................................... 1
  **Tips for Success** ...................................... 2
  **General Preferences** ............................... 4
    Saving Files ............................................. 5
    Display & Cursors .................................... 5
    Transparency & Gamuts ........................... 6
    Units & Rulers ......................................... 6
    Guides & Grid .......................................... 6
    Plug-Ins & Scratch Disks ......................... 7
    Image Cache ............................................ 7
  **Color Settings** .......................................... 8
    RGB Setup ............................................... 8
    Monitor Setup ......................................... 9
    CMYK Setup .......................................... 12
    Grayscale Setup ..................................... 12
    Profile Setup ......................................... 13
    Working Spaces ..................................... 14
    Embedding Profiles ............................... 14
    Legacy Files .......................................... 14
    Missing Profiles .................................... 15
    Opening The First Image ...................... 15
  **Review** .................................................... 16
**Recovery Strategy** ................................... 17
  Recovery Options ................................... 18
  History Palette ........................................ 19
  Creating Snapshots ................................ 20
  Snapshot Tips .......................................... 21
  Using Snapshots ..................................... 22
  History State and Snapshots ................. 23
  **Review** .................................................... 24
**Masking Basics** ........................................ 25
  Selections Tools ...................................... 26
  Working with Selections ....................... 28
  Selections to Channels .......................... 30

Displaying Channels .......................... 31
Channel Viewing Options .................. 32
Naming and Inverting Channels ........ 33
Feathering .......................................... 34
Quick Mask ....................................... 36
Paths .................................................. 38
Using Paths to Create Selections ...... 40
Silhouetting & Clipping Paths ........... 41
**Review** .............................................. 42
**Reproducing Grayscale Images** ............ 43
  Image Reproduction Process ............ 44
  Measuring Tools ............................... 46
  Levels ................................................ 48
  Curves ............................................... 50
  Histograms ........................................ 52
  Page Setup ........................................ 53
  Sharpening Filters ............................. 54
  Degrading Filters .............................. 55
  Line Image Tools .............................. 56
**Methodology** ..................................... 58
How to:
  Identify Image Characteristics .......... 60
  Adjust Highlights and Shadows ........ 62
  Adjust Midtones ............................... 64
  Sharpen the Image ............................ 65
  Save the File ..................................... 66
  More About Midtones ...................... 68
  Make Corrections ............................. 70
**Review** ................................................ 74
**Retouching Basics** ................................ 75
  Retouching Strategies ....................... 76
  Snapshot vs Selections ..................... 77
  Toning Tools ..................................... 78
  Cloning ............................................. 79
**Review** ................................................ 80

**Layers** ..................................................... 81
  Layers Basics ........................................ 82
  Managing Layers .................................. 85
  Layer Mask ........................................... 86
  Adjustment Layer ................................ 88
  Text and Layers .................................... 89
  Shadows on Images ............................. 90
**Review** .................................................. 92
**Photoshop Tips** ...................................... 93
  Color to Grayscale Options ................. 94
  Ghosting ............................................... 97
  Creating Extraordinary Contrast ........ 98
  No More Moirés! .................................. 99
  Cropping ............................................ 100
  Scaling ............................................... 102
  Actions Basics ................................... 104
  Actions-Batch Processing .................. 106
  Creating a Mirror Image ................... 108
  Extending Backgrounds .................... 110
  Dust Busting ...................................... 112
  Line Images ....................................... 113
**APPENDIX A:** Image Resolution ............ 114
**APPENDIX B:** Calibration Tips ............... 119
**APPENDIX C:** Scanning Tips ................... 124
**APPENDIX D:** Scanner Calibration ........ 126
**APPENDIX E:** At-A-Glance Index ........... 130
**GLOSSARY** ............................................. 132
**BIBLIOGRAPHY** ..................................... 135
**INDEX** .................................................... 136

# GETTING STARTED

**Tips for Success** ..........................................2
**General Preferences** ..................................4
Saving Files ...................................................5
Display & Cursors .........................................5
Transparency & Gamuts ..............................6
Units & Rulers ...............................................6
Guides & Grid ................................................6
Plug-Ins & Scratch Disks .............................7
Image Cache ..................................................7
**Color Settings** ............................................8
RGB Setup .....................................................8
Monitor Setup ................................................9
CMYK Setup .................................................12
Grayscale Setup ..........................................12
Profile Setup ................................................13
Working Spaces ..........................................14
Embedding Profiles ....................................14
Legacy Files ................................................14
Missing Profiles ..........................................15
Opening The First Image ...........................15
Review ..........................................................16

# TIPS FOR SUCCESS WITH THE PHOTOSHOP GRAYSCALE BOOK

## ITEM LOCATOR
To aid in finding the needed tools, we have added a guide to the headings. When you see a heading like this:

**GENERAL** `File: Preferences`

It indicates that the item, General, is found under the menu bar using the selection **File** and then **Preferences**.

## WILLINGNESS TO EXPERIMENT IS CRITICAL
People learn by doing. Experimentation with Photoshop tools and techniques is critical for learning all aspects of working with black and white images in Photoshop. In all computer applications, it is important to learn the mechanics of the software. Repetition and testing are the key ingredients to learning Photoshop tools and functions. Once your mechanical skills with Photoshop tools are developed, it is easier to focus on specific imaging tasks with Photoshop.

## PHOTOSHOP DIFFERENCES: MAC VS WINDOWS
While there are not many differences between how Photoshop works on Macintosh and Windows 95, 98, and NT operating systems, here are the most obvious ones we found respective to the Macintosh and Windows keyboards.

- The Macintosh Command key is equivalent to the Control key on Windows. To indicate the difference between Macintosh and Windows, we will use **Cmd/Cntrl**.
- The Macintosh Option key is equivalent to the Alt key on Windows. To indicate the difference between Macintosh and Windows, we will use **Opt/Alt**.
- The Macintosh Delete key is equivalent to the Backspace key on Windows. To indicate the difference between Macintosh and Windows, we will use **Delete/Backspace**.
- The Macintosh Return key is equivalent to the Enter key on Windows. To indicate the difference between Macintosh and Windows, we will use **Return/Enter**.

To ensure success in the use of this book, be familiar with the operating system of your computer.

- Master the basic skills: start up, point, click, drag, Open, Close, Save, Save As, Save a Copy, Undo/Redo, and shut down.
- Organize your computer applications and folders.

  Each user has individual ideas and needs for organizing his or her computer system.

  Determine names, letters, numbers, or a combination that will be used for files or folders. Create easy-to-understand file names or a file identification system that is user-friendly. This will avoid problems in retrieving a file when it is misplaced.

  DO NOT USE - Untitled 1, 2, etc. as a file name.

- Learn how to use computer utilities such as "Find" to locate lost or misplaced files.

Have basic knowledge of Photoshop menus and tools.

- Be able to open or scan an image into Photoshop.
- Learn the basic menu structure and features of Photoshop as well as the mechanics of the important and frequently used tools.
- Know how to back up your work routinely and do it frequently. Use Photoshop's Save, Save As, or Save A Copy feature to create an exact duplicate of a file with a different name. If necessary, use handwritten notes kept in a notebook that is stored in a safe place as a backup to keep track of key imaging parameters and preference settings.
- Learn how to use keyboard shortcuts. Identify the Photoshop keyboard commands for the most frequently used computer short cuts.

  It is especially useful to learn important Photoshop Tool Palette shortcuts that are initiated by pressing one or two keys.

## THE TOOL PALETTE AT A GLANCE
Each tool has a single keyboard key that will activate that particular tool. Using keyboard shortcuts is critical to success with Photoshop.

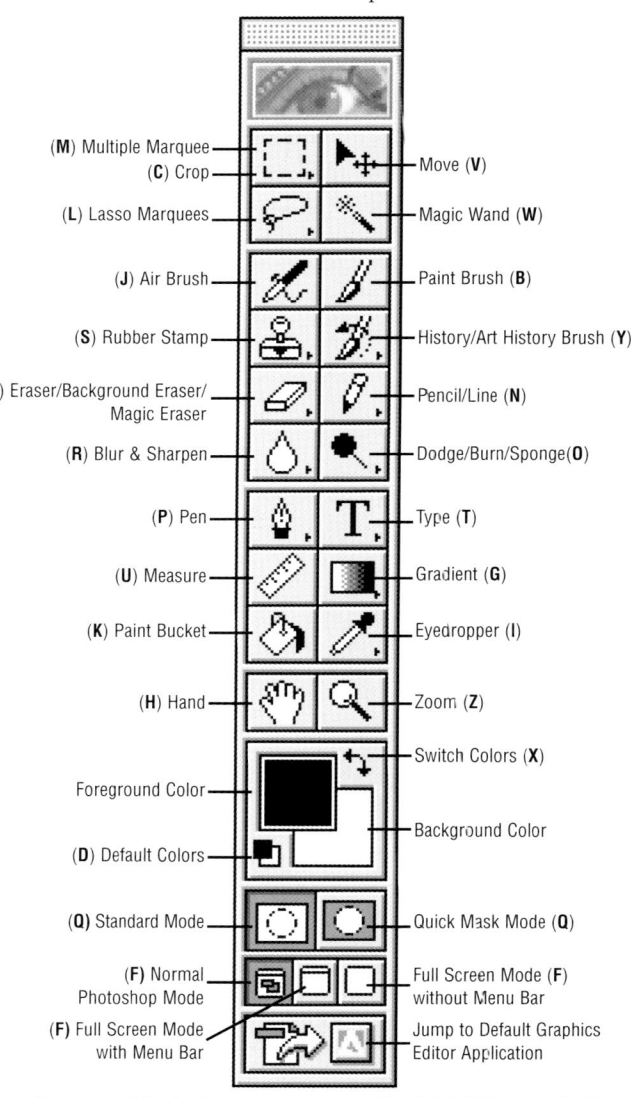

- (**M**) Multiple Marquee
- (**C**) Crop
- Move (**V**)
- (**L**) Lasso Marquees
- Magic Wand (**W**)
- (**J**) Air Brush
- Paint Brush (**B**)
- (**S**) Rubber Stamp
- History/Art History Brush (**Y**)
- (**E**) Eraser/Background Eraser/Magic Eraser
- Pencil/Line (**N**)
- (**R**) Blur & Sharpen
- Dodge/Burn/Sponge (**O**)
- (**P**) Pen
- Type (**T**)
- (**U**) Measure
- Gradient (**G**)
- (**K**) Paint Bucket
- Eyedropper (**I**)
- (**H**) Hand
- Zoom (**Z**)
- Switch Colors (**X**)
- Foreground Color
- Background Color
- (**D**) Default Colors
- (**Q**) Standard Mode
- Quick Mask Mode (**Q**)
- (**F**) Normal Photoshop Mode
- Full Screen Mode (**F**) without Menu Bar
- (**F**) Full Screen Mode with Menu Bar
- Jump to Default Graphics Editor Application

**For more of the keyboard shortcuts, use the Quick Reference Card that comes with the software.**

## QUICK REFERENCE TO TOOL PALETTE SHORTCUTS AND POP-UP MENUS OPTIONS

Each tool in the Palette has a number of options that expand and control its functions. These keyboard shortcuts make it easy to access the options and improve productivity. It is difficult to remember all these shortcuts, so you should learn the four or five that are used daily, then add to these as you work along.

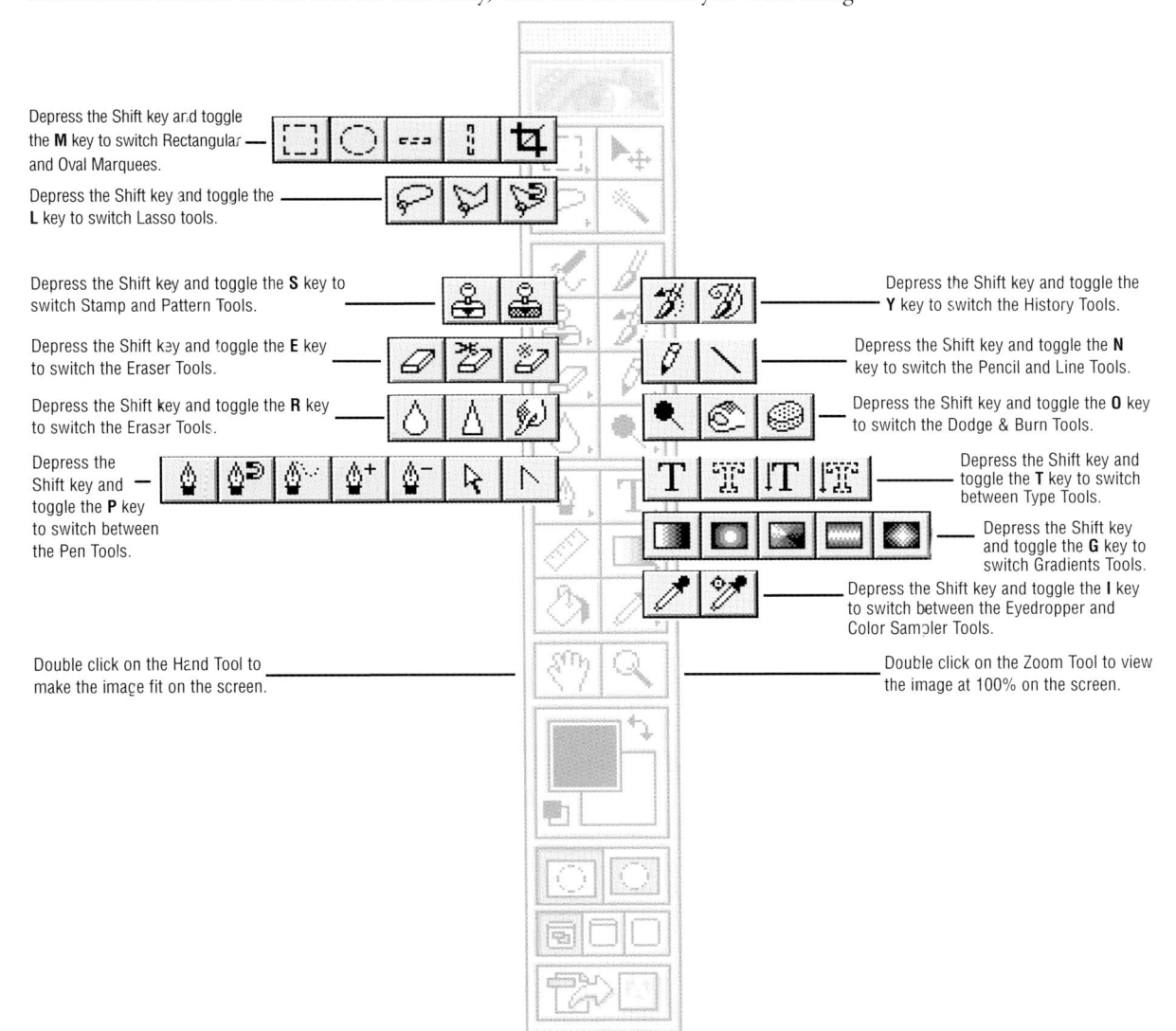

Depress the Shift key and toggle the **M** key to switch Rectangular and Oval Marquees.

Depress the Shift key and toggle the **L** key to switch Lasso tools.

Depress the Shift key and toggle the **S** key to switch Stamp and Pattern Tools.

Depress the Shift key and toggle the **E** key to switch the Eraser Tools.

Depress the Shift key and toggle the **R** key to switch the Eraser Tools.

Depress the Shift key and toggle the **P** key to switch between the Pen Tools.

Double click on the Hand Tool to make the image fit on the screen.

Depress the Shift key and toggle the **Y** key to switch the History Tools.

Depress the Shift key and toggle the **N** key to switch the Pencil and Line Tools.

Depress the Shift key and toggle the **O** key to switch the Dodge & Burn Tools.

Depress the Shift key and toggle the **T** key to switch between Type Tools.

Depress the Shift key and toggle the **G** key to switch Gradients Tools.

Depress the Shift key and toggle the **I** key to switch between the Eyedropper and Color Sampler Tools.

Double click on the Zoom Tool to view the image at 100% on the screen.

## OTHER SHORTCUT TIPS

**General Computer Shortcuts**

- **Cmd/Cntrl + S** Saves or updates an image.
- **Cmd/Cntrl + Z** to Undo or Redo the last command.
- **Cmd/Cntrl + X** Cuts all or part of an image to the computer's clipboard.
- **Cmd/Cntrl + C** Copies all or part of an image to the computer's clipboard.
- **Cmd/Cntrl + V** Pastes all or part of an image to the computer's clipboard.

**Photoshop Navigation Shortcuts**

- Press the Space Bar for the Hand Tool.
- Press **Cmd/Cntrl** + Space Bar to Zoom In.
- Press **Opt/Alt** + Space Bar to Zoom Out.
- Press the Tab key to show or hide all palettes.
- Press Shift + Tab to show or hide all palettes but the main Tool Palette.

**Resetting Dialog Box Shortcuts**

- The **Opt/Alt** key is used for resetting almost all Photoshop dialog box commands. This will change the Cancel button into a Reset button.

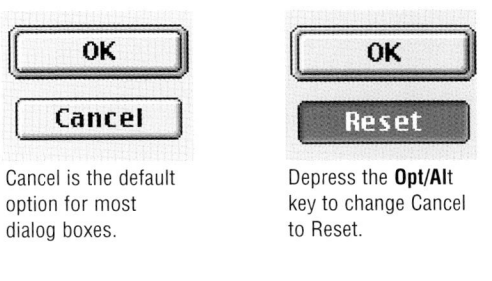

Cancel is the default option for most dialog boxes.

Depress the **Opt/Alt** key to change Cancel to Reset.

**Image Processing Shortcuts**

- Press **Cmd/Cntrl + M** to enter Curves.
- Press **Cmd/Cntrl + L** to enter Levels.

3

# GETTING STARTED

## PREFERENCES

### GENERAL

This section identifies the essential preferences you will need to know when producing and refining black-and-white images with Photoshop.

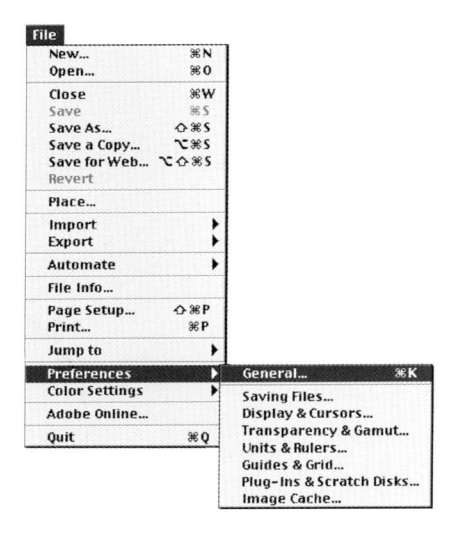

**Note:** The eight General Preference settings are numbered based on their position in the General Preferences menu. Use **Cmd/Cntrl** 1-8 as keyboard shortcuts to make these preference settings easier to access.

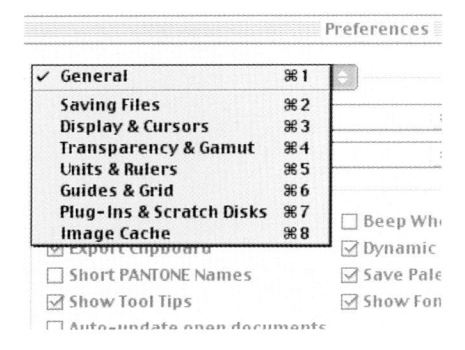

## GENERAL  File: Preferences

General Preferences contains several setting choices that affect the reproduction of grayscale images. Be sure to select the *Photoshop ColorPicker* or you will be unable to select the K value (black) in the CMYK value boxes in the Color Pickers. Set the *Interpolation to Bicubic* for more accurate cropping and transformation calculations. The General Preferences dialog box has nine options to set up Photoshop General Preferences.

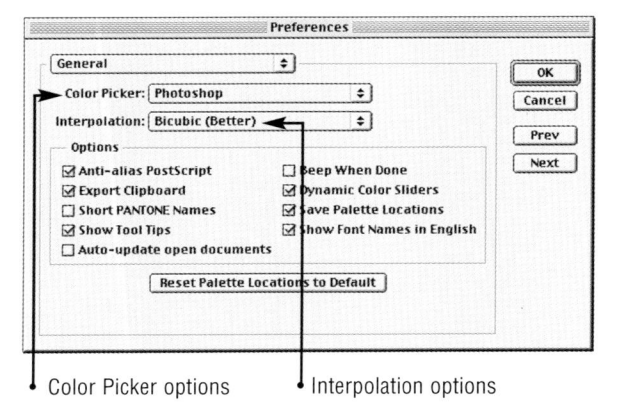

• Color Picker options   • Interpolation options

The illustration above shows the Color Picker and Interpolation settings in the General Preferences Dialog box.

- **Anti-alias PostScript** - This should be turned on. This permits Photoshop to import objects such as Illustrator or Freehand graphics with the use of paste, Drag-n-Drop, or by importing. When this is checked, Photoshop provides the best smooth edge it can around objects. If it is not checked, objects will have jagged edges.

- **Export Clipboard** - This should be turned off. This option tells Photoshop to transfer whatever image it has in its own clipboard to the operating system clipboard. This usually slows down the computer system. While this might sound like a good idea, Photoshop transfers clipboard data anyway, so you can paste images into other applications.

- **Short Pantone Names** - Usually this should be turned off. Most all of the recent desktop publishing applications support the current Pantone color names. If you are using older Desk Top Publishing (DTP) applications, then this feature might have to be turned on.

- **Show Tool Tips** - If you do not have much experience in Photoshop, this is a good feature to guide you. On the other hand, if you have experience in Photoshop, turning this off can save time because then you will not be distracted.

- **Auto-update open documents** - This is a subjective option. This instructs the computer to beep every time an operation with a Progress window is finished in Photoshop. We find it annoying, so it is turned off.

- **Beep When Done** - This is an subjective option to alert you every time an operation is done. We find this annoying also, so it is turned off.

- **Dynamic Color Sliders** - This should be turned on. This options allows you to dynamically preview the effects of the slider bars of the Color Palette.

- **Save Palette Locations** - This should be turned on. This feature permits you to return to an exact set of previously setup palettes. If you do not turn this feature on every time when Photoshop is restarted, it resets all the Palettes to their default position.

- **Show Font Names in English** - If you work with English text, this should be turned on.

## SAVING FILES — File: Preferences

These Preference options make it possible to specify and include the following features when saving files.

- **Image Previews**

  This allows preview options for Macintosh and Windows systems. Pop-up menus include:

  Never Save, Always Save, Ask When Saving. Always Save offers check boxes for Icon, Full Size, Macintosh, and Windows Thumbnail. Unchecking the Icon boxes will make the files slightly smaller.

- **Append File Extension**

  This provides an option to add upper or lower-case three-character file extensions to the end of file names indicating file formats. This is necessary for files that are being transferred to the Windows and Unix environments.

- **File Compatibility**

  *Include Composited image with Layered Files* - This should be turned off. This option was created for cross-application compatibility and for use with Adobe Illustrator. If it is turned on, native Photoshop files can increase dramatically in size. In some cases, file size can double.

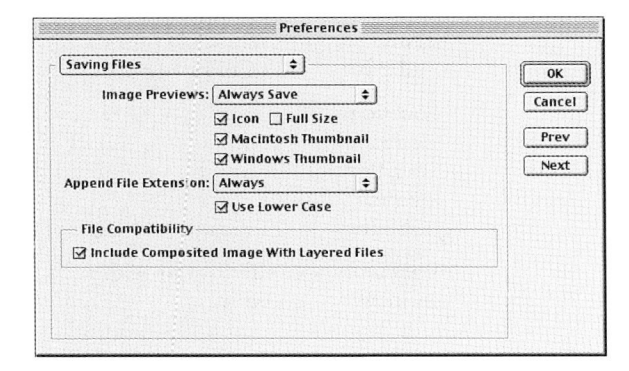

## DISPLAY & CURSORS — File: Preferences

- **Video LUT Animation**

  Make sure the Video LUT (Look Up Table) Animation is turned on. If your video board cannot use Video LUT Animation, use the Preview button to view changes to the image on screen. Check with your video card manufacturer if you have specific questions about LUT Animation.

- **Color Channels in Color**

  This should be turned off. This allows you to view color channels as grayscale files not as color channels.

- **Use System Palette**

  This should be turned off. This has to do with computer systems that use 8-bit monitors that can only display up to 256 colors.

- **Use Dither**

  This should be turned on. This option also has to do with old computer systems that use 8-bit monitors that can only display up to 256 colors. If your computer system is capable of displaying more than 256 such as thousands or millions, then it will not matter if this option is on or off.

- **Painting Cursors**

  This should be set to Brush Size. When this is set to Standard, Photoshop displays the tool icon. You cannot tell exactly how large the brush of the painting tool is unless the Brushes Palette is open. Setting it to the Brush Size makes it easier to see the actual brush size icon on each image.

# GETTING STARTED

## PREFERENCES
### SAVING FILES
### DISPLAY & CURSORS

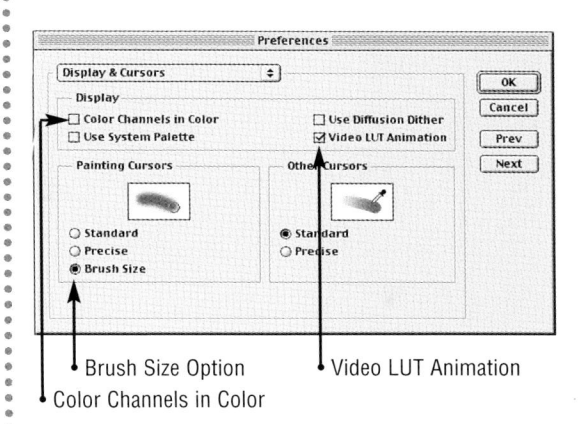

• Brush Size Option
• Color Channels in Color
• Video LUT Animation

5

# GETTING STARTED

## PREFERENCES
## TRANSPARENCY & GAMUTS
## UNITS & RULERS
## GUIDES & GRID

**ORIGINAL IMAGE WITH 100% OPACITY**

The image above shows the effects of transparency on an image. A 40% opacity was used with a medium grid size and a dark grid color.

## TRANSPARENCY & GAMUTS  File: Preferences

These settings are subjective and allow you to customize the Grid in Layers when viewing Transparency. The Gamut color adjustments only work on color images not grayscale.

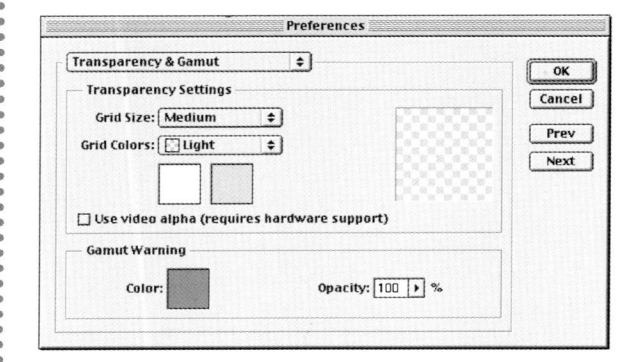

The image on the left represents the light grid color and small grid size background indicator for Transparency.

The image on the left represents the medium grid color and medium grid size background indicator for Transparency.

The image on the left represents the dark grid color and large grid size background indicator for Transparency.

## UNITS & RULES  File: Preferences

These Preferences permit altering the measurement units you wish to use throughout Photoshop.

- The Ruler allows you work in inches, points, picas, pixels, centimeters, or percent.
- The Column options allow you to specify the width and gutter sizes of pages.

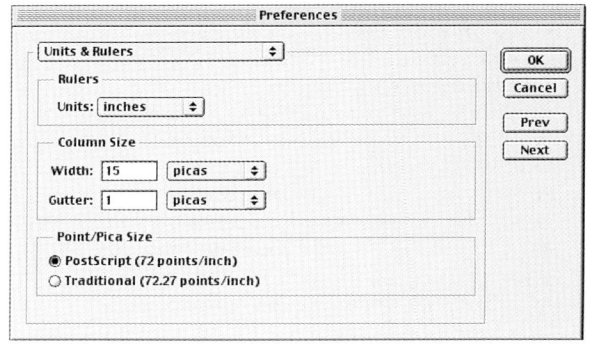

## GUIDES & GRID  File: Preferences

These settings are for customizing the color and size of the Guides & Grid lines. These Photoshop Guides can be dragged out of the rulers onto an image.

6

## PLUG-INS & SCRATCH DISKS  `File: Preferences`

- **Plug-Ins**

  Photoshop allows you to use either the current Plug-Ins folder that is located in the Photoshop folder or to create a new folder with Plug-Ins and place it any where on your computer system. If you do change the Plug-Ins folder, use the new folder to identify it.

- **Scratch Disk**

  Virtual memory operations take place on the computer's hard drive when Photoshop is performing operations and the computer system runs out of Random Access Memory (RAM). The hard drive is called the scratch disk. This version of Photoshop (5.0.2 and above) can now use up to four disk drives as scratch disks for its virtual memory system. The rule of thumb for setting up a computer system with multiple hard disks is to allocate an empty hard disk as the primary scratch disk. Typically, second and third hard disk drives will run applications and be used for saving files. Allocate the second and third hard disk drives as the second and third scratch disks. This is the most efficient way to work with Photoshop's virtual memory system. If virtual memory of the primary hard disk becomes full during an operation, then secondary disks will be used. As this happens, the computer system becomes less efficient, and the computer slows down because Photoshop's virtual memory system is competing for non-contiguous disk space. We recommend *not* using removable media for scratch disks.

  If Plug-Ins & Scratch Disks options are altered, close Photoshop and then restart it.

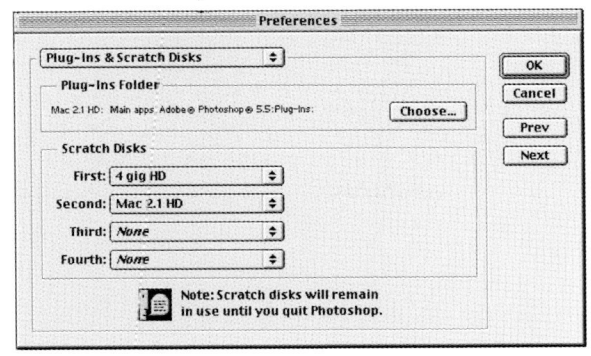

## IMAGE CACHE  `File: Preferences`

- **Image Cache** is used to make viewing images faster and is based on the amount of RAM in your computer system and workflow. There is no absolute rule for setting this up, only these guidelines. If your computer system has a large amount of RAM, say over 100 megabytes, and you work with large images, say over 25 megabytes, set the cache value to 8. This will take some of the allotted RAM away from processing images in Photoshop, but the previews will become faster. If your computer system uses a small amount of RAM, say 32 megabytes, set the cache value to 1 or 2. This will give Photoshop more RAM for processing.

- **Use Cache for Histograms**

  When Levels or Threshold image processing tools are selected, Photoshop generates a Histogram. This option uses the information from the cached image to generate a Histogram. If this option is checked *on,* it creates a faster and less accurate Histogram. If accuracy if preferred, then check it *off.* It will then take longer to create the Histogram. We suggest you check the Use Cache for Histograms *on.* If you are really concerned about the quality of a Histogram, then do not check this option.

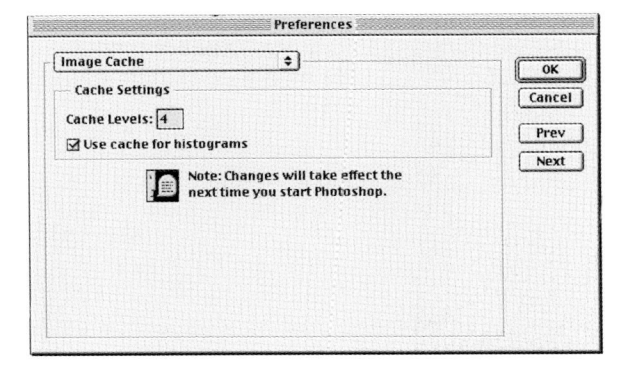

**Tip:** A shortcut to change the Plug-Ins & Scratch Disks options without quitting and restarting Photoshop is to hold down the **Cmd/Cntrl** and **Opt/Alt** keys during Startup of Photoshop.

# GETTING STARTED

## PREFERENCES
### PLUG-INS & SCRATCH DISKS
### IMAGE CACHE

#### RAM STANDS FOR RANDOM ACCESS MEMORY

It is one of the key ingredients for making Photoshop a fast image-editing program. RAM is much faster than the computer's hard drive/scratch disk. RAM may be expanded by adding memory chips or memory boards. Photoshop is a RAM-hungry program, so our rule of thumb is the more RAM, the better. It is not uncommon for computer systems to use 512 megabytes to 1 gigabyte of RAM with Photoshop high resolution images.

#### MEMORY SET UP TIP

If you are working on a Macintosh that has RAM added to it, be sure to turn off virtual memory in the control panels. This will allow you to take advantage of the computer's system RAM. Then alot RAM to Photoshop.

#### THE SCRATCH DISK IS FULL. WHAT SHOULD I DO?

This error message means your computer's hard disk is full and that Photoshop does not have any disk space left to perform operations. The only solution is to remove and delete images or other data that is taking up hard disk space on your computer.

A key strategy is to use removable storage media such as: Zip, Jazz, tape, or CD. These are low-cost solutions for image storage and backup of image data.

7

# GETTING STARTED

## COLOR SETTINGS

### RGB SETUP

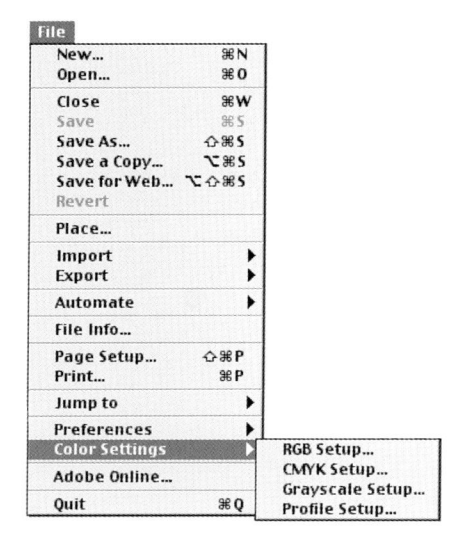

**USE THE CORRECT VERSION OF PHOTOSHOP**

If you do not already have it, we suggest that you download the free Photoshop update for version 5.0.2 from Adobe's website (www.adobe.com). This will make it easier to understand the discussion on the next few pages about Working Spaces and Color Settings.

**ICC VS ICM PROFILES**

*ICC* designates International Color Consortium profiles used with the Macintosh operating system.

*ICM* designates Integrated Color Management profiles used with the Windows operating system.

*ICC* and *ICM* profiles are interchangeable (cross platform) between either operating system. The only difference is that, if an *ICC* profile is going to be used with the Windows operating system, it must have a file extension of *.ICM*.

## ABOUT COLOR SETTINGS AND PHOTOSHOP CALIBRATION

The Color Settings menu in Photoshop 5.0.2 and 5.5 allows two basic methods of calibration. One method uses International Color Consortium (ICC) profiles, and the other uses older methods without ICC profiles. ICC profiles provide calibration for a complete imaging system. That is, calibration for scanner(s), monitor(s), digital proofer(s), and printing presses. ICC profiles are typically created with third-party applications and measuring tools. Their purpose is to correct for the deficiencies and varying color spaces of scanners, monitors, and printers.

Profiles are like correction filters. By passing files through a filter, you can correct for the discrepancies of a device (at least theoretically). Is the ICC profile system perfect? No. Using ICC profiles correctly in various types of workflows is a major drawback. Since 1999, all types of profiles (scanner, monitor, and printer) can be created relatively easily and economically. The problem we find is that operators sometimes apply the profile incorrectly in the workflow and achieve the incorrect results. Even with this drawback, there are positive benefits for using ICC profiles. Profiles make it possible for various output devices to achieve better color-matching capabilities. If your ICC profiles are created and implemented correctly, you can send the same file to many different printers and have the images come close to an exact visual match. This is a critical outcome that makes an ICC workflow practical and cost effective resulting in less wasted time and materials.

If you do not have access to quality ICC printer profiles, the second approach to calibration that has been popular for years is the closed-loop approach. This is where the end-user has to recognize the visual relationships between images, monitors, proofs, printing, and the numerical values that created the final results. This method of calibration is based on systematic experimentation where the operator keeps track of many system variables. Calibration is maintained with various techniques where each system component is characterized and adjusted by the end-user with vendor-supplied tools within the closed imaging system.

Another problem with ICC profiles is that grayscale images are not supported by ColorSync 2 and the majority of third party profiling applications do not offer grayscale printer profiling capabilities. This limitation makes it almost impossible to work efficiently with ICC profiles and grayscale images in Photoshop.

Our general approach in this book is to use the *go-by-the-numbers* method to reproduce grayscale images. Along the way, we will outline how to establish the Color Settings for use with and without profiles.

### RGB SETUP — File: Color Settings

While the scope of this book is about grayscale images, it is pertinent to discuss its Color Settings. In Photoshop version 5.0.2 and 5.5, the RGB setup option defines a *Working Space* for editing RGB images. The *Working Space* model is a change from earlier versions of Photoshop. There are ten built-in RGB color space options plus an option for custom spaces. Each of the color spaces has its own Gamma, White Point, and Primary settings as well as custom options for fine-tuning the Working Space. The RGB Setup dialog box also provides support for displaying the current monitor profile for RGB images, as defined by Apple's ColorSync or Adobe's Gamma monitor calibration profile or any third party monitor calibration programs that creates ICC profiles.

The RGB Setup options do not have a major effect on how grayscale images are reproduced in print.

Our advice is to standardize your *Working Space*. The rule of thumb is to try one of three RGB color spaces.
- Adobe RGB (1998) for print & non-print work.
- Use ColorMatch RGB for newspaper applications.
- Use SRGB for Internet imaging.

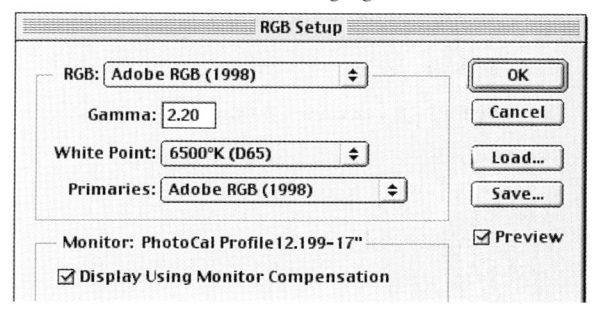

## PRELIMINARY SETUP OF THE MONITOR

To set up Photoshop and the monitor on your computer system to view grayscale images, create a profile that will be used in the RGB setup dialog box.

Before this profile can be created, some preparation has to be done to ensure the monitor will perform at its best. Environmental conditions will affect equipment performance.

1. **Evaluate your monitor to be sure it is bright enough.**

   Monitors can lose their brightness over time and, ultimately cannot be calibrated accurately. The rule of thumb to determine if the monitor has enough brightness is to turn up the brightness control all the way. View some images to see if they are brighter than is expected. If they are, then your monitor is good. If not, then it is time to replace it.

2. **Let the monitor warm up for at least 30 minutes.**

3. **Standardize the monitor's manual controls.**

   Some monitors have analog knobs, others, digital features. Typically, the monitor's controls are adjusted to make the screen look white (no color casts) and bright. After the controls are setup, tape or lock them to avoid accidental re-adjustment. If they are changed, the calibration will be inaccurate.

4. **Control the surrounding viewing environment.**

   To get the most accurate and consistent results, the monitor should be in an area with controlled and subdued lighting. There should be a designated area next to the computer for properly viewing black-and-white originals and proofs. To create this situation, it is necessary to use a standard 5000K (Kelvin) overhead and transparent light box. Window shades are a practical alternative in rooms with windows to create a better viewing environment.

5. **Use a neutral gray background on your monitor.**

   Color backgrounds are distracting and are a cause of a poorly calibrated monitor. If your computer's operating system (such as the Mac OS 8.6) does not come with a neutral background, use Photoshop to create one.

## TIP: CREATING A NEUTRAL GRAY BACKGROUND

1. **In Photoshop, create a new file.**

   Make the file size 72 x 72 pixels, select 72 resolution, and choose grayscale.

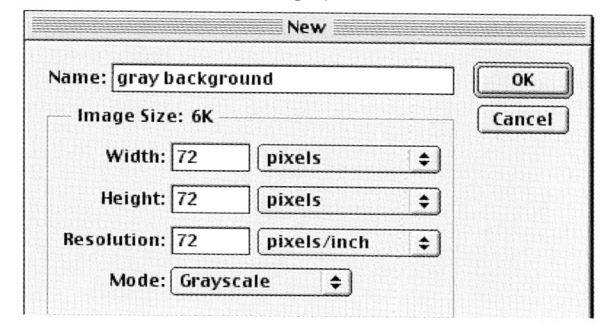

2. **Click on the Background color in the Tool Palette.**

   Adjust the RGB values to 200. The 200 value is subjective. We could have made the neutral gray lighter or darker.

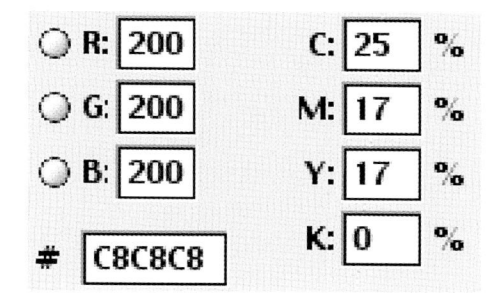

3. **Select All of the new image file.** Use **Cmd/Cntrl A**.

4. **Fill the Selection with the Background Color.**

   To fill the Selection, depress the Delete/Backspace key.

5. **Copy the Selection to the computer's clipboard.** Use **Cmd/Cntrl C**.

6. **Go the Macintosh Control Panel, choose Appearance, and select the tab titled Desktop.**

   Use Paste to place the neutral gray image into the patterns column. Select the neutral gray pattern, and set the Desktop.

# GETTING STARTED

## COLOR SETTINGS
### MONITOR SETUP

**NEUTRAL GRAY BACKGROUNDS AT-A-GLANCE**

1. In Photoshop create a new file.
2. Adjust the background color of the Tool Palette.
3. Select All of the new image file.
4. Fill the Selection with the Background Color.
5. Copy the Selection to the computer's clipboard.
6. Paste the neutral gray image into the Appearance dialog box. Select the neutral gray pattern and set the Desktop.

9

# GETTING STARTED

## COLOR SETTINGS

### CREATING A MONITOR PROFILE

#### HOW A MONITOR PROFILE IS CREATED

There are two ways to create a monitor profile:

- With a hardware measuring instrument such as a colorimeter. A measuring instrument is the most accurate method to use. This approach is usually used with third-party applications that allow measuring a monitor's critical values.
- Without any measuring equipment, using your visual judgment.

The following discussion outlines how to use the visual approach to create a monitor profile. This method is available in all recent versions of Photoshop (5.0.2 and 5.5).

#### BE AWARE OF THIRD-PARTY VIEWING APPLICATIONS

Various workflows and third-party applications can interact with Adobe Gamma settings to change the viewing conditions on the monitor.

For example, a digital photography workflow uses a third-party viewing application. Adobe Gamma is set to a 1.8 Gamma as per our guidelines. After Adobe Gamma is set up, the viewing conditions of the monitor becomes inaccurate in the third-party application.

To overcome this problem of the interaction between Adobe Gamma and the third-party application, we experimented with some of the Adobe Gamma settings. Changing the Gamma value in Adobe Gamma to 2.2 resolved the viewing problem.

You should be aware there are a number of workflows where the monitor calibration procedure we have outlined might not work. Our advice in that situation would be to contact the manufacturer of the third-party viewing application.

1. **Go to the Help Menu.**

   Open the Color Management Assistant, and then open Adobe Gamma.

2. **Choose the step-by-step Wizard.**

   There are two alternatives in this method: (1) the step-by-step wizard or (2) use of the control panel. This discussion will review the step-by-step wizard. See the side bar about the control panel.

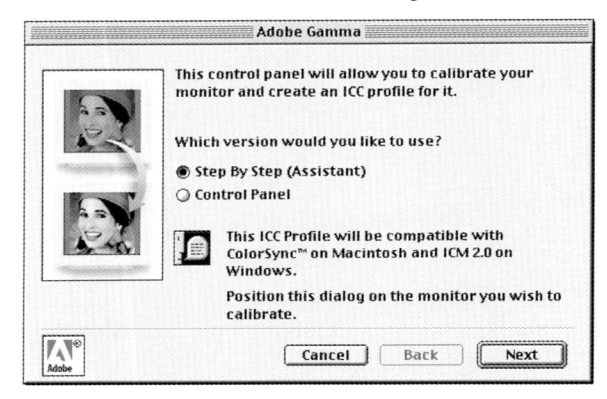

3. **Select the starting-point profile.**

   You have a choice of using the default profile or choosing a new one. On the Macintosh, the ColorSync System Profile is the default; on Windows 95/98, the default is the ICM profile; and on Windows NT, the default is a profile installed by Photoshop.

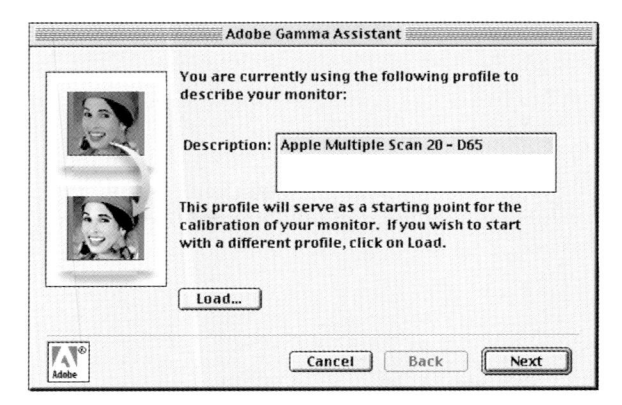

4. **Set the monitor's brightness and contrast.**

   These settings should already be close to accurate if the preliminary setup has been done correctly. This option should fine-tune it. Follow the instructions in the dialog box to adjust the brightness levels.

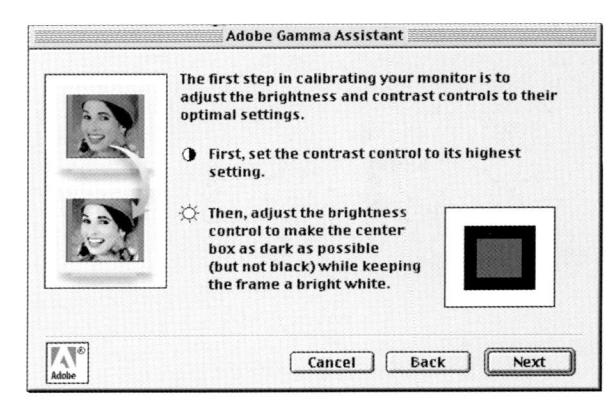

5. **Select the type of phosphors your monitor uses.**

   To find this information, check the documentation that came with the monitor or contact the vendor. It is possible to change the phosphors by going into Custom. This will permit changing the XY chromaticities of the monitor's phosphors.

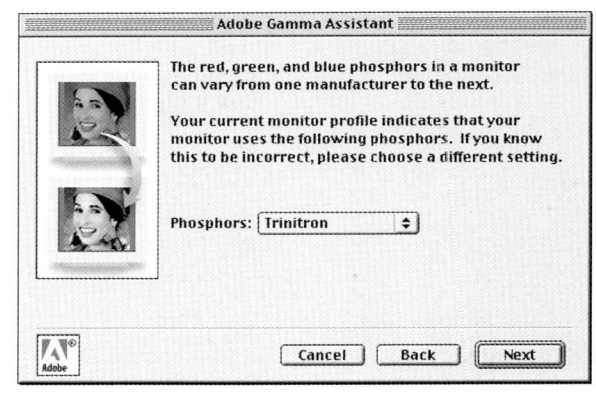

6. **Set the Gamma.**

   Use the three Gamma sliders. This is a more refined way to adjust the monitor. Do not use the single Gamma slider. Most experts agree on 1.8 Gamma for the Macintosh and 2.2 Gamma for Windows.

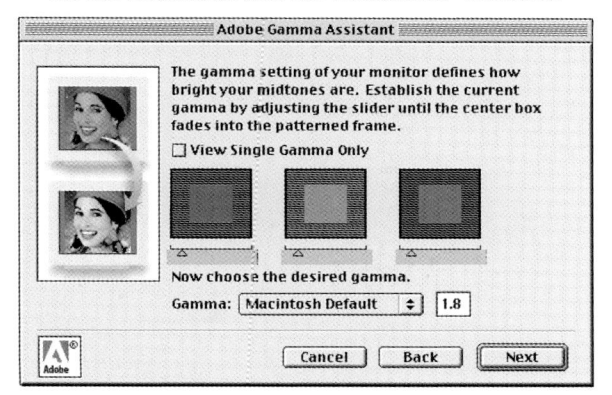

7. **Set the White Point values for your monitor.**

   This set of options is a little tricky. To determine where to set the White Point, it is necessary to experiment. Try D50 and D65. If D50 dims the monitor too much, use D65. If you choose to measure your monitor by selecting Measure, you will have to make estimated visual choices by selecting gray patches that become available in this part of the Adobe Gamma program. During this process, use a piece of white paper that your images are printed on. Use the Adobe Gamma set of tools to make the monitor's white match the paper as close as possible.

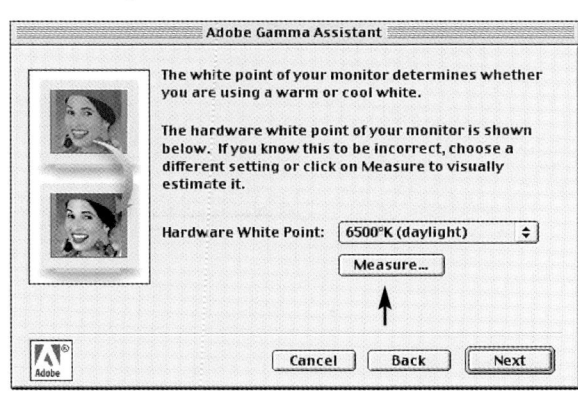

Next, you must make the choice of keeping these values or adjusting the White Point. Unless, you are expert with measuring the White Point, we suggest using the *Same as Hardware* values.

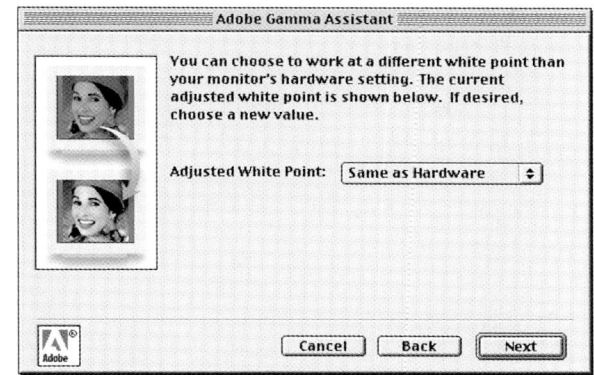

8. **Save the profile.**

   Give it a name that makes sense to you, such as GS Monitor Profile 11.3.99 (the current date). On the Macintosh, the profile will automatically be placed in the ColorSync profile folder. On Windows, save the profile manually in the color directory.

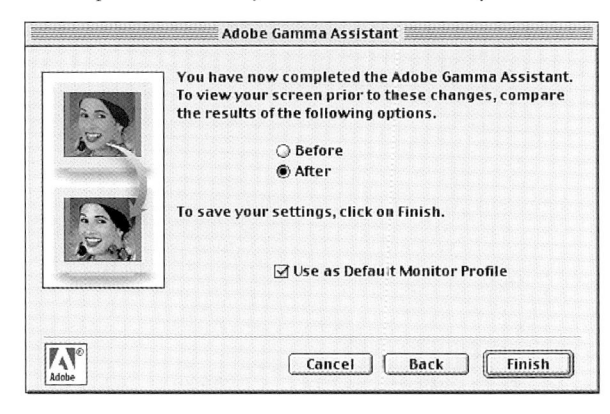

# GETTING STARTED

## COLOR SETTINGS

### CREATING A MONITOR PROFILE

**USING ADOBE GAMMA AT-A-GLANCE**

1. Go to the Help Menu, and open the Color Management Assistant.
2. Choose the step-by-step Wizard.
3. Select the starting-point profile.
4. Set the monitor's brightness and contrast.
5. Select the phosphors for your monitor.
6. Set the Gamma.
7. Set the White Point values of your monitor.
8. Save the profile.

The example below shows a monitor profile being saved with a descriptive name and date.

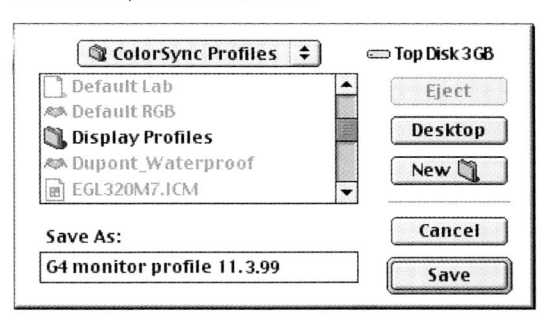

11

# GETTING STARTED

## COLOR SETTINGS

### CMYK SETUP

### GRAYSCALE SETUP

**ADJUSTING DOT GAIN FOR GRAYSCALE IMAGES**

The method we recommend for altering the dot gain characteristics of grayscale images is to use image processing tools such as Levels, Curves, or Transfer Curves. These tools are used to apply a known adjustment to manually compensate for the effects of dot gain.

For more about Dot Gain, see APPENDIX B Calibration.

**TIP: DETERMINING DOT GAIN VALUES**

The best method to determine dot gain values is to consult with your printer or service provider. A good printer will address your concerns and will have run tests that identify different dot gain values for their different printing presses.

However, if you are setting up dot gain for a digital printer and there is no one to consult, here is a place to start.

- Run some tests by printing out a grayscale image with different dot gain adjustments using Curves. Be sure the digital printer is outputting consistent results and is not drifting. Methodically use Curves with different midtone adjustments to identify a good midtone setting for images being printed. Use the Load and Save feature to apply the Curve when an image is ready for printing.

- Examine the printed results and visually compare them with different dot gain values to the original. This method is based on visual comparisons and how closely prints match the original. This will determine the dot gain value. In this process, make sure the printed image has correct highlight and shadow target value settings.

## CMYK SETUP   File: Color Settings

The CMYK Setup dialog box combines the previous versions of Photoshop Color settings, Printing Inks Setup, and the Separations Setup into one dialog box. This dialog box has three options for the CMYK Mode: Built-in, ICC, and Color Separation Tables.

### Built-in Mode

The built-in mode is the native portion of the updated Photoshop 16-bit-per-channel color separation engine.

In this mode, the Dot Gain settings in the CMYK mode will only affect the view of the grayscale file, not the actual values in the file itself.

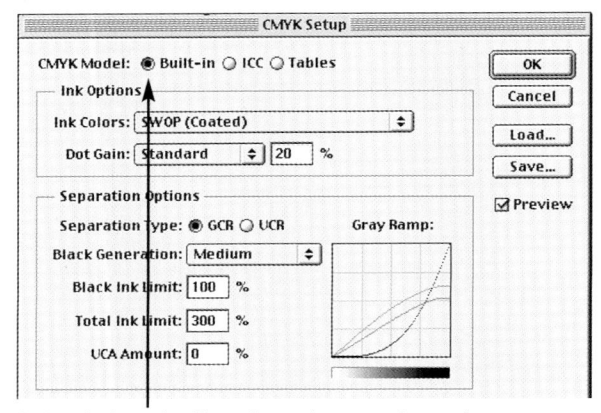

Built-in is the native Photoshop color separation engine.

### ICC Mode

The ICC mode is for working with ICC profiles.

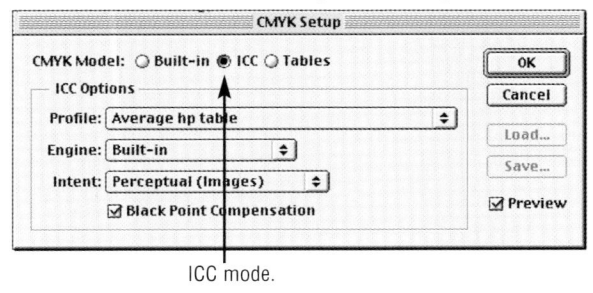

ICC mode.

### Color Separation Tables

Photoshop color separation tables are for making consistent image conversions of RGB to CMYK. These tables do not affect grayscale image reproduction.

## GRAYSCALE SETUP   File: Color Settings

The Grayscale Setup dialog box contains two simple options, *RGB* and *Black Ink*.

- The RGB option is for working on grayscale images that will be used for non-print applications, such as the World Wide Web, as well as as digital photography and CD-ROM publishing.

When this option is selected, the Gamma setting in the RGB setup affects how grayscale files are viewed on your monitor.

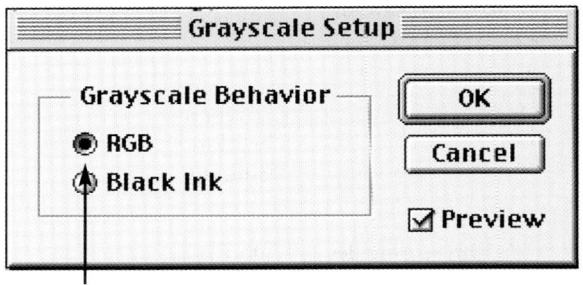

Click this button on for grayscale non-print applications.

- The *Black Ink* option is for print-oriented applications. Selecting the *Black Ink* option is like enabling the *Use dot gain for grayscale images* checkbox in previous versions of Photoshop Printing Inks Setup dialog box.

When this option is selected, the CMYK Setup Dot Gain Settings affects the viewing of grayscale files on your monitor.

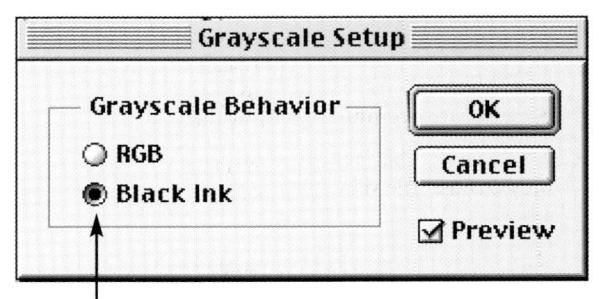

Click this button on for grayscale print applications.

## PROFILE SETUP `File: Color Settings`

Profile Setup is a flexible way to set up Photoshop for different workflows. One of the purposes of *Color Settings>Profile Setup* is to warn the operator if a file is going to be altered from its original rendering intent.

This dialog box provides three areas of control.

**1. Embed Profiles.**

This controls options for embedding ICC profiles into RGB, CMYK, Grayscale, or LAB images files when they are saved. Use the check mark to embed profiles, and leave the box unchecked if you do not want to embed profiles.

If you do not want to attach profiles to a grayscale image, you can turn it off. To do this, click the check mark off on the Embed Profile box. This ensures that profile embedding is off.

**2. Assumed Profiles.**

This feature provides four choices for opening grayscale images:

It defines various options for opening or acquiring images with or without ICC profiles.

- *None.* Using the None option will ignore any attached profiles when opening an image. This is a safe method for opening files, but it does not let you know if any profiles were previously attached to the image.

- *Ask When Opening.* This warns the operator about any conversions that might take place before the file is open. This is the best option to use to avoid mistakes when opening a grayscale image because you will be alerted to any changes that might take place before beginning work in Photoshop.

- *1.8 Gamma.* This is a viable option to use because it only changes the values in the file by approximately 1% overall.

- *2.2 Gamma.* This option changes the values in the file by 9% at the 50% value. This is not a good option to use, especially for print applications.

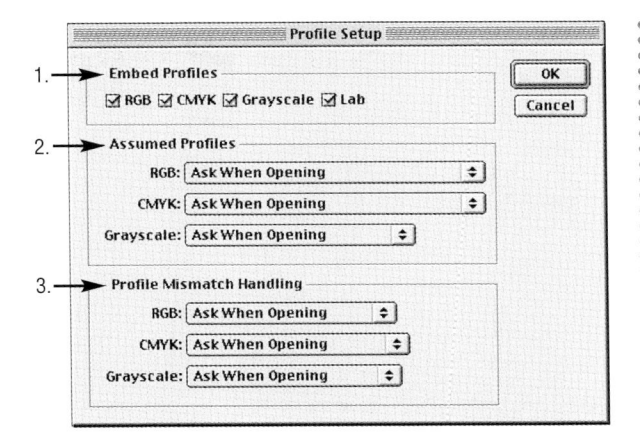

**3. Profile Mismatch Handling.**

This feature is one of the keys to opening and managing image files with or without ICC profiles attached. It has three areas for controlling grayscale images.

- *Ignore.* This disregards telling the operator if there are embedded profiles when a file is open. This is not recommended for use because it is too easy to open a file and have it change without knowing that a change took place. Plus, this option will ignore any embedded profiles that someone may have attached to an image.

- *Ask When Opening.* This is the best option to use to avoid mistakes when opening files. This option will always alert you if there is a change between a file and the current Color Settings.

- *Convert to Grayscale.* This option will automatically convert the file to the parameters of the profile. This option will convert a color file to grayscale on the fly.

**Warning:** When a Photoshop profile is embedded, it is considered to be a complete ICC profile, and, because it is attached to the file, it also increases the file size. For print this is not critical, but for non-print purposes like the web, it might make the file larger and, therefore be slow in opening on a web site.

Using the *Save for Web* dialog box should prevent this from happening. It removes the attached profile unless you tell it to embed it in the image.

# GETTING STARTED

## COLOR SETTINGS

### PROFILE SETUP

**FILE FORMATS THAT SUPPORT EMBEDDED PROFILES**

- Native Adobe Photoshop or PSD
- Portable Document Format or PDF
- Tagged Image File Format or TIFF
- Encapsulated PostScript or EPS
- Joint Photographic Experts Group or JPEG
- PICT

13

# GETTING STARTED

## COLOR SETTINGS
## WORKING SPACE
## EMBEDDING PROFILES
## LEGACY FILES

Below are the Profile to Profile menu and its dialog box.

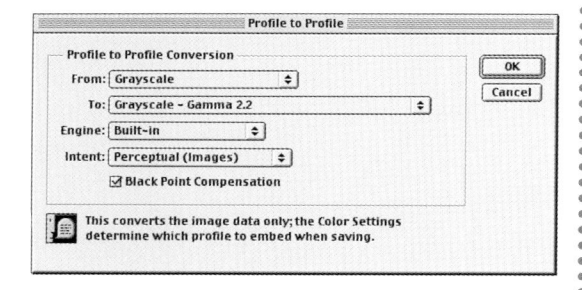

**Tip:** The Grayscale option in the Profile to Profile Menu produces the same results as using the **Image>Mode>Grayscale** option.

## THE WORKING SPACE FOR GRAYSCALE IMAGES

Adobe's solution for grayscale image editing is to use either the 1.8 Gamma or the 2.2 Gamma Working Space options.

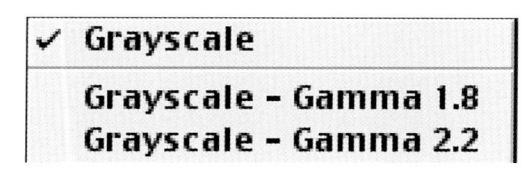

Below is an example of how ICC profiles would work in Photoshop. In this ICC workflow, we are using accurate scanner, monitor, and printer profiles.

### Scanning

Some scanning applications support profiles and others do not. If the scanning program does not support profiles, the profile is applied in Photoshop by using the *Profile to Profile* option under the Mode Menu. The options in this dialog box allow using the scanner Profile to Profile option. Select:

- *From* the scanner profile
- *To* the Photoshop *Working Space (2.2 Gamma)*

In this scenario, use the RGB scanner mode and the RGB scanner profile for scanning both grayscale and color originals. Then use Photoshops 2.2 Gamma for grayscale. When the file is saved, the profile is attached. The 2.2 Gamma offers the largest working space for editing grayscale images.

### Image Editing

After the scanner profile is applied to the image, it is edited or retouched with Photoshop tools such as Levels and Curves.

### Printing

There are a number of options for printing. Here is one if an ICC grayscale printer profile is available. Be sure your grayscale file is open.

- Go to the Print menu and set up the printer options. The printer options include the Photoshop color spaces. Each printer driver will have its own options for loading ICC profiles.
- Select the correct ICC grayscale printer profile that was made for your printer and then print.

## Embedding Profiles

- Theoretically, if grayscale images were supported by page layout programs such as Quark or PageMaker one workflow option would be to embed the profile in the image file.
  In this workflow, use Profile to Profile. Select:
- *From* the *Working Space (2.2 Gamma)*
- *To* the ICC printer profile

  This workflow creates a new image file that is placed in a page layout program.

  Unfortunately, grayscale images are not currently supported in page layout programs. While page layout programs do not offer support for grayscale profiles, we believe it is important to apply ICC profiles to grayscale files. Our reasoning is that using ICC profiles allows you to capture the optimum scanned image data that benefits both ICC and non ICC workflows.

## LEGACY FILES AND WORKING SPACES

What are Legacy files? Legacy files are previously created images that have not yet been opened and resaved in Photoshop version 5.0.2 or 5.5. Legacy files affect how the Color Settings are established. If the Color Settings are not adjusted properly when opening a Legacy file, the contrast of a grayscale file can be ruined.

For example, you might want the Legacy file to reproduce the same as it did the last time it was used. If, when opening a Legacy file, the Color Settings and the *Working Space* are not set correctly and the incorrect opening options are selected, the Legacy file's pixel values will change. This can make the file reproduce poorly.

When working with Legacy files, there are two *Working Space* choices for the grayscale images, 1.8 Gamma and 2.2 Gamma. The 1.8 Gamma is the only practical option. When 1.8 Gamma is chosen, the image changes overall by 1%. Choosing 2.2 Gamma changes the image by 9% at the 50% values.

A third choice and the most practical is to adjust the *Profile Setup* options so that the message *Do Not Convert* displays upon opening a grayscale file. This will ensure the grayscale file does not change from its original state.

# GETTING STARTED

## COLOR SETTINGS
### MISSING PROFILES
### OPENING THE FIRST IMAGE

## MISSING PROFILE

This Missing Profile dialog box might appear when opening Legacy files for the first time. Here are two ideas to consider if that happens:

- If planning to use the Working Space with Legacy files, then it is best to choose 1.8 Gamma.

- If you are **not** planning to work with profiles, select *Don't Convert* when opening the file.

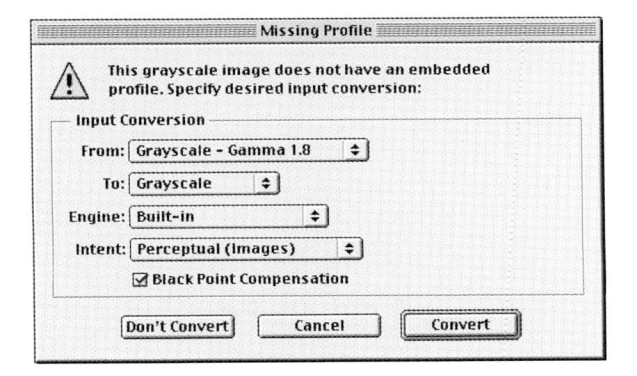

**Tips for Setting up Photoshop without Profiles**

- Turn off profile embedding.

- Adjust the Profile Mismatch Handling options to *Ask When Opening* for all options. This will avoid mistakes when opening files.

- If you are going to print, make sure that the Grayscale Setup option is set on Black Ink.

- Always use *Do not Convert* the grayscale image when prompted. This approach will ensure the file is opened in its original state.

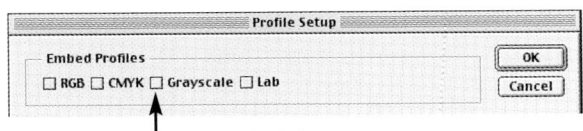

Embed Profile options are unchecked

This example above shows the Profile Setup dialog box with the Embed Profile options unchecked. It is therefore turned off and will not embed a profile to the image when it is saved.

## OPENING AN IMAGE THE FIRST TIME IN PHOTOSHOP 5.0.2 OR 5.5

Before opening or acquiring a file for print or non-print applications, we suggest that you always adjust the Profile Setup for grayscale images. Make sure the *Assumed Profiles* and *Mismatch Handling* settings are adjusted to *Ask When Opening*. This will alert you if the file contains an embedded profile.

**When to use *Do not Convert***

- Use *Do not Convert* when you are **not** planning to use profiles and you want the file that is being opened to retain its original state. This is a common way to work with grayscale Legacy files.

- Use *Do not Convert* when an image does not match your Color Settings. The file will open without any type of conversion.

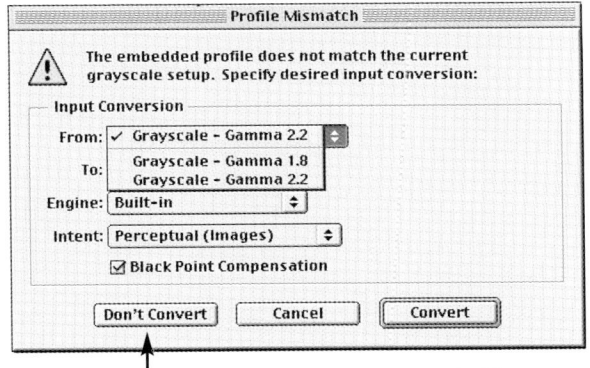

Use this option when you do not want to convert the file.

**When to use *1.8 Gamma*.**

- Use *1.8 Gamma* with Legacy files that are going to be used in an ICC or ICM workflow.

15

# GETTING STARTED

## REVIEW

Here is an example of how to use keyboard shortcuts.

If you do a lot of retouching work, learn how to enter brushes and how to change brush size and opacity. While there are at least six brush choices, only one or two probably will be used. The tip is to remember the important shortcut keys.

(1) B for the Paintbrush.

(2) D to Default the Foreground and Background Colors.

(3) X to Switch the Defaulted Colors.

(4) Bracket Keys to change brush sizes.

(5) Single number keys to change the Opacity or Pressure of a brush.

(6) Undo/Redo. Cmd/Cntrl Z.

### RGB SETUP AND WORKING SPACE GUIDELINES

- Use Adobe RGB (1998) for print & non-print work.
- Use ColorMatch RGB for newspaper applications.
- Use SRGB for Internet imaging.

---

The Getting Started section covered where to begin in using Photoshop.

- **Tips for Success**

  These tips provide the essentials of navigation shortcuts that make it easier to use the Photoshop Tool Palette. Learn the keys that you would commonly use in each Photoshop working session. While there are dozens of choices, focus on five or six shortcuts. See side bar example.

- **General Preferences**

  The General Preference settings ensure you have the basic program set up so Photoshop is optimized for your computer system as well as the particular type of work you are doing. While it is important to have all eight of the General Preference Settings correct, there are two settings of the eight that are critical. Be sure the Preference Settings are adjusted for:

- *Display and Cursors* - Be sure Video LUT animation is turned on and that the Color Channels in Color option is turned off.

- *Plug-ins & Scratch Disk* - Make sure the Scratch Disk is set up correctly so that Photoshop's virtual memory system works efficiently as possible. See page 7.

- **Color Settings**

  It is important to have all Color Settings adjusted correctly for efficient and constant use of images in Photoshop. Consider this question about about calibration: should you use ICC profiles or not?

  In general, we think using ICC profiles is a good idea, but the only problem today is that using ICC profiles with grayscale images are not well supported. So the only practical solution is to go by the numbers. Having stated that, it is still possible to use ICC profiles to capture optimum image data and convert the file to grayscale. See page 14 for this scenario. Then use the go-by-the-numbers approach. That is, use the Info Palette to identify the values that you have gotten good results with for setting highlights, midtones, and shadow settings.

  Our belief is that all Photoshoppers will use RGB, CMYK, and grayscale images at sometime. So be sure to adjust the Setups for RGB, CMYK, and grayscale. To that end, here is our advice:

- **RGB Setup**

  Try to use one of the particular RGB working spaces for your type of work. See sidebar of this page.

- **CMYK Setup**

  The Dot Gain settings affect the way grayscale images are viewed. We cannot suggest specific settings, but we recommend that you find a dot gain that provides the best representation of your type of images on your computer's screen. To do this, run some tests to verify those settings. In this situation images are proofed or printed and then compared to the same images on the computer's screen. The final CMYK Dot Gain settings should make the images appear close to the proofs.

- **Grayscale Setup**

  For non-print applications, select **RGB**.
  For print applications choose **Black Ink**.

  If you are working with profiles, use the Grayscale Working Spaces of *2.2 Gamma*.

  If using Legacy files in conjunction with ICC profiles, use *1.8 Gamma*.

  If you are not planning to use ICC profiles with new images or Legacy files, be sure the Profile Mismatch Setup is adjusted to: (1) *Ask When Opening* and that (2) *Profile Embedding is turned Off*.

  So when you open a file that does not match your Color Settings, you will select *Do Not Convert*.

- **Profile Setup**

  After you have determined your RGB and Grayscale Working Spaces, adjust the Profile Setup for all types of images RGB, CMYK, and grayscale to *Ask When Opening*. This will alert you when opening a file that does not match your Color Settings.

- **Monitor Setup**

  The most accurate way to create an ICC profile is to use a measuring tool such as a Colorimeter with a third party application. The other method is to use Adobe Gamma that is supplied with Photoshop. See page 11 for the step-by-step instructions.

# RECOVERY STRATEGY

Recovery Options ..................................18
History Palette........................................19
Creating Snapshots ..............................20
Snapshot Tips........................................21
Using Snapshots ...................................22
History State and Snapshots ..................23
Review...................................................24

# RECOVERY STRATEGY

## RECOVERY OPTIONS

While the History Palette and its array of tools are a tremendous help, there is no one method that covers all the imaging situations, especially for correcting errors when using grayscale images in Photoshop. The bottom line is that it does not matter which tool is used to recover from an imaging error. Our experience indicates these methods help all levels of operators learn recovery strategies that allow them to keep on working in a skilled and creative way as the image area is being restored.

### HISTORY BEHAVIOR TIPS

- The History Palette does not keep track of changes made to the palettes, color settings, actions, and Preferences since they are not changes to a specific image's State.
- Closing a document removes all the States. States in the History Palette are only available while the image is open in a working session.
- History States and Snapshots can be dragged and dropped between images. They show up in the History Palette of each image.

The History Palette is accessed from the Window Menu.

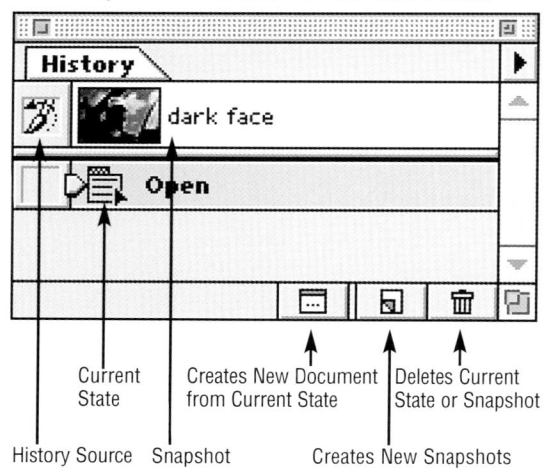

Current State · History Source · Snapshot · Creates New Document from Current State · Deletes Current State or Snapshot · Creates New Snapshots

## RECOVERING FROM IMAGING MISTAKES

There are a number of ways to recover from an imaging mistake with Photoshop. These methods are important to master so an environment can be created where it is possible to recover the right image data with little or no loss. The first one is Revert, the second is Undo/Redo, and the third is the History Palette.

### REVERT

One of the most obvious and easiest ways to recover from a mistake in Photoshop is the Revert command. It forces you to return to the last saved version of your document. You might have found out already, the Revert feature is not a very elegant solution to fix an error, but it may be the only option you have.

Revert is slightly different in version 5.0.2 than version 5.5. When Revert is activated in version 5.0.2, a dialog box asks if you are sure you want to OK the Revert. In version 5.5, Revert does not use a dialog box, so you can undo Revert.

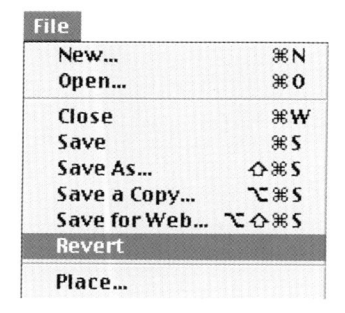

### UNDO/REDO - CMD/CNTRL Z

The Undo Command found under the Edit menu. This option is the most obvious and the easiest way to recover from a mistake, that is, of course, if you catch the mistake before you have made more than one extra key or brush stroke.

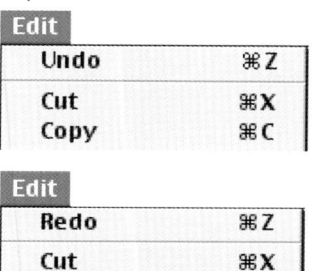

Use Cmd/Cntrl Z to examine before (use undo) and after (use redo) image processing effects such as Curves, Levels, or Filters.

### THE HISTORY ERASER TOOL

The History Eraser Tool offers an option for painting image data back to the original image information. This has been a feature of Photoshop for years, only it was called the Magic Eraser. Be careful not to confuse it with version 5.5's new Magic Eraser Tool.

In versions 5.0.2 and 5.5, the History Eraser now uses a Snapshot that is created in the History Palette when an image is opened.

For the History Eraser Tool to work, the History Options need to be set to *Create a Snapshot* when Opening an image. See page 20.

**The History Eraser Tool is used in two basic ways.**

1. To erase pixels to the Background color (of the Tool Palette) or if you are working on a Transparent Layer you can erase the image to become Transparent.

2. Use the History Eraser Option.

   This allows you to paint back pixel values from the last saved image (the Snapshot that was created in the History Palette).

   To activate the History Eraser Tool feature, hold down the **Opt/Alt** key or Check the Erase to Saved option in the History Eraser Tool Palette.

- The shortcut for the History Eraser Tool is the E key.
- The History Eraser Tool has four different types of brushes offering a tremendous amount of flexibility for changing brush sizes and image opacity.

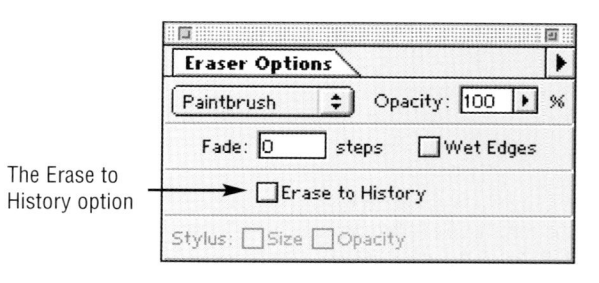

The Erase to History option

## HISTORY PALETTE OPTIONS

States of an image are created from the top of the History list moving down. This makes the last State in the list the most current State. Each item in the list is named for a feature that was used to create that particular State. **Moving Between States = multiple undos.** There are two basic ways to move up and down to different States.

1. Use the mouse to click on a specific State in the History list. *See the shortcuts in the History Palette Pop-out menu.*
2. Use the keyboard: for Macintosh use **Shift/Command/Z** to move up, **Option/Command/Z** to move down.
   Use the keyboard: for Windows use **Shift/Control/Z** to move up, **Alt/Control/Z** to move down.

**Linear and Non-Linear States.**
When History Options are set to the Linear feature, any State below the selected State will dim and be unavailable. A way to avoid the lower States from becoming inactive is to use Non-Linear States.
These options permit moving to any State and not having the lower States become dim or unavailable.

**Linear States**
The default setting for using States in the History Palette is Linear. The *Allow Non-Linear History* is Unchecked.

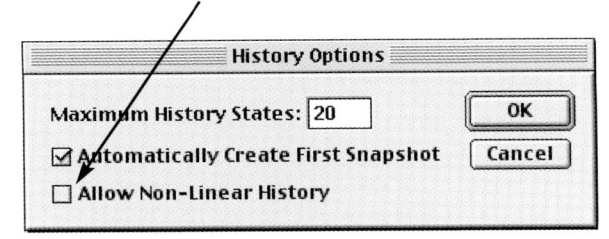

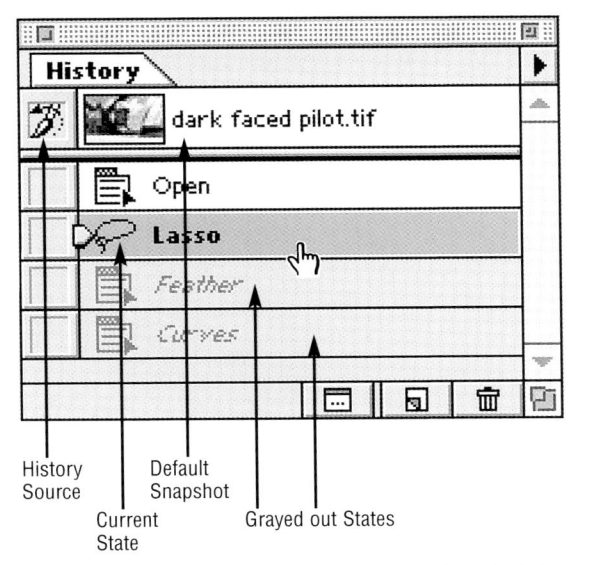

**Non-Linear States**
Use the Non-Linear State setting in the History Palette for access to all States when working to keep current States from dropping off the bottom of the list when a previous State is selected.

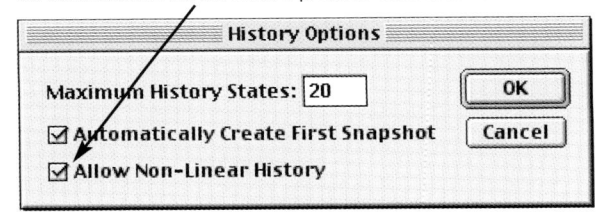

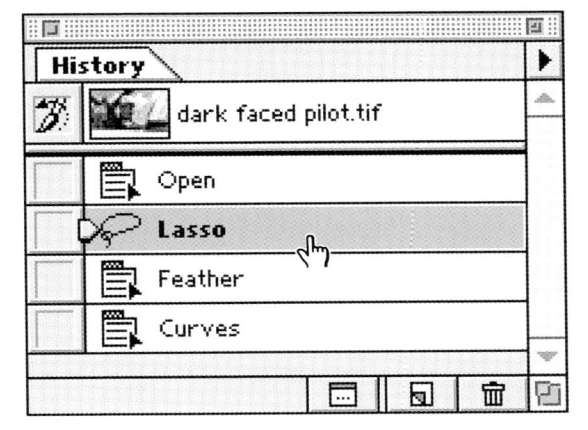

History Source
Default Snapshot
Current State
Grayed out States

The History Palette above shows what happens when a State is selected and when Histories is set to its Linear Options. Note the grayed out States.

Be aware that while the History Palette can help prevent costly imaging errors, once the image is saved and closed all of the History data is gone.

The History Palette above shows the palette behavior when Histories is set to the Non-linear Options. Note that none of the States are grayed out.

# RECOVERY STRATEGY
## HISTORY PALETTE OPTIONS

**HISTORY POP-OUT MENU**

1. Step Forward  ⇧⌘Z
2. Step Backward  ⌥⌘Z
3. New Snapshot...
4. Delete
5. Clear History
6. New Document
7. History Options...

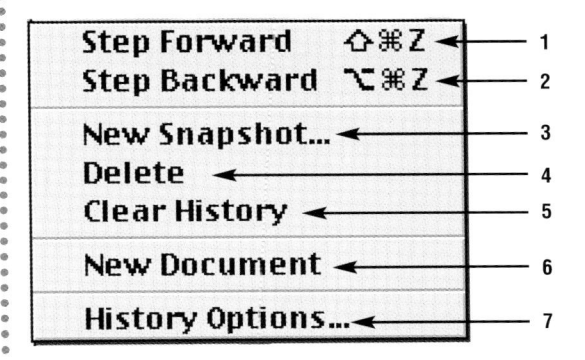

1. **Step Forward** - This allows moving down the History list.
2. **Step Backward** - This allows moving up the History list.
3. **New Snapshot** - This creates a Snapshot in the History list.
4. **Delete** - To use Delete, click on the State you wish to remove. Then delete one State at a time.
5. **Clear History** - Removes all of the States in the History list.
6. **New Document** - The New Document option from the Pop-out menu permits creating a new document with all the previous edits applied to it. This feature permits making a new Photoshop file from the last current State of the image. This can be a useful strategy to recover and combine a certain State of a file.
7. **History Options** - This feature permits setting the number of History States, creating or not creating a Snapshot when a file is open, and using Linear or Non-Linear States.

# RECOVERY STRATEGY

## CREATING SNAPSHOTS

### THE SNAPSHOT OPTION

Snapshot is one of our favorite tools for recovering from mistakes and retouching images. After you learn the History Palette and Brush Tool options, you will find the Snapshot feature easy to use. More important, the Snapshot is flexible and powerful for complex imaging work.

### THE LAST STATE IN THE HISTORY LIST

The last State in the History list has all the previous States' functions embedded in it. This becomes important when a limited number of States are used to make the computer system more efficient.

For example, the History Palette has been setup to use eight States. During the working session, over 20 States are created. After nine States are created, the previous States are overwritten.

If every State is important to you in a working session, create Snapshots frequently to ensure none of the States are overwritten.

## SNAPSHOTS

A Snapshot is a History Palette feature that lets you make a temporary copy of the image you are currently viewing on your computer screen. A Snapshot becomes part of the History list that resides above its States. A Snapshot preserves the exact state of an image when the Snapshot was created. To create a Snapshot, use the History Palette Pop-out menu. The default History Options settings will automatically create the First Snapshot.

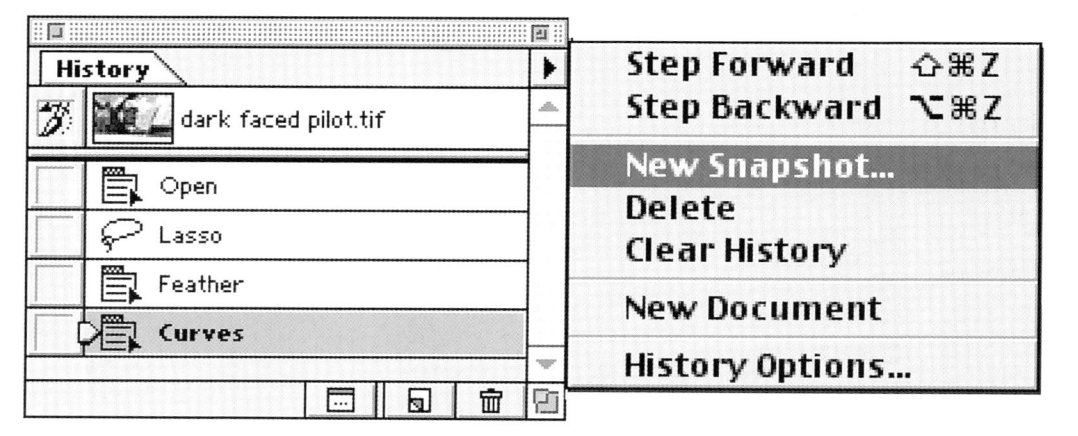

The example above shows the History list with four States and one Snapshot.

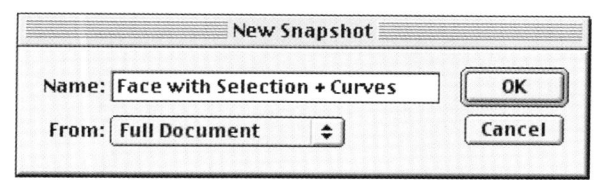

The Snapshot dialog box.

The image above shows the results of this working session. In this exaggerated correction the image has a Feathered Selection that was corrected with Curves.

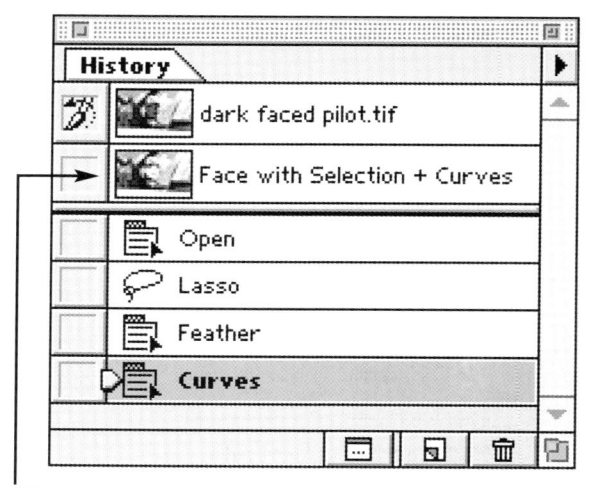

The example above shows the History list with a new Snapshot of the image that has a Feathered Selection with a Curves correction.

## HISTORY AND SNAPSHOT SUCCESS TIPS

■ **Create and name a Snapshot.**
Use the History Pop-out menu and select the Snapshot option. This takes you to the New Snapshot menu where a name can be given to the Snapshot. Give it a meaningful name.

For example, if you are using the Snapshot with Gaussian Blur or Dust & Scratches, call it Fuzzy1, or if making tone corrections, name it based on the area that is being corrected such as face, etc.

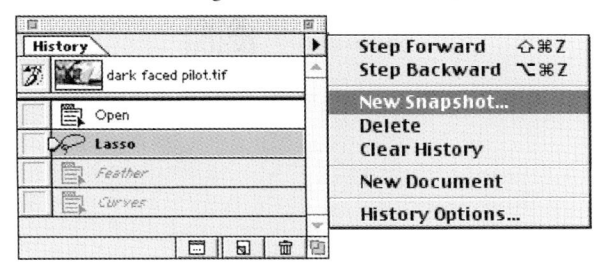

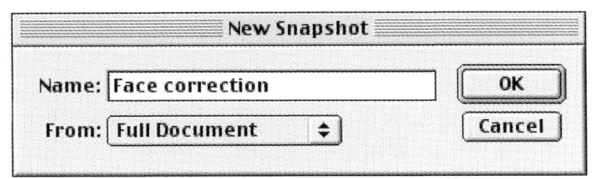

■ **Change the History Source.**
Using the mouse to click on a Snapshot or States Source permits painting from a specific Snapshot or State from the History list with the History brush. To change the Source, click on another Snapshot or State on the left side of a Snapshot or State. The Source of the Snapshot or State becomes a History Brush Icon and must be selected in order to paint from it.

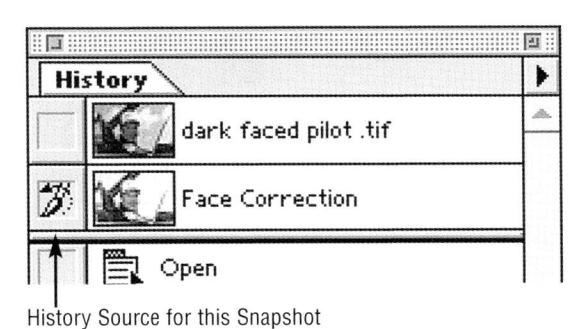

History Source for this Snapshot

■ **Click on the correct Snapshot or State.**
To change the Snapshot or State, click on another Snapshot or State on the right side of that particular State or Snapshot. The Snapshot or State then becomes highlighted. The highlighted Snapshot or State is the image information that becomes viewed on your computer screen. The example below illustrates the last State of the image that had Curves applied to it.

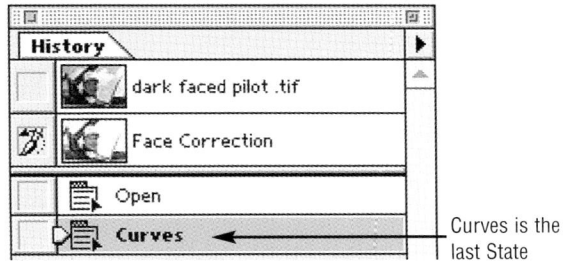

Curves is the last State

■ **Use the History brush from the Tools Palette.**
To Select the History Brush from the Tools Palette, depress the Y key. Also be sure that you have chosen the correct History brush and not the Impressionist Brush.

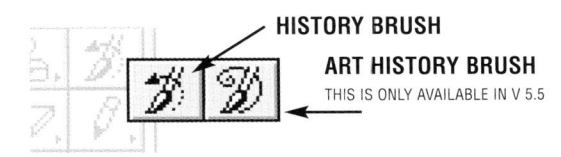

HISTORY BRUSH
ART HISTORY BRUSH
THIS IS ONLY AVAILABLE IN V 5.5

■ **Work with different brushes and opacity.**
When the History brush is selected:
• Use numbers 1 through 0 to change opacity.
• Use the Bracket keys to change the Brush sizes.

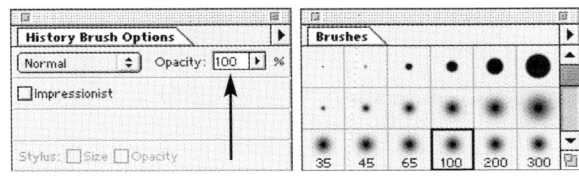

Be sure the History Brush Option palette is selected. Then type in a number such as 5. This will change the History brushes opacity to 50%. If the History brush palette is not selected, you will change the Layers opacity.

# RECOVERY STRATEGY
## SNAPSHOT TIPS

### HISTORY TOOL

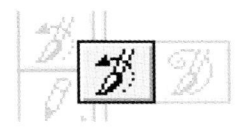

#### SNAPSHOT TIP

To keep a specific State unchanged throughout a working session, use the Snapshot option. If necessary, a Snapshot can be turned into an image by creating a New Document.

#### MORE STATES CAN SLOW DOWN THE COMPUTER

A strategy we suggest is limiting the number of States to 5 or 10 except for special situations where you might need to go back dozens of steps.

Although the maximum number of States is 99, the greater the number of States, the more the computer's speed potentially slows down. This happens when Photoshop has to use the scratch disk. The speed of Photoshop depends on the size of the file being worked on, the amount of RAM in the computer, and the computer's speed.

For example, if you are working with small images and your computer has a lot of RAM, Photoshop and the computer system will not slow down.

To figure out how many States affect the speed of the computer, experiment with different size files, allotting more RAM to Photoshop and adjusting the number of States in the History options.

The rule of thumb is that the fewer States that are used, the less RAM is needed which makes the computer system respond faster.

In this section the History options for v 5.5 are shown. We mention this because it is slightly different from v 5.0.2.

21

# RECOVERY STRATEGY

## USING SNAPSHOTS

### SNAPSHOT AT-A-GLANCE

1. Correct or alter the image overall.
2. Take a Snapshot. Then use Undo (optional).
3. Select the Source of the new Snapshot.
4. Click on the Top Snapshot on the right side area.
5. Select the History Brush from the Tools Palette and correct the image.

### SNAPSHOT PAINTING TIP

If possible use long brush stokes. Then use Undo **Cmd/Cntrl**/Z. This makes it easier to see exactly what has or has not been painted in the image.

## USING THE SNAPSHOT

There are a variety of techniques for using the History Palette, Snapshots, and States. The next few pages illustrate some of the simpler, yet powerful, ways to work. The History Palette used with an image processing tool is one of the easiest and most productive methods for correcting image areas that are poorly exposed, require selective corrections, or have dirt and blemishes embedded in them. This method is used with the History default setting so a Snapshot is automatically created.

**1. Correct the image overall.**

Use Curves, Levels, or a filter to adjust the image overall. This Snapshot makes the correction for a specific image area.

Original Image that requires retouching.

**2. Take a Snapshot.**

Use History Palette Pop-out menu.

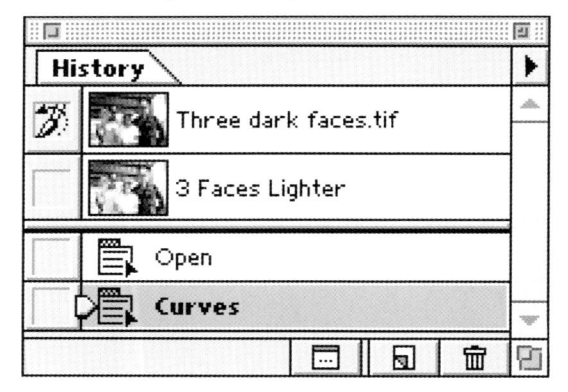

The above example shows the History Palette with a new Snapshot. In this example, the Snapshot information is the overall image that has been corrected by using Curves.

**3. Select the Source of the new Snapshot.**

The Source of the Snapshot is in the little square area on the left side of the History Palette.

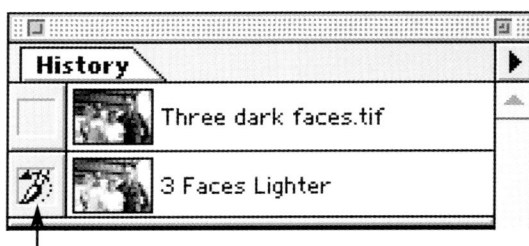

Source for the new Snapshot

**4. Click on the Top Snapshot.**

Be sure to click on the name of the right side area. This will make the Snapshot active.

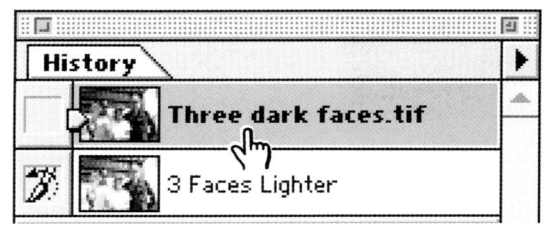

**5. Select the History Brush from the Tools Palette.**

Set the brush size and opacity, then correct the faces. Now paint with the lighter image in the areas that need it.

This example illustrates how powerful and easy the Snapshot method is. It allows you to make varying tonal adjustments to image areas because you can use different opacity values with the History brush. In this example, different opacities were used to even out the dark areas on each of the retouched faces.

## USING HISTORIES, BUT... THERE IS NO ORIGINAL SNAPSHOT

Sometimes the History Options are set up so there is not an original Snapshot. If you have begun your working session and find that there is no option to paint back to the original image, here are some alternatives for what can be done.

**1. Do a Save As on the file.**

In this example this Saved As file will be called file #2.

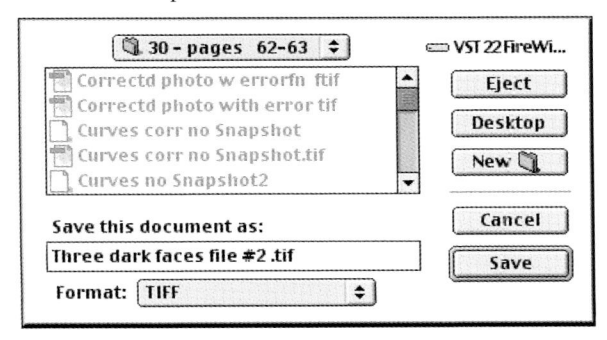

**2. Reopen the original file and take a Snapshot.**

The example above shows the Snapshot that is available from the original image.

**3. Drag-n-Drop the new Snapshot to file #2.**

This will place the new Snapshot in the History Palette of file #2. Then click on the Source of the new Snapshot from the original file and be sure you are in the History brush with the correct brush size and opacity. Paint back to the original.

**History Palette without Snapshot example**

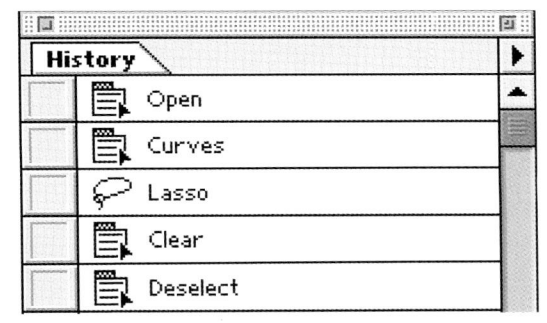

The example above shows there is no Snapshot just States of a working session in the History Palette.

**History Palette with Snapshot Example**

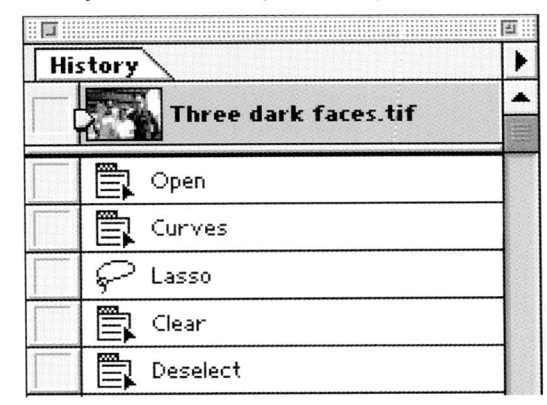

The example above shows the Snapshot from image #1 was Dragged-n-Dropped onto the file #2 image. For this technique to work, the original file and the file without the Snapshot have to be the same resolution and have the same vertical and horizontal dimensions. See sidebar about why recovery methods fail.

# RECOVERY STRATEGY
## HISTORY STATES AND SNAPSHOTS

### WHY RECOVERING METHODS FAIL

Sometimes when working with Histories, a warning Icon appears that indicates the Snapshot or States will not work with the History brush options. The reasons usually are:

1. The image resolution has been changed with either Cropping or Image Size.
2. The Canvas Size has changed.
3. The Mode has been changed.
   To avoid these type of problems, make back-up versions of the image after changing the cropping and changing resolutions, the Mode, or Canvas Size. Then recovering from a mistake becomes manageable.

**Tip:** Be aware when working with the History Palette that it is sometimes unforgiving especially when the Linear Option is selected. The History remembers all the States of an image. This can make it difficult to recover from an error. If that situation happens, then use the Pop-out menu from the History Palette and create a New Document of the image you are viewing. Once the new document is created, it is possible to Drag-n-Drop previously created States to new documents.

23

# RECOVERY STRATEGY

## REVIEW

The Recovery section covers three fundamental ways to recover from making imaging errors.

1. **Revert.** This simple method takes you back to the last saved version of the file.

2. **Undo/Redo.**

   This is one of the most common ways to recover. However, this only takes you back one step in the process.

   Another effective way to use **Undo/Redo** is to make a change to a file, such as a tone correction to an image, and then use **Undo/Redo.** This strategy allows you to toggle between the original view of the file and the correction.

3. **History Options.**

   The History options are Photoshop's solution for multiple undos. The key to success with the History Palette is to learn its behavior. The History Palette uses States and Snapshots.

**States Behavior**

- States represent a Photoshop menu option or tool that was applied to an image.

- The History Palette creates a list of States, so the last State becomes the most current State.

- Linear and Non-Linear States makes the History list very easy to use as recovery options. This is done just by using the mouse to click on the History Palettes list of States.

- Non-Linear States provides the greatest number of recovery options.

**Snapshot Behavior**

- Snapshots can be created from an opened image during a working session.

- Snapshots are a temporary copy of the image you are currently viewing.

- Snapshots make it easy to recover. They make it possible to paint back to the original image file that the Snapshot represents. See page 22.

**States and Snapshot Behavior**

- Each State and Snapshot has a Source. The Source area is on the left side of the State or Snapshot.

- States and Snapshots can be duplicated to become a New Document that is an image.

- Be aware that States and Snapshots are only available during the working session. When the image is saved and closed, the working session is over and the States and Snapshots disappear.

# MASKING BASICS

Selections Tools ..................................26
Working with Selections ........................28
Selections to Channels .........................30
Displaying Channels ............................31
Channel Viewing Options ......................32
Naming and Inverting Channels .............33
Feathering .........................................34
Quick Mask .........................................36
Paths .................................................38
Using Paths to Create Selections ...........40
Silhouetting & Clipping Paths ................41
Review...............................................42

# MASKING BASICS

## SELECTION TOOLS

### ANTI-ALIASING

Anti-Aliasing is an option in all of the Photoshop Selection Tools. The anti-aliasing technique is used to reduce, eliminate, or smooth the jagged edges (jaggies) of a diagonal line or curve of a Selection. To avoid the jaggies, *Anti-aliased* should always be checked on.

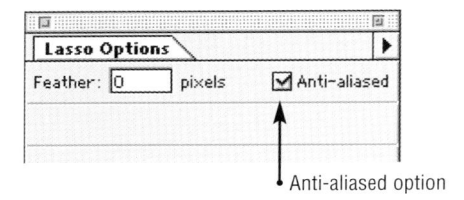

• Anti-aliased option

### HOW TO DESELECT A SELECTION.

The Deselect option is a command to remove the Selection from the image. Deselect can be accessed through the Select Menu or by the keyboard shortcut **Cmd/Cntrl Shift D**. This is one of the most practical ways to Deselect a Selection.

**Tip:** An option when making the first Selection with this tool is to hold down the **Opt/Alt** key for straight line Selections by clicking and moving the mouse to the next point and then clicking again to create the next point.

## MAIN SELECTION TOOLS

- The Rectangle or the Oval Marquee are activated by clicking and holding on the tool or by using the shortcut, the **M** key. Use the **Shift + M** key to toggle between Marquee options.

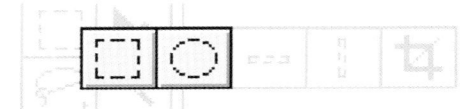

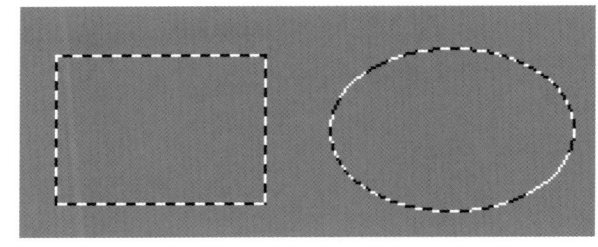

The above example shows Rectangular and Oval Selections.

- The Lasso icon is activated by clicking on the Tool Menu icons or by using the keyboard shortcut, the **L** key. Use the Shift + **L** key to toggle between Marquee options.

**The Lasso Tool has three options.**

1. **Free-form Lasso that allows freehand drawing of Selections.**

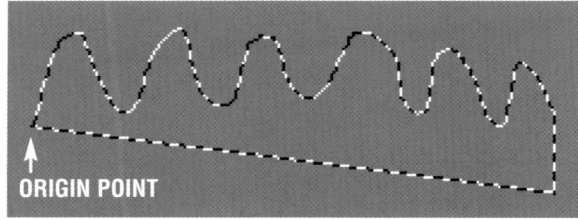

ORIGIN POINT

The example above shows a freehand drawn Selection. Note the lower right side and how the Selection becomes a straight line. The mouse button was released. This causes the Lasso to return to its origin point to finish the Selection.

2. **The Polygon Lasso is used to create straight line Selections.**

   Click on single points to start a Selection and continue Selections. Double click to end the Selection.

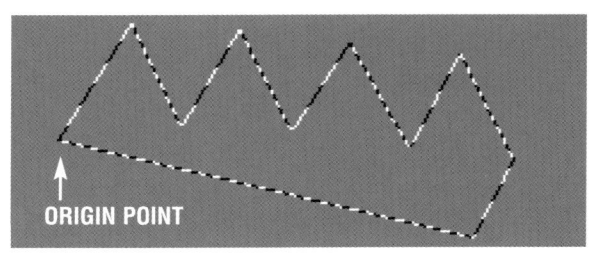

ORIGIN POINT

The above example shows a Selection Created with point-to-point segments using the Polygon Lasso. Note the lower right side and how the Selection becomes a straight line. Double clicking on the mouse button caused this to happen. The Polygon Lasso returned to its origin point to finish the Selection.

3. **The Magnetic Lasso has options for automatically making Selections on the edges of images.**

   Testing is an important part of this tool because it can be confusing sometimes. Our advice is to keep it simple when using the Magnetic Lasso. We mean, after the settings are adjusted, move the Magnetic Lasso around the image areas you want to make a Selection. Double click to end the Magnetic Lasso Selection or use **Return/Enter**.

26

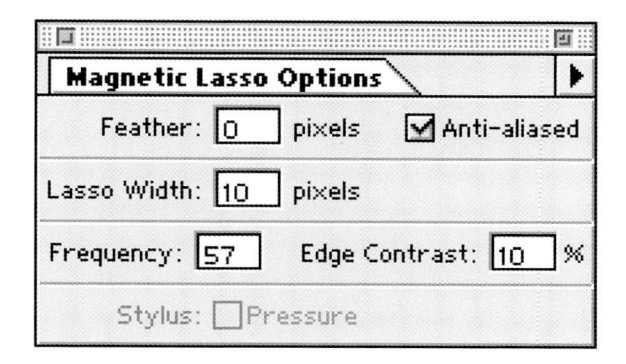

**MAGNETIC LASSO OPTIONS:**

These options make it possible to determine how to draw Selections automatically on an image area.

- **Feather** - This defines the softness of a Selection's edge.
- **Lasso Width** - This determines how close to move the cursor to the edge of an image area where you want to create a Selection.
- **Frequency** - This determines the rate at which points are created that guide where the Selection is created on the image.
- **Edge Contrast** - This determines how much contrast is needed between each image's edge areas so Photoshop can make an accurate selection.

The two examples above shows the Magnetic Lasso points (on the left) and the resulting Selection (on the right).

- The **Magic Wand** icon is activated by clicking the Tool Menu icon or by using the keyboard shortcut, the **W** key.

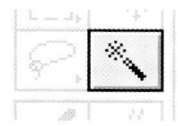

The Magic Wand creates Selected areas that are based on the pixel value of the point that was clicked on in the image and the Tolerance value in Magic Wand Options.

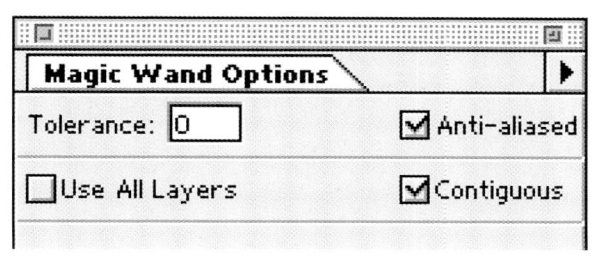

To make sense out of the Magic Wand Tool, here are two examples that use gradients to explain Tolerance:

In the first gradient, we clicked on a pixel value of 100 and used a Tolerance value of 10. In this situation, a Selection was created with pixel values ranging from 90 to 110.

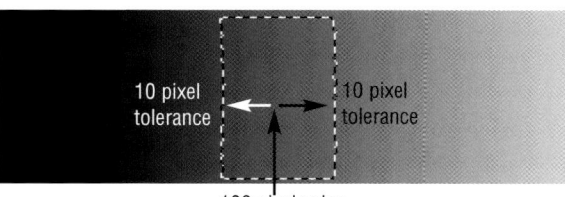

In the second gradient, we clicked on a pixel value of 100 and used a Tolerance value of 50. In this situation, a Selection was created with pixel values ranging from 50 to 150.

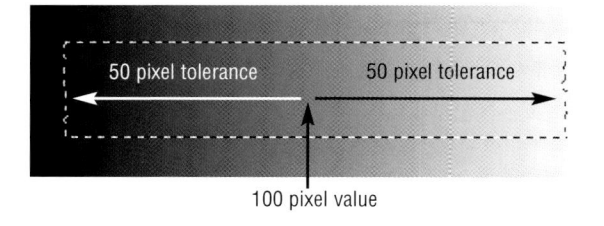

# MASKING BASICS
## SELECTION TOOLS

**EXPANDING SELECTIONS**

Another method to expand the size and shape of Selections is to use Grow and Similar options under the Select Menu.

- Grow will enlarge contiguous areas of the Selection.
- Similar expands the Selection in non-contiguous image areas.

This method works with all of the Selection Tools. The Tolerance settings in the Magic Wand Tool affects the amount the Selection expands.

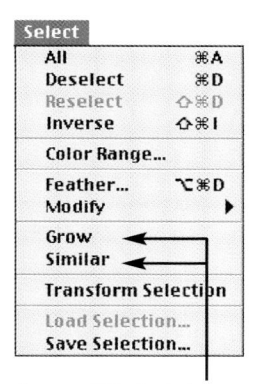

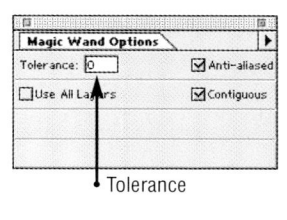

Grow and Similar helps expand Selections

**Magic Wand Reminder:**

- All Selections including the Magic Wand use the **Shift** key to add to a Selected image area.
- To subtract the Selected area, hold down the **Opt/Alt** key.

27

# MASKING BASICS
## WORKING WITH SELECTIONS

### PRACTICE, PRACTICE, PRACTICE
Practice and experimentation are the best ways to learn about Selections. These are the fundamentals to work on.

1. Creating a basic Selection.
2. Adding and subtracting from Selections.
3. Inversing a Selection's active and non-active areas.
4. Saving Selections as Channels.
5. Loading Selections onto an image.

### SELECTIONS VS MARCHING ANTS
Marching Ants is another way to describe a Selection.

The Channels Palette is accessed from the Window Menu.

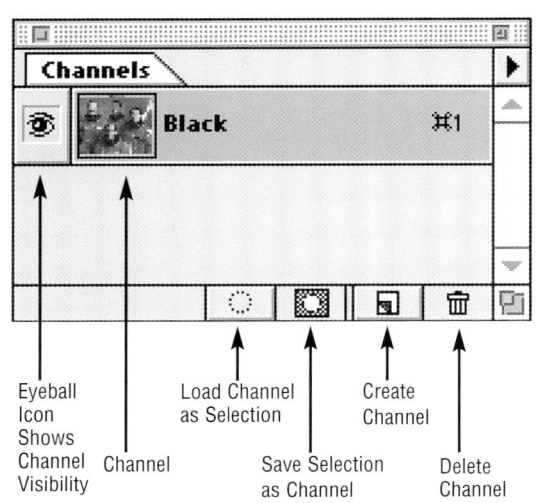

Eyeball Icon Shows Channel Visibility
Channel
Load Channel as Selection
Save Selection as Channel
Create Channel
Delete Channel

Selections are tools used to mask or isolate specific image areas. Think of the white area of a Channel as the active portion of the Selection and the black area of the Channel as the non-active portion of the Channel. To gain experience using Selections and Masking, familiarize yourself with the five critical Selection and Channel topics listed in this section.

### 1. HOW TO CREATE A SELECTION
The Tool Palette provides access to the Rectangle and Elliptical Marquees, the Lasso, and the Magic Wand.

- When using the Rectangle or Elliptical Marquees, click and drag the mouse over the image to scroll the Rectangle or Elliptical Selection over a specific area. Holding down the **Shift** key constrains your selection to a square or a circle.

- The Lasso Tool and its options allows freehand or point-to-point drawing of Selections by holding down the mouse button. Another Lasso Selection option for creating straight-line segments is to hold down the **Opt/Alt** key while clicking the mouse along successive points. This method only works when there are no Active Selections or using the Polygon Lasso Tool.

- The Magic Wand Tool creates a selection based on a chosen pixel value and a Tolerance value. Double click on the Wand Tool to activate the Magic Wand Options Palette. In the Magic Wand Options Palette select the Tolerance value, then go to the image and depress the mouse button over the image area where you wish to create a Selection. For more about the Selection creation, see page 26.

### ACTIVE AREAS
When a Selection is created, the Selected area becomes the **Active Selected areas.** This is the area within the boundaries of the Selection and is the image area that can be affected by image processing tools.

### NON-ACTIVE AREAS
The Non-active areas are outside of the Selected area.

**Tip:** If you are new to working with Selections, take some time to experiment with adding and subtracting Selections. Work with a tool like the Rectangular Marquee. Then practice using the **Shift** key to add and the **Opt/Alt** key to subtract.

### 2. ADD AND SUBTRACT FROM SELECTIONS
There are many instances when working with Selections that it is necessary to create more than one or to add or subtract from one.

- Hold the **Shift** key down to add to a Selection.
- Hold the **Cmd/Cntrl** key down to subtract from a Selection.

The above example shows the cause and effect of Adding and Subtracting Selections and then making a correction.
Two Rectangular Marquees were made by holding down the Shift key. Then the Lasso was used to Subtract an irregular portion of a Selected area. An extreme contrast correction was made with Curves to illustrate how the Selection was created.

The above example illustrates how a Selection works.
A Rectangular Selection was created, then the Active area was dramatically adjusted. The Non-Active areas were unaffected by the adjustment.

## 3. HOW TO INVERSE SELECTIONS

The Inverse option is a command to flip or reverse the sense of the Selection. Inverse can be accessed through the Select Menu or by the keyboard shortcut **Cmd/Cntrl/Shift/I.**

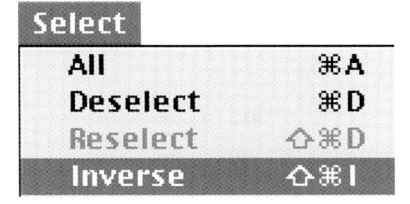

**Tip:** To understand how Selections work, make a Selection and then use the **Delete/Backspace** key. This will load the Background color into the Selection or delete the image data if it is on a Layer. Use the keyboard shortcut, the **D** key to set the Background color's default values to white. After you have seen the cause and effect of Loading the Background Color, apply Undo/Redo, **Cmd/Cntrl** Z.

This example shows what an image might look like when the Background Color is loaded into a newly created Selection.

This example illustrates what an image might look like when the Background Color is loaded into the Inversed Selection.

## 4. HOW TO SAVE SELECTIONS

When a Selection is saved, it becomes an Alpha Channel. This is a good way to save a difficult Selection you might want to use again later. This can be seen by displaying the Channel's Palette.
To create an Alpha Channel:

- Create a Selection on a grayscale image.
- Go to the **Select** *Menu>Save Selection* Option.
- OK it as a New Channel.

An option is to type in a name into this dialog box and then OK it.

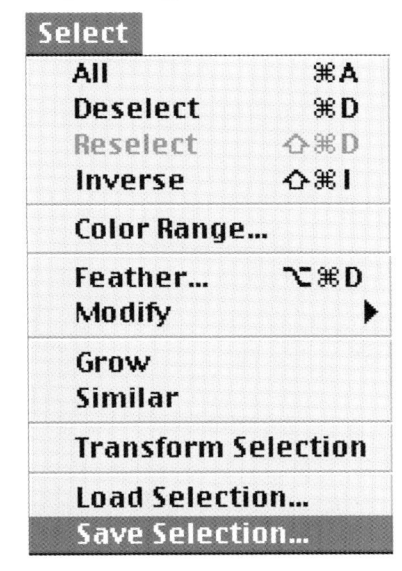

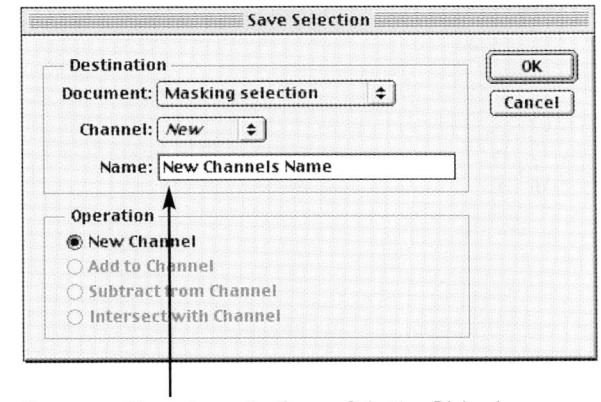

To name a Channel; use the Save a Selection Dialog box.

# MASKING BASICS
## WORKING WITH SELECTIONS

When Saving Selections as Channels, note the Channel's Palette before and after you OK the New Channel.

Before Channels Palette

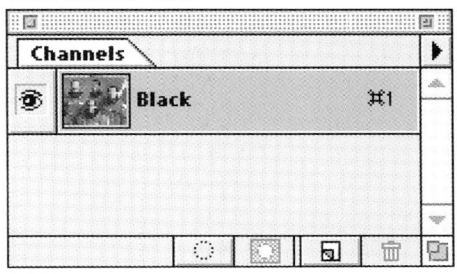

Channels Palette with a new Channel

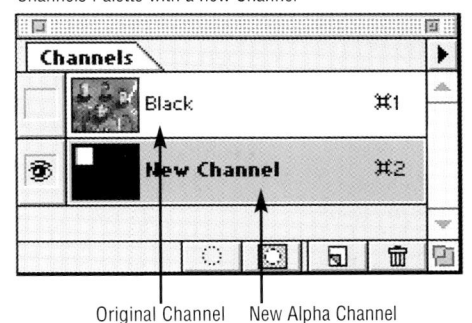

Original Channel    New Alpha Channel

### 24 IS THE MAXIMUM NUMBER OF CHANNELS

While this might not seem like a lot of storage for masks, we have seen only a few situations where more masks are required. If more masking storage is required, then it is possible to use Layers for loading Selections. See pages 82-85 about Layers Basics.

# MASKING BASICS
## SELECTIONS TO CHANNELS

### UNIVERSAL WAY TO LOAD SELECTIONS

In Photoshop, there are standard and easy-to-use ways to load Selections from the Channels, Layers, and Path Palettes.

- Hold down the **Cmd/Cntrl** key and Click on a particular **Channel**, **Layer**, or **Path** in the respective Palette to load the **Channel**, **Layer**, or **Path** information as a Selection.

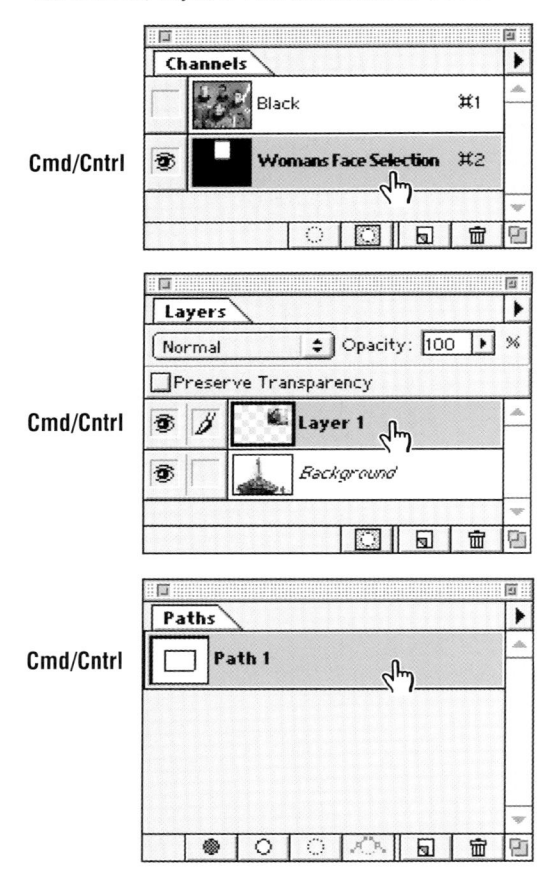

### MAKING THE CONNECTION BETWEEN SELECTIONS AND CHANNELS

Selections and Channels are part of Photoshop's masking system to isolate specific image areas. When a Selection is saved, it becomes a Channel. If a Channel has been created, it can be Loaded as a Selection.

### 5. HOW TO LOAD A SELECTION

There are a number of ways to load a Selection from Channel information.

1. **Use the Select Menu.** (This is usually the way novices get started with Loading Selections.)

    Go to the **Select Menu** after the Selection has been created and choose the Load Selection option while the Selection is highlighted in the Channels Palette.

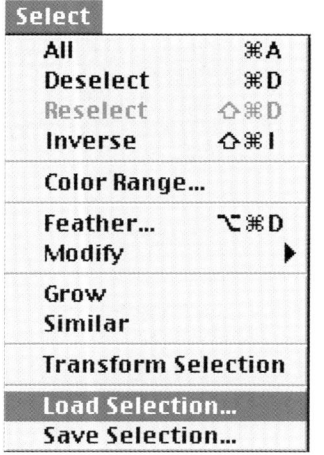

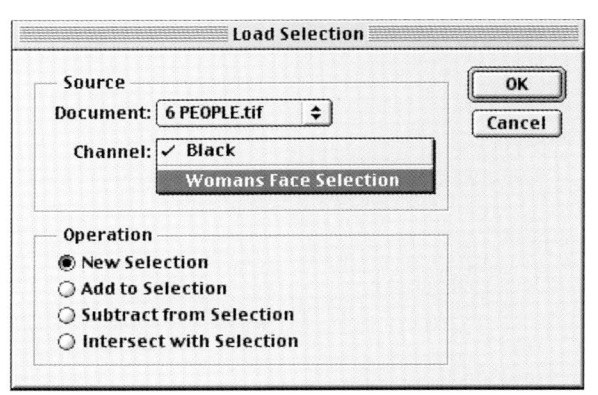

The above dialog box appears when using the Select Menu for loading a Selection from Channel data. Note the Pop-out menu and the other options when loading a Selection from a Channel to an image.

2. **Use the Channels Palette.**

    Drag-n-Drop the new Channel from the Channels Palette to the lower left icon of the Channels Palette.

    To better use this option, become familiar with the features of the Channels Palette.

Before beginning, be sure the image you wish to work on is displayed on your computer screen.

30

Learning to work with Channels can be difficult, so it is important to learn how to display Channels. Click on the Channel you wish to display. Be careful to avoid clicking on the Channel Eyeball icon that is well to the left of the Channel Thumbnail or you will hide or reveal the Channel. If the Channel Eyeball icon is turned, it will make learning and working with Channels confusing. See the sidebar.

# MASKING BASICS

## DISPLAYING CHANNELS

### DISPLAYING A CHANNEL

Click once on the Channel in the Channels Palette will display that particular Channel on your computer screen.

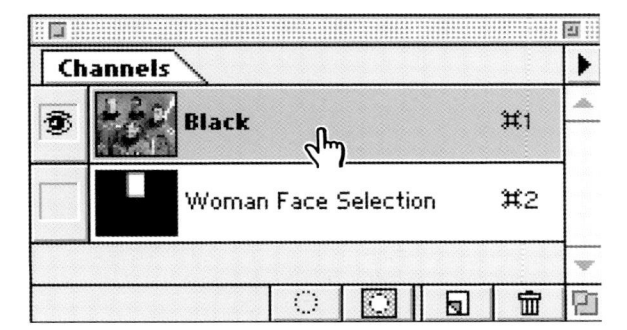

### DISPLAYING A CHANNEL MASK

Click once on the Channel Mask icon or its name in the Channels Palette will display the Channel on your computer screen.

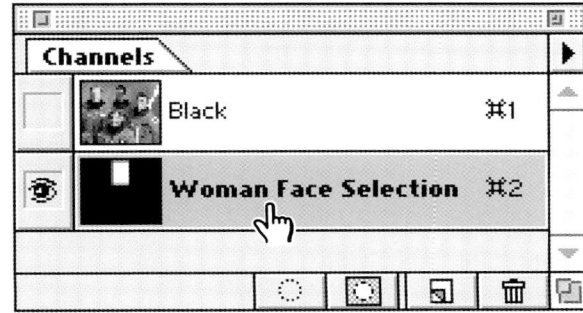

### WARNING! WARNING!

Clicking on an Alpha Channel Eyeball icon when the image Channel is visible on your computer screen will cause a red partially opaque mask (Quick Mask) to display on the image. This can be confusing. If you accidentally click on the Alpha Channel Eyeball and turn on the Quick Mask, click on it again to turn it off.

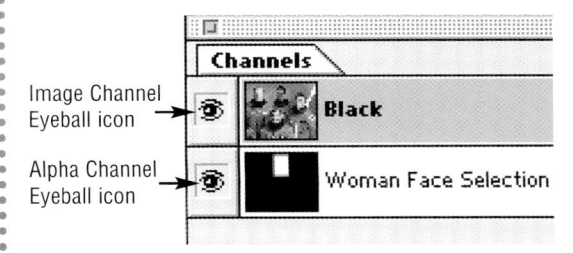

Image Channel Eyeball icon

Alpha Channel Eyeball icon

The above example illustrates the result of clicking on the Channel that represents the image.

The above example illustrates the result of clicking on the Channel that represents the mask.

**TIP:** A way to think about a Channel Mask is that the white areas allow the light or active area through to be worked on and the Black areas protect the image from being worked on (hey, its a mask).

The image above represents what happen when both Eyeballs in the Channels Palette are activated.

31

# MASKING BASICS
## CHANNEL VIEWING OPTIONS

### VIEWING IN QUICK MASK

There are two ways to enter and exit the Quick Mask Mode: (1) Click on the Quick Mask Mode Icon in the Tool Palette. (2) Depress the Q key.

When viewing in the Quick Mask Mode, the Masked Areas and Selected Areas Options affect the way Quick Mask is viewed. See page 36 for more about Quick Mask.

The above example shows how the *Masked Areas* affects the way Quick Mask is viewed on an image.

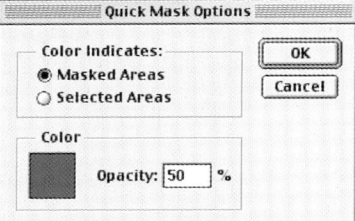

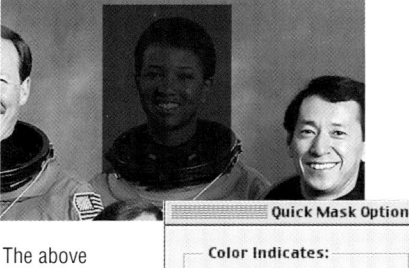

The above example shows how the *Selected Areas* affects the way Quick Mask is viewed on an image.

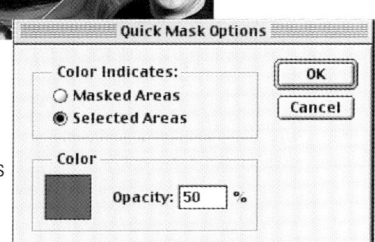

### CHANNEL VIEWING OPTIONS IN BLACK OR WHITE

After double clicking on a Channel in the Channels Palette, the Channels options menu becomes available. In this dialog box are the Masked Areas and Selected Areas options. These affect how Channels and Quick Masks are displayed.

When the Masked Area option is selected, the Active areas of a Channel appear as white and the Quick Mask Active areas appear as being clear.

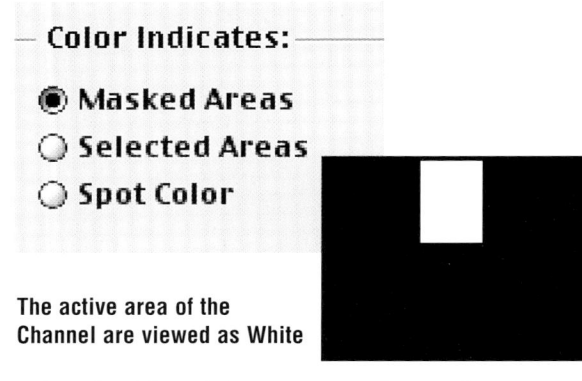

**The active area of the Channel are viewed as White**

When the Selected Area option is chosen, the Active areas of a Channel appear black and the Quick Mask Active area appears as a color.

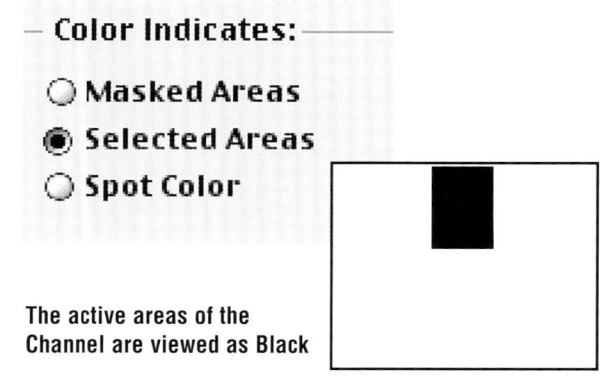

**The active areas of the Channel are viewed as Black**

Channels masks work the same way with either viewing option. The only difference is the way high contrast masked areas are viewed on the monitor.

### WHICH CHANNEL VIEWING OPTION IS BEST?

This is a tough question to answer and depends (1) on your previous experience with Photoshop, (2) other types of high-end imaging tools you have worked with, and (3) your current workflow.

We believe it is better to learn and use the Masked Areas option until Channels are completely understood and then change to the Selected Areas option. Two reasons for this are that the Masked Areas option is the most logical way to (1) teach and (2) view Channel masks. The Masked Areas option fits best with the Masking metaphor. The white areas of the mask are the Active image area that are going to be corrected and the black areas (the Mask) protect the image. A third reason to use the Masked Areas option is because it is the only way a Layer Mask can be viewed (see page 86).

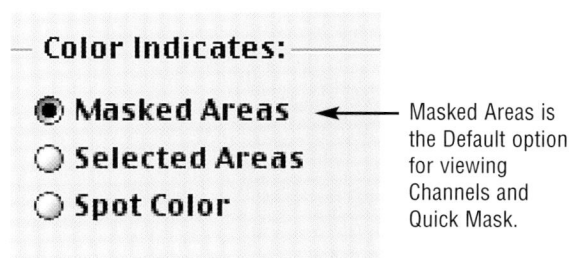

Masked Areas is the Default option for viewing Channels and Quick Mask.

## ANOTHER OPTION FOR NAMING CHANNELS

Double click on the Channel in the Channels Palette. This takes you to a dialog box to type in a name.

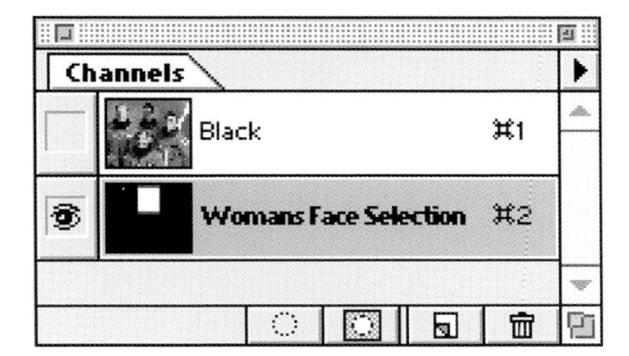

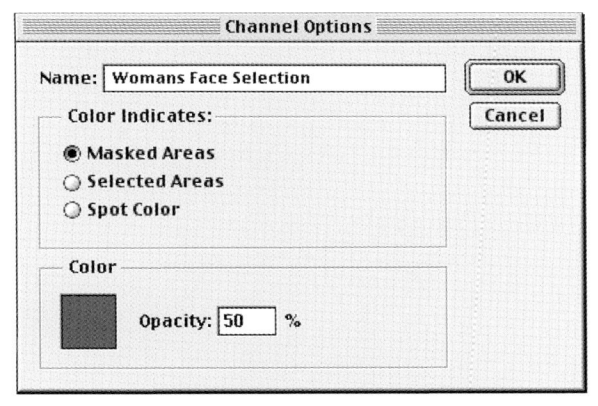

## ALWAYS NAME CHANNELS

No matter how many Channels are being used, it is always best to give them a descriptive name. This makes it possible to identify how the Channel mask was originally used.

## INVERT CHANNELS

A saved hard-edged Selection (a Channel) has two areas, white and black:

### White areas
The white areas are a visual representation of the Selection's active area.

### Black areas
The black area is a visual representation of the Selection's non-active area.

When a Channel is Inverted, it changes the white areas to black and black areas to white. Practically speaking, this is another method to Inverse the Selection.

This technique becomes important when working on a Channel. To Invert a Channel, the Channel needs to be displayed. To display the Channel, click on the Channel in the Channels Palette. Go to *Image>Adjust>Invert*.

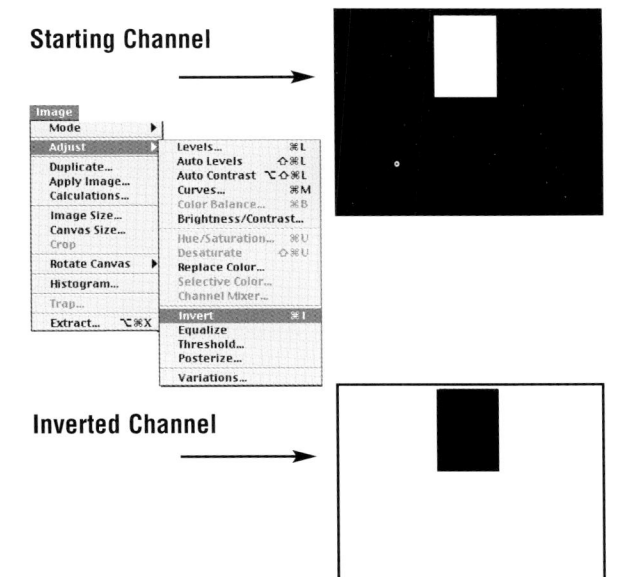

**Starting Channel**

**Inverted Channel**

# MASKING BASICS
## NAMING AND INVERTING CHANNELS

### BE CAREFUL WITH INVERT AND INVERSE

*Invert* is an image processing feature that changes the tones of an image. Remember, a grayscale image is just a Channel with variable tones.

*Inverse* is a Selection option that flips or reverses the direction of the Selection.

The image above is a normal image.

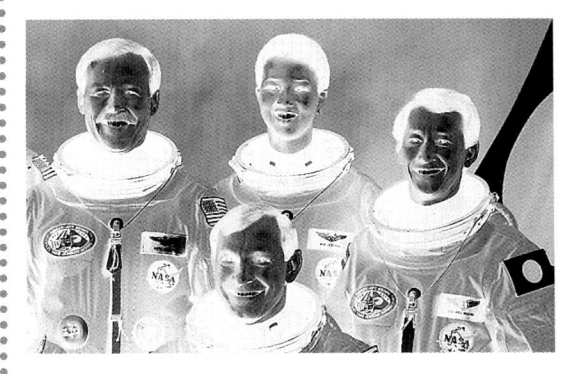

The image above has been Inverted. The tones become the exact opposite of the normal image. The white tones become black and black tones become white.

33

# MASKING BASICS

## FEATHERING

This example illustrates one way to use Feathering, a Selection to create a soft-edged vignette.

1. Use the Rectangular Marquee to create a Selection.

2. Apply Feathering to the Rectangular Marquee Selection. The Feather amount depends on the effect desired and the image's resolution.
   - Notice how the corners of the Selection have become rounded.

3. Inverse the Selection. Use **Select>Inverse**.

4. Fill the Inversed Selection. Use **Edit>Fill>Select White**.

## FEATHERING A SELECTION IS A METHOD TO CREATE A SOFT-EDGE ON A SELECTION

Soft-edged Selections are used to create transitions between masked image areas. A soft-edged Selection is typically used when selective corrections are made to grayscale images. In this process, an image mask is made with a Selection, then Levels or Curves are used to adjust the image's tones within the active Selected area. In a lot of correction situations, hard-edged Selections can cause a harsh or undesirable effect around the edges of the Selection. Soft-edged or Feathered Selections are used to avoid this problem. Here are two ways to create a Feathered Selection.

### SOFT-EDGED SELECTION OPTION 1

1. **Create a hard-edged Selection with a Selection Tool.**

   In this example, the Lasso Tool was used to create a hard-edged Selection of the image area (the woman's head) that are to be selectively corrected. (for more about Quick Mask, see page 36).

2. **Use the Feather option in the Select Menu.**

   The keyboard shortcut is **Cmd/Cntrl, Opt/Alt D**. Keyboard in a value to soften the Selection's edge. 1 to 5 pixels are typical for 300 dpi images. We used 3 pixel Feather to soften the Selection's edges.

3. **Use Levels or Curves to correct the image in the active Selection area.**

Use 1-5 pixels for 300 dpi images to soften the Selection's edge.

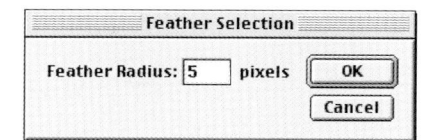

### COMPARING SOFT AND HARD EDGED SELECTIONS

In the examples below, we did two things out of the ordinary to illustrate the positive effects of feathering: (1) The tone correction was exaggerated and (2) the Selection was not totally accurate.

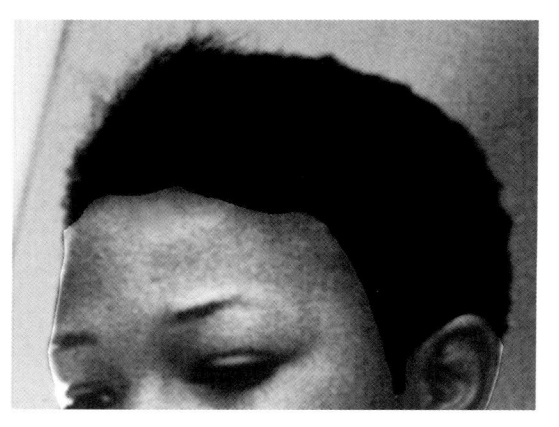

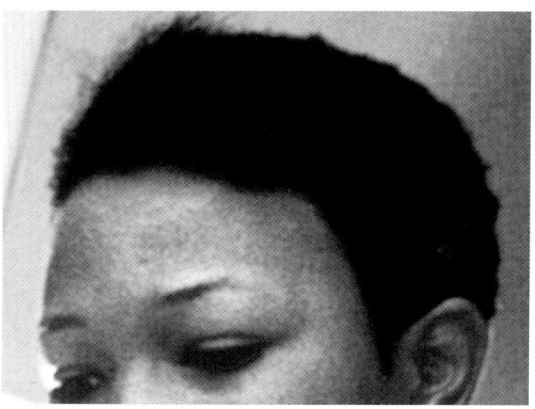

- The top image used a hard-edged Selection. Note the rough edges of the silhouette around the face and hair areas.
- The bottom image used a Selection with a five pixel feather. Notice the smooth transitions around the head and hair area.

## SOFT-EDGED SELECTION OPTION 2.

This option is a flexible method for customizing a mask to create a soft-edged Selection.

1. **Create a hard-edged Selection.**

   Save it as a Channel or use a Channel that is already saved.

2. **Blur the Channels edges.**

   Use Gaussian Blur to soften this Channel. Other filters can be used, but Gaussian Blur is the most flexible and powerful one. Gaussian Blur values ranges from 0.1 to 250 pixels. There are no typical values for creating soft-edges because each image has a different resolution. Experiment with different settings such as 3 to 5 pixels for close-cut silhouettes.

3. **Load the Selection onto the image.**

4. **Use Levels or Curves to correct the image in the active selected area.**

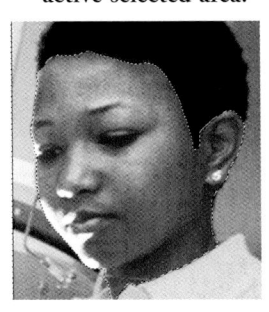

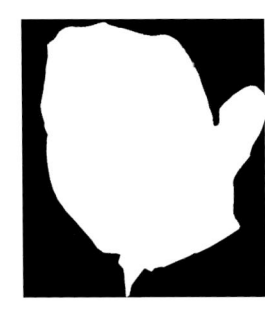

The left image above shows the Selection. The right image above is the Channel of that saved Hard-edged Selection.

The above left image is the Channel that has 5 pixel Gaussian Blur applied. The right image has been corrected using the mask.

## FEATHERING PART OF A CHANNEL

One good reason to know how to work with Selections and Channels is to selectively correct portions of an image area with and without soft-edges. Here is an example.

1. **Create a hard-edged Selection.** Save it as a Channel or use a Channel that is already saved.

2. **Display the Channel.** Click on the Channel icon. Make a Selection over the part of the Channel that you wish to be come feathered or soft.

3. **Apply a Blur.** Use the *Blur Filter>Gaussian Blur* to soften the area inside the Selection. We used 3 pixels.

4. **Display the main image.** Load the newly created Selection onto the image.

5. **Use Levels or Curves to correct the image in the active selected area.**

soft-edge areas   hard-edge areas   soft-edge areas

The above image is an extreme example to show how soft-edged portions of a mask effect an image.

# MASKING BASICS
## FEATHERING

### SELECT ALL

The *Select All* option (**Cmd/Cntrl** A) creates a Selection around the complete image areas. This is one of the easiest methods to Select an entire image.

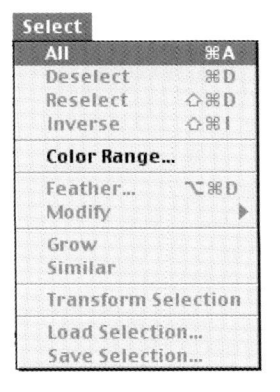

| Select | |
|---|---|
| All | ⌘A |
| Deselect | ⌘D |
| Reselect | ⇧⌘D |
| Inverse | ⇧⌘I |
| Color Range... | |
| Feather... | ⌥⌘D |
| Modify | ▶ |
| Grow | |
| Similar | |
| Transform Selection | |
| Load Selection... | |
| Save Selection... | |

**Feather Tip:** While we suggest Feather values between 1-5, the only way to determine the correct amount of feather/softening is to experiment with different Feather values on various types of images.

# MASKING BASICS

## QUICK MASK

### USE SELECTIONS WITHIN QUICK MASK

As experience is gained, most Photoshoppers work with both Selections and Quick Mask to create and fine-tune Selections. A typical scenario is to use the Lasso or the Magic Wand to create the basic Selection. Use Quick Mask to refine the edges of the Selection with different size brushes. Small brushes are used to paint or unpaint Selections in hard-to-draw image areas and bigger brushes are used to paint or unpaint Selections in easy-to-access image areas.

### CREATE A SOFT EDGE WITH QUICK MASK

Soft edges such as vignettes are created with the Feather command. The results of using this feature is often difficult to visualize. These steps help you see soft edges on Quick Mask.

- Create a hard-edged Selection.
- Enter the Quick Mask Mode.
- Use Gaussian Blur.

Example of Quick Mask Mode with Gaussian Blur applied.

## QUICK MASK SUCCESS TIPS

The Quick Mask feature is an extension of the Selection and Masking tools. The Quick Mask feature is a visual tool that uses brushes to add or subtract from the Quick Mask areas. A combination of brushes can be use to create soft-edged or hard-edged Selections. When you finish working on the Quick Mask, the painted Quick Mask areas become the Selection.

If you have never worked with the Quick Mask mode before, it takes some experimentation to learn how to enter and exit the Quick Mask mode and how to paint with different kinds of brushes. Practice the keyboard shortcuts. See the Quick Mask Success Tips below.

### 1. ENTER QUICK MASK.

To enter the Quick Mask mode, use the mouse to click on the Quick Mask mode icon or use the keyboard shortcut and type **Q**.

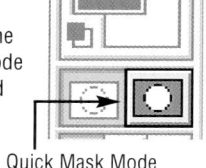

Quick Mask Mode

### 2. CRITICAL QUICK MASK KEYBOARD SHORTCUTS.

- Use the D key to default the foreground and background to black and white.
- Type the X key to toggle between them. This tip will allow painting and unpainting in the Quick Mask Mode.

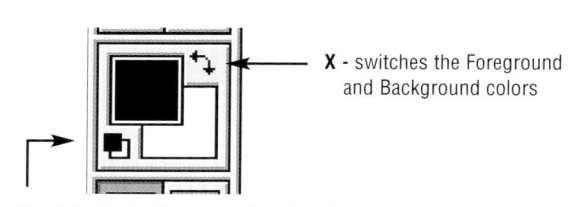

**X** - switches the Foreground and Background colors

**D** - Defaults the Foreground and Background colors to black and white.

### 3. WATCH THE CHANNELS PALETTE.

This is another method to determine if you are in or out of the Quick Mask Mode.

### 4. LEARN THE BRUSHES.

Once in Quick Mask mode, learn how to use the brushes to paint or unpaint the Mask on the image you wish to selectively correct.

The Eraser Tool offers easy access to four brush options for painting or unpainting the Quick Mask:

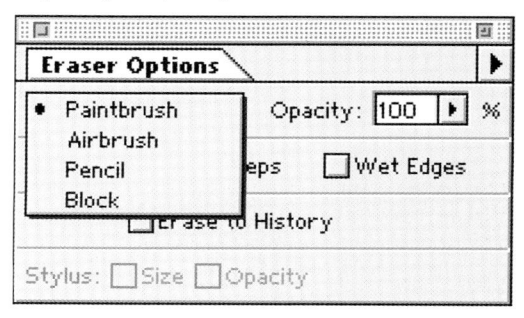

**Tip:** Use the keyboard numbers 0-9 to change painting opacity in 10% increments or type in two digits for more accuracy.

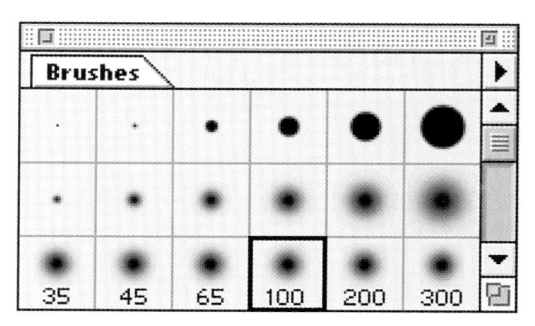

**Tip:** Use the Bracket keys to increase and decrease brush sizes.

### 5. EXIT QUICK MASK.

To enter the Quick Mask mode use the mouse to click on the Quick Mask mode icon or use the keyboard shortcut **Q**.

## QUICK MASK BASICS

1. **Make the Quick Mask easier to see.**

   Create a Selection on the image.

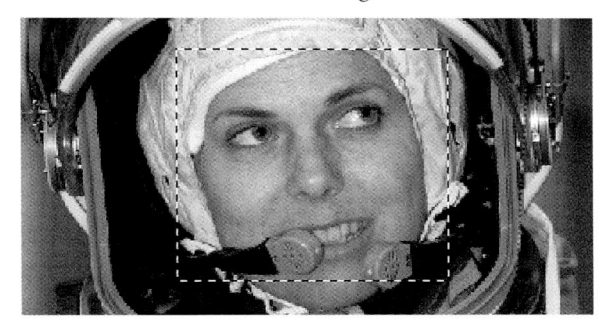

   The above example shows the Rectangular Marquee before entering the Quick Mask Mode.

2. **Enter the Quick Mask mode.**

   Use the mouse to click on the Quick Mask mode icon or use the keyboard shortcut **Q**.

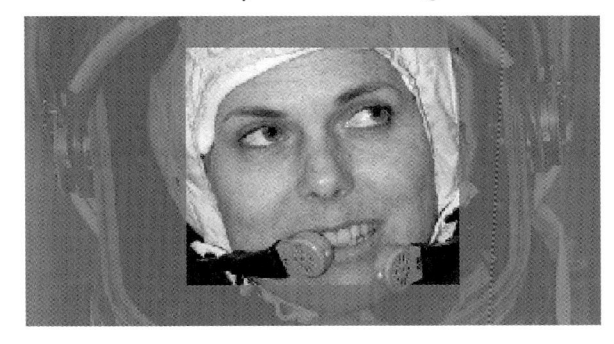

   The above example is of the effects of entering the Quick Mask Mode. The Selected area changed to a Mask that represents the Rectangular Marquee.

3. **Select a brush. Set up the brushes in Quick Mask.**

   The brushes are used to paint or unpaint the Mask on the image areas you wish to selectively correct. Painting and unpainting is done by using the X key to switch the defaulted (black and white) Foreground and Background colors.

   - Select a brush and set it to 100% opacity. If the opacity is less than 100%, then the image will only be partially Selected.

   **Brush Tip:** Experiment with different Brush edges to create soft edges when painting the Quick Mask. To change the edge of the brush, double click on the Brush in the Brushes Palette or use the Palettes Pop-out menu.

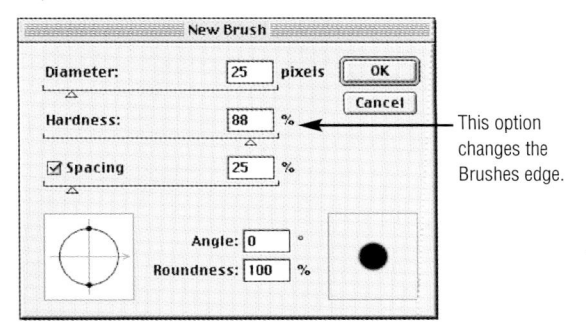

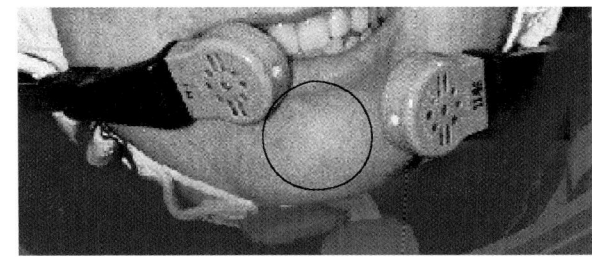

   This option changes the Brushes edge.

   The above example shows the effects of using Quick Mask and a Brush. The circle in the image represents the size of the brush that is painting or unpainting the Quick Mask.

4. **Finish the mask and exit the Quick Mask mode.**

   Use the mouse to click on the Standard Photoshop mode icon or use the shortcut **Q**.

   An Option after exiting the Quick Mask Mode is to Save the Selection as a Channel. This will allow loading the Selection from the Channel data. See sidebar.

# MASKING BASICS
## QUICK MASK TIPS

### DISPLAY A CHANNEL WITHIN QUICK MASK

In some Quick Mask situations, you will want to view the Quick Mask as a high contrast Channel. Press the Tilda Key ~ when in Quick Mask Mode. This will display the Quick Mask as a Channel. In this Display mode, you can work on the high contrast Channel with Brushes, Filters, Image Processing, and Selection tools. To exit this option, press the Tilda Key ~ to return to Quick Mask.

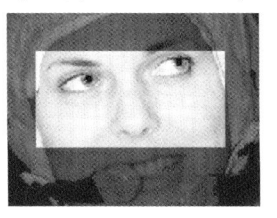

Example of Quick Mask Mode changed to a temporary Channel.

This technique is useful for cleaning up a dirty Quick Mask. For example, a Selection was originally created using the Magic Wand Tool and many small pixel size image areas did not get Selected. In this situation, it is hard to visually see these types of non-Selected areas on a colored Quick Mask. Displaying a Channel within the Quick Mask makes it easier to see and clean up the small pixel image areas with a brush or by filling a Selection with black or white.

### QUICK MASK SAVED AS A CHANNEL

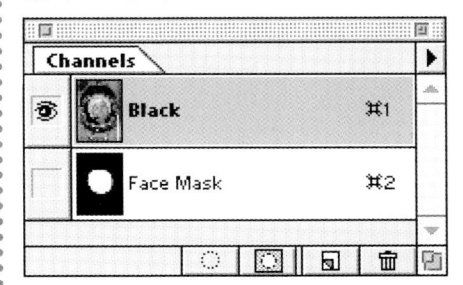

The example above shows the final Channel after the Quick Mask was created and then saved.

37

# MASKING BASICS
## PATHS

If the Pen Tool is new to you, it will take some experimentation to be come familiar with how it works. Use it to draw straight or curved lines, move Paths, add, subtract, and straighten Path points.

The Paths Palette is accessed from the Window Menu.

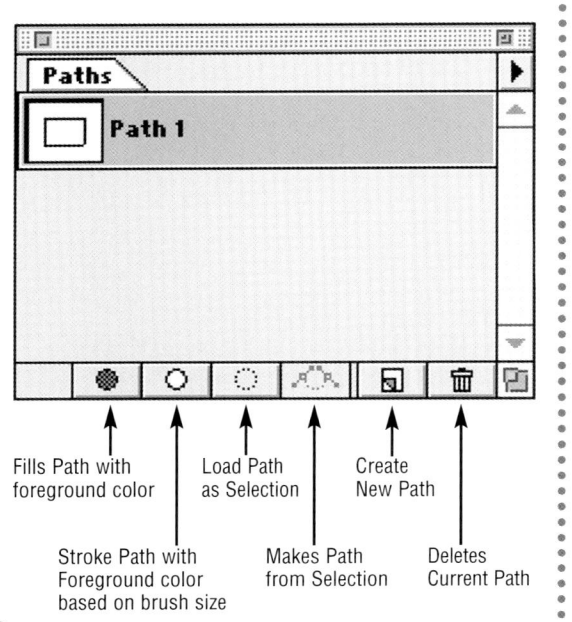

Fills Path with foreground color

Load Path as Selection

Create New Path

Stroke Path with Foreground color based on brush size

Makes Path from Selection

Deletes Current Path

The Pen Tool is the most precise way to create a Path, an outline around an image area, and then create a Selection from that outline. This tool has migrated from drawing programs such as Adobe Illustrator, Macromedia Freehand, or CorelDraw into Photoshop. The most common way to create a Path with Photoshop is to start with the Pen Tool.

The **Pen Tools** offers five ways to create anchor points.

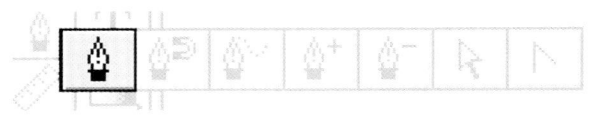

The **Pen Tool** is used to draw straight line segments or smoothed-edged points of a Path. Here are two methods for working with this tool.

1. **Straight Path Points.**

   To draw straight line segments, click with the mouse to create a Path point by depressing and releasing it. Then move the mouse to the next point on the image. Click with the mouse again by depressing and releasing.

2. **Curves Paths Points.**

   To draw curved lines, click the mouse to create a Path point, but do not release the mouse, then drag the handle on the Path point.

- To end a Path after part of an image area has been isolated, place the tip of the Pen Tool over the first Path point (an icon will appear on the lower right side of the Pen Tool).

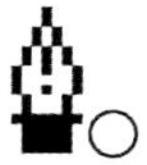

The above icon shows what the Pen Tool looks like when the tip of the Pen is placed over the first Path point. This is how a Path can be finished.

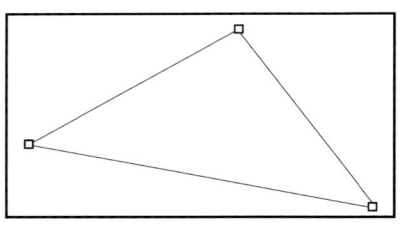

The above example shows the results of straight line path segments by using the mouse to click and create a point and then release the mouse button.

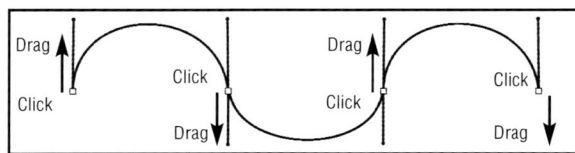

The above example shows the results of curved path segments using the click and drag method.

**The Magnetic Pen Tool** is used to create or draw smooth-edged points along the Path.

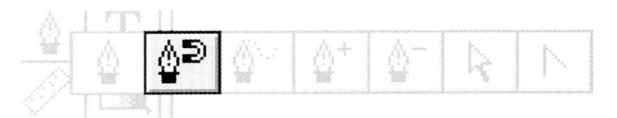

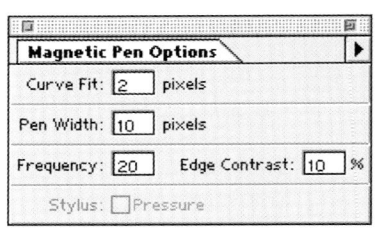

Double click on the Magnetic Pen tool for the options Palette.

### THE MAGNETIC PEN TOOL OPTIONS INCLUDE:

- Curve Fit - This options controls the smoothness of the Path. The values range between 0.5 and 10. Lower values make it possible to follow edges more carefully and higher values provide few Path points and smoother transitions between points.

- Pen Width - This determines how close to move the Pen to the edge of an image area where you want to create a Path. The values range between 1 and 40. Lower values make it possible to create smoother edges and higher values make possible to follow edges more carefully, but the Path point transitions are not smooth between the points.

- Frequency - This determine the rate at which anchor Path points are created on the image. The values range between 5 and 40. The lower values mean fewer points and higher values mean more points.

- Edge Contrast - This determines how much contrast is need between each image area so Photoshop can make an accurate Path. The values range between 1 and 100. The lower values allow the Path to distinguish between image contrast.

# MASKING BASICS
## PATHS

**The Free form Pen Tool** is used to create Paths with a drawing motion instead of using the point-click-and-release or a click-and- drag method.

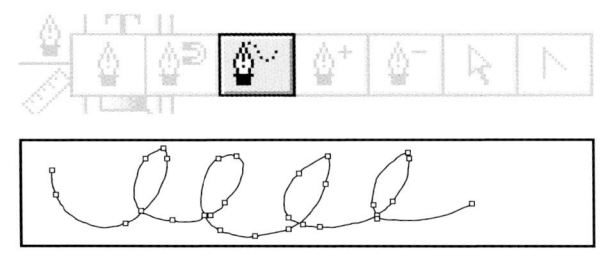

Example of Bezier Path

### Add a Point to the Path Pen Tool

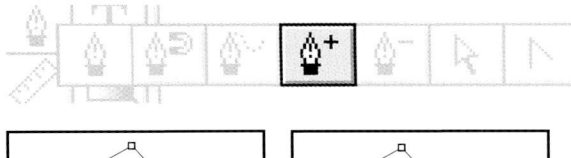

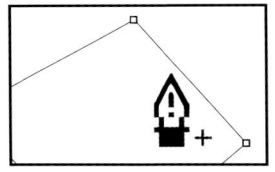

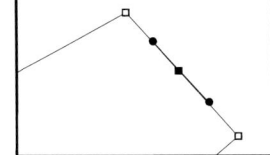

The Add-Anchor-Point Tool was used to click on the center area of the Path and added a curved Path point (the image on the right).

### Subtract a Point from the Path Pen Tool

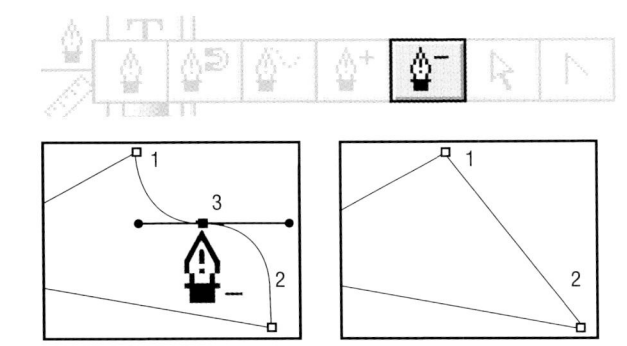

The Subtract-Anchor-Point Tool was used on the above left example. It clicked on the center Path Point. The point was removed. The results are seen on the right image.

**The Direct-Selection Tool** is used to select and move the Path or parts of the Path. This is also called the Hollow Point Tool.

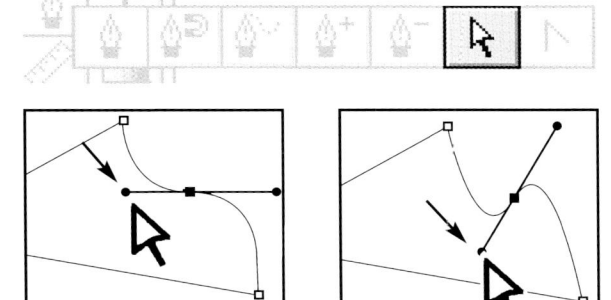

This tool works by moving it over a Path, Path points, and or Path Handles. Depressing the mouse button will permit moving the Path, Path points, and Path Handles. The above image on the right had the handle turned with this tool.

**The Convert-Anchor-Points Tool** is used to straighten curved anchor points along the Path or to add a curve to straight anchor points.

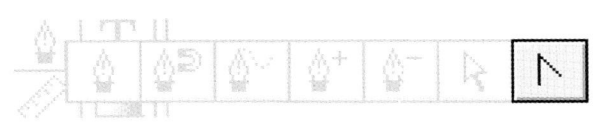

This tool works by moving it over curved or straight Path points. Clicking on a curved Path point will make a straight point. Clicking-and-dragging on a straight point will make the point become curved.

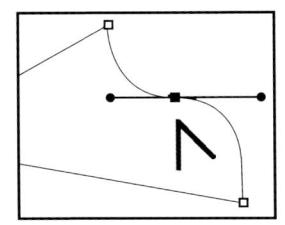

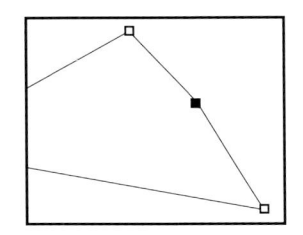

We started with the curved Path point (the image on the left), The Convert-Anchor-Points Tool was used (on the image on the right) to click on the center of the Path point. The curved Path point was converted to a straight Path point.

# MASKING BASICS
## USING PATHS TO CREATE SELECTIONS

### CONVERTING PATHS TO SELECTIONS
### AT-A-GLANCE
1. Create a Path and save it.
2. Convert the Path. Use the Path Palette Pop-out menu to convert the Path into a Selection on the image.
   A. Create a hard-edged Selection.
   B. Create a soft-edged Selection.
      Use the Feather Option.

### PATHS AND SELECTIONS

The Pen Tool is one of the most accurate methods for creating silhouettes in Photoshop. Paths offers a variety of flexible features:

- Paths are adjustable with the Pen Tool options.
- Paths do not make an images file size grow dramatically as does a Channel.
- A Path can be made into a Selection.
- A Selection can be made into a Path.

### CONVERTING PATHS TO SELECTIONS

1. Create a Path and save it.

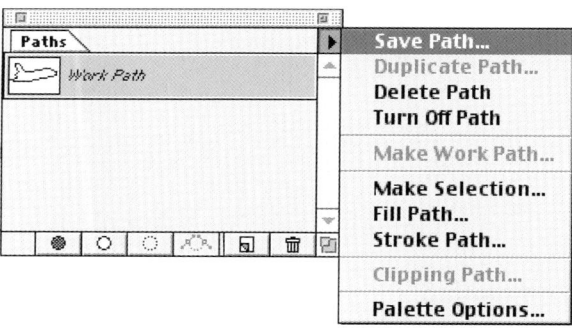

When a Path is initially created, it becomes titled a Working Path. Using the Save Path option, the Path can be renamed.

**2A. Convert the Path into a Selection.**

Use the Path Palette Pop-out menu.
This turns the Path into a hard-edged Selection.

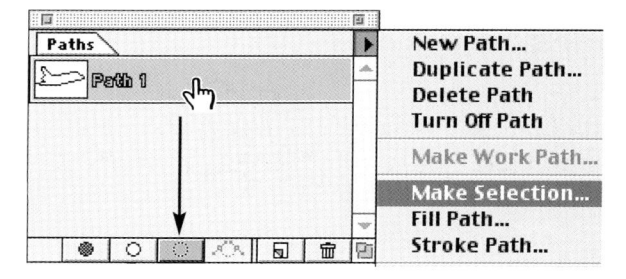

There are two basic ways to create a hard-edged Selection from a Path:

- Use the Pop-out menu of the Path Palette to select *Make Selection*.
- Drag-n-Drop the Path you want to become a Selection using the lower Palette and the fourth icon from the right. This is the easy way to create and load an accurately made Selection.

**2B. Use the Feather Option to feather the Selection.**

- Use the Make Selection dialog box or
- Use the Feather option in the Select Menu (the keyboard shortcut is **Cmd/Cntrl, Opt/Alt D**).

Keyboard in a value to soften the Selections edge. 1 to 5 pixels is typical for 300 dpi images.

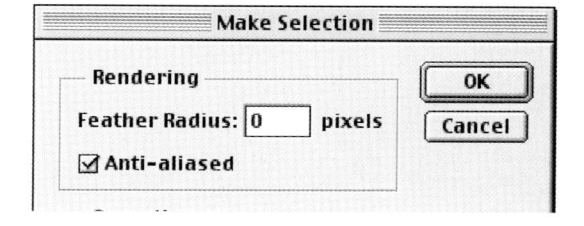

## PATHS AND SILHOUETTES

The Pen Tool is also used to silhouette an image that will be used in a page layout or drawing program. In Photoshop terms, a silhouette is called a Clipping Path. Clipping Paths are created by drawing a Path and saving it as a Clipping Path. The advantage of a Clipping Path is to allow an image to have Transparency in the background areas when it is placed in a page layout application or a drawing program.

To create a **Clipping Path** follow these steps:

1. Use the Pen Tool to draw a Path around the part of the picture you want to silhouette.

The above example shows the original Path created around part of the image.

2. Save the Path.

   Use the Path Palette arrow Pop-up, select the Save Path option, and name the new Path.

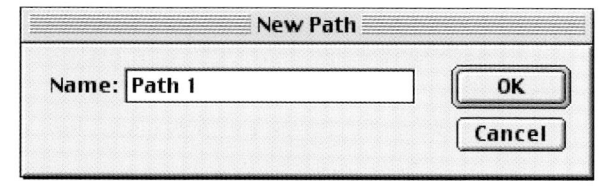

3. Choose Clipping Path from the Paths Palette menu.

   Select the Path you want to use and designate a Flatness value.

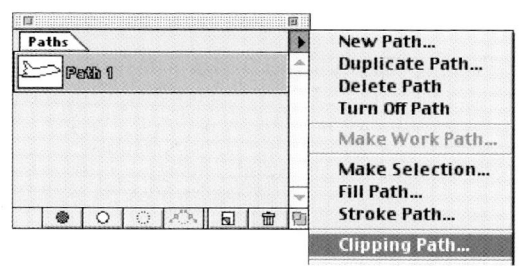

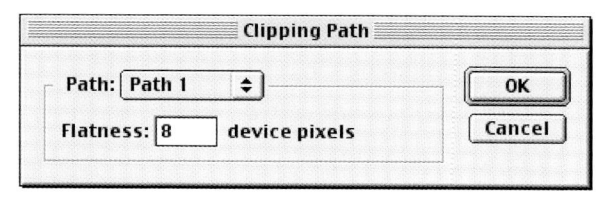

The Flatness value is determined by testing the Raster Image Processing (RIP) and resolution capabilities of the output device. See the sidebar for more about Flatness.

4. Save the file in the EPS format.

   EPS is the most common file format for saving Clipping Paths, but other file formats, such as TIFF and JPEG, now support Clipping Paths.

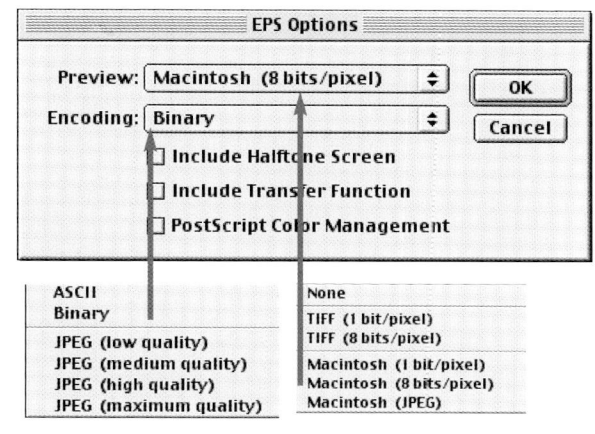

For more about these options see page 66.

# MASKING BASICS
## SILHOUETTES & CLIPPING PATHS

### HOW TO CREATE A CLIPPING PATH AT-A-GLANCE

1. Use the Path Tool to draw a Path around the part of the picture you want to silhouette.
2. Choose Save Path from the Path Palette Pop-up menu.
3. Choose Clipping Path from the Paths palette menu.
4. Save the image as an EPS file with the Clipping Path.

### WHAT IS FLATNESS?

The flatness setting values are in pixels. They define the length of a Path's straight-line segments so the Path can approximate a curve when it is rendered. The higher the flatness value the less accurate the curve will reproduce.

Rules of thumb for flatness.

- Low resolution devices use a setting of 3.
- High resolution devices use a setting of 8.
- Depending on the resolution range of the device, the higher the Flatness value, the straighter lines of the Path will be.
- Use a number between 1 and 4 for more accurate Paths.

The above example illustrates how Clipping Paths work when an image is placed in a page layout program. The areas outside of the Clipping Path become transparent and allow the pages background to show through.

**41**

# MASKING BASICS
## REVIEW

The Masking Basics section covers tools and methods for creating various types of masks in Photoshop.

### Selections

Selections are the main tools for creating masks. They are created from the Rectangular and Oval Marquee, the Magic Wand, and the Lasso with its three Selection options: the Free-form Lasso, the Polygon Lasso, and the Magnetic Lasso.

Our teaching experience shows us that typically Photoshoppers will use Selections approximately 30% of the time during a working session. This is why it is important to learn how to use Selections.

**This section stresses the fundamentals of how to work with Selections.**

- Creating a basic Selection.
- Adding and subtracting from Selections.
- Inversing Selections.
- Saving Selections.
- Loading Selections onto an image.

### Soft-edged and Hard-edged Selections

Typically, when a Selection is first created, it has a hard edge. Feathering a Selection is a way to create a soft edge. Another soft-edge creation method is to work with Channel Masks and Gaussian Blur. This permits creating more refined soft-edged Selections.

### Quick Mask

Quick Mask is another way of working with Selections. Quick Mask is a visual method for viewing and using brushes to paint or unpaint on a colored mask that represents a Selection.

### Paths

The first few times a new Photoshop user tries to create a Path can be disconcerting and down right difficult. But if you want an accurate mask, the Pen Tool is the best method for creating a Path.

One of the keys to becoming successful with Paths is learning how to create Straight and Curved Path Points.

- Straight Path Points are created with the Pen Tool by using the mouse with a click and release of the mouse button.
- Curved Path Points with a click and drag of the mouse button.

### Paths, Selections, and Clipping Paths

- Paths can be converted into Selections. See page 40.
- Selections can be converted into Paths but this method does not produce an accurate Path.
- Paths are also used to create Clipping Paths.
- Clipping Paths are used to Silhouette an images that requires the area outside of the Clipping Path to become transparent when it is placed into a page layout program. See page 41.

# REPRODUCING GRAYSCALE IMAGES

Image Reproduction Process ..................44
Measuring Tools ....................................46
Levels ...................................................48
Curves ..................................................50
Histograms ...........................................52
Page Setup ...........................................53
Sharpening Filters ................................54
Degrading Filters ..................................55
Line Image Tools ..................................56
**Methodology** ............................................58
**How to:**
Identify Image Characteristics ................60
Adjust Highlights and Shadows ..............62
Adjust Midtones ....................................64
Sharpen the Image ................................65
Save the File .........................................66
More About Midtones ...........................68
Make Corrections ..................................70
Review ..................................................74

# HOW TO REPRODUCE GRAYSCALE IMAGES - INTRODUCTION TO THE BLACK AND WHITE IMAGE REPRODUCTION PROCESS

The image **reproduction process** usually starts after an original scene is captured on continuous-tone film (the material you load into your camera). The continuous-tone film is converted, with an input scanner, into a digital signal that represents the original black-and-white image. The black-and-white digital information is optimized, converted into a file for viewing, or is typically output to halftone film and a proof is generated.

After the review process, the proof is approved or is sent back to the workstation for adjustments. Once the adjustments are approved, printing plates are made from the halftone film. The plates are placed on a printing press and the image is printed.

**Images** are available with two types of characteristics: (1) continuous tone and (2) line work.

**Continuous-tone images** have a broad range of tones that do not use screened dots. They can be black-and-white (grayscale) or color and can come from transparencies, reflection originals, or digital cameras.

**Transparent originals** are available in two forms: positives or negatives. Positive transparencies allow light to pass through and they appear similar to the original scene (like slides). Positive film comes in different sizes from 16 mm to over 20" x 24". Negatives are the transparent plastic strips you get back from the store with your prints that show a reverse of the image.

Black-and-white and color **reflective** originals reflect light off their surfaces. We're talking about standard photographic prints. Much like transparencies, photographic reflection prints or originals come in many different sizes. Reflection originals range in size from 35 mm contact prints to any size painting or artwork.

**Line Work images** have two tonal values (black and white) and are suitable for reproduction without a halftone screen.

**Graphic arts scanners** are specialized high resolution drum and flatbed devices. Graphic arts scanners can provide the necessary features such as the final resolution (dpi), screen frequency (LPI), and sharpness functions necessary to reproduce black-and-white images. This group of scanners provide options for the final image to be output directly to final halftone film or as an electronic file for use at a workstation.

**Desktop and Plug-'n-Play Scanning** involves more than the scanner. It includes the use of a workstation with specialized software (Adobe Photoshop!) and an imagesetter. The purpose of the desktop scanner is to capture grayscale or color digital data that can be adjusted and optimized at the workstation and output via an imagesetter.

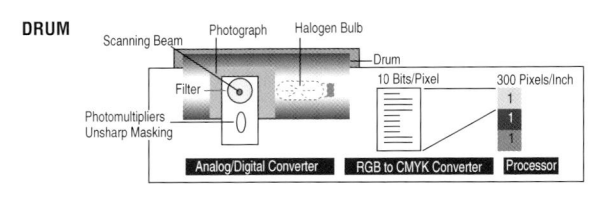

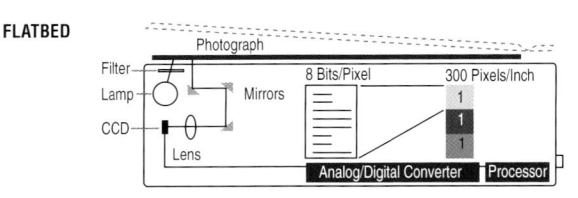

**DRUM**

**FLATBED**

**Scanners** output RGB (Red, Green and Blue) and CMYK, (Cyan, Magenta, Yellow, and Black) or grayscale digital data. RGB data values are measured in levels from 0-255. CMYK and grayscale data are measured in % of dot values ranging from 0% to 100%. Each level equals 0.39 of a dot %. In a grayscale reproduction, the RGB levels are equal to each other.

A bit is the smallest unit of data a computer uses. It has 2 states: 1(on) or Ø (off) (1 Bit)

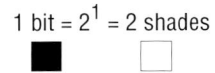

$1 \text{ bit} = 2^1 = 2 \text{ shades}$

With 8 bits and 2 states you can make 256 combinations of the 8 bits.

10101111(8 Bits)

In an 8 bit file each pixel (picture element) can contain 1 of the 256 shades or RGB levels.

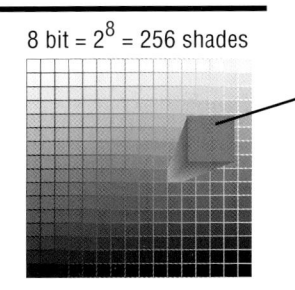

$8 \text{ bit} = 2^8 = 256 \text{ shades}$

**Digital Data** gathered during input scanning or with a digital camera describes the original's tonal characteristics and resolution. The data is stored as a series of bits that define pixels for display on a computer monitor. The number of bits identifies the scanner sensor's capability to capture tonal information. To reproduce a grayscale continuous-tone image, 8 bits per pixel (256 levels) are required. Line art only requires 1 bit per pixel (two levels).

**Laser Proof**- adequate for concept and position.

**Contact Print** - Used as contract proof but does not reflect dot gain.

**Matchprint™/Cromalin™** - Used as contract proof. Can show effects of dot gain. Produced from film.

**Digital Proof** - Used as contract proof. Can show effects of dot gain. Made before film.

**Proofs** are a visual "best guess" of the expected final reproduction. Some proofs are closer to the final end product than others. The more exact the proof, the more expensive it is to produce. The more exact proofs are usually saved for the end of the reproduction process. They can be created digitally or made with the film output from the imagesetter. When a client "OK's" the proof, it becomes a contract between them and the party that supplied the proof (you). When you "OK" the proof to the printer, the same implied contract exists.

44

**Tone Compression** occurs because the range of reproducible tones in the printing process is smaller than the range of tones in the original image. The original image contains a smaller range than you see in real life. Due to the effects of tone compression, images with average, light, or dark characteristics have their own special adjustments applied during the scanning process or on the desktop to achieve optimum results.

**Dot Gain** causes halftone dot sizes to increase. Dot gain can come from imagesetter mis-calibration, varying paper qualities, and mechanical limitations of the printing process. Dot gain can adversely change the look of your final printed image.

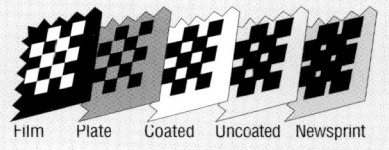

Film  Plate  Coated  Uncoated  Newsprint

**PPI (Pixels Per Inch), DPI (Dots Per Inch), and LPI (Lines Per Inch)** are all units of measure. These units apply to digital data and relate to the ability of specialized hardware to capture and use that digital data. Monitors display individual dots of light or Pixels (picture elements) on screen to form an image. An image needs to have a higher DPI for printing than it does to look good on a monitor. DPI represents the resolution of a device. Typical resolutions are 72-77 DPI for a monitor, 72-3000+ DPI for digital cameras, scanners, and imagesetters. DPI and PPI are often used interchangeably. LPI refers to a line screen ruling used in halftone reproduction to simulate various shades of gray.

**Calibration** occurs when all hardware and software components throughout the process predictably produce standardized values and measures. In other words, you get no (or very few) surprises when you compare your proofs to the final printed image. During the reproduction process, digital camera or scanned image values, values in the workstation, and image output values interrelate and agree. Calibration is the process by which the input and output values are adjusted to compensate for mis-calibrated imagesetters, the varying properties of paper and ink, and different printing presses (see Dot Gain).

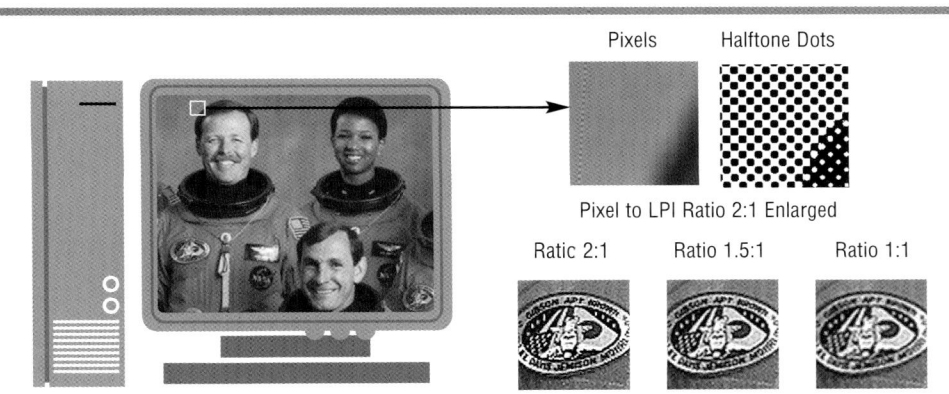

Pixels  Halftone Dots

At 300 DPI a 133 LS yields 5 shades of gray

At 1200 DPI a 133 LS yields 81 shades of gray

At 2400 DPI a 133 LS yields 256 shades of gray

300 DPI Laser Printer

600-3000+ DPI Imagesetter

RIP

Pixel to LPI Ratio 2:1 Enlarged

Ratio 2:1    Ratio 1.5:1    Ratio 1:1

Best Quality  Good Quality  Some Uses

To ensure the best reproduction quality, the line screen (LS) and imagesetter resolution should be chosen to produce 256 shades of gray, the maximum addressable in the PostScript language.

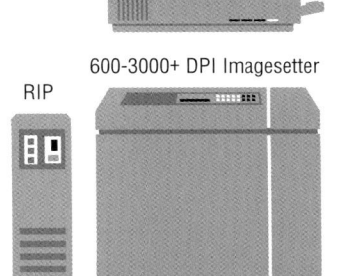

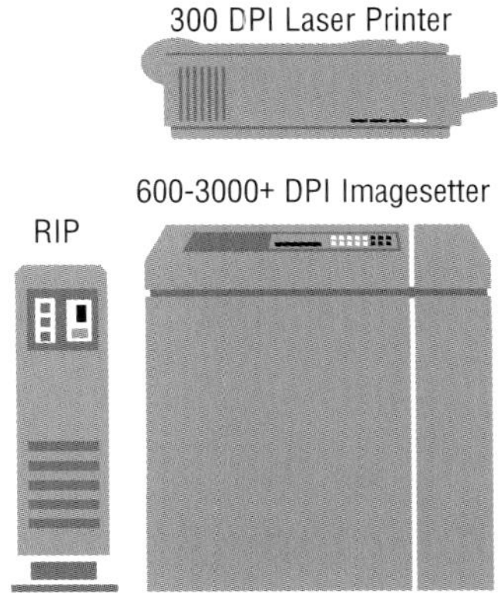

**Workstations** are powerful computer systems that enable the user to make adjustments to digital images to optimize their reproduction and to perform imaging functions like cloning, airbrushing, and retouching. Workstation platforms include Unix, IBM-PC and compatibles, and Apple Macintosh.

**Halftones** are used to reproduce continuous-tone images on a printing press. A halftone line screen (LS) divides an image into patterns of different-sized dots that create an optical illusion of continuous shades of gray. To get the best results, an image needs to process through the imagesetter twice as many screen pixels as halftone dots at final image size. To produce the maximum levels of gray and reduce banding effects, the correct line screen and imagesetter resolution combination must be used. The number of available shades of gray is determined by the formula: # of shades = (Imagesetter output DPI/halftone screen LPI)$^2$+1.

The **RIP** (Raster Image Processor) converts the digital data into the bitmap data the **Imagesetter** uses to render line work or halftone information to film or paper. A 300 DPI laser printer is a low resolution imagesetter.

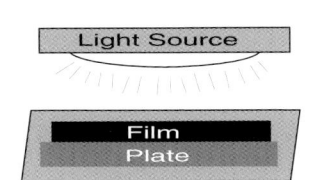

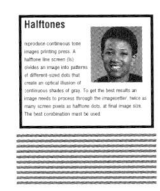

Light Source

Film
Plate

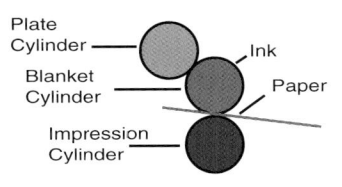

Plate Cylinder
Blanket Cylinder
Impression Cylinder
Ink
Paper

Original    Random Proof    Printed Piece

**Printing** involves rendering the image data to a substrate such as paper. In the traditional printing process of offset lithography, halftone film generated by imagesetters is photographically imaged onto printing plates. A plate is placed on a press, inked, and the halftone image is transferred to paper.

**The Review Process** is essential to determining if the reproduction is optimized. You do this by visually inspecting originals, proofs, and printed results and making judgments about the degree of success you wish to achieve in reproducing the image. If the image is not optimized, you can make future adjustments based on this inspection. Remember, experience is your best teacher.

# REPRODUCING GRAYSCALE IMAGES

## MEASURING TOOLS

### OPTIONAL EYEDROPPER CURSOR

By locking the Shift key down when using this tool, a target point cursor is displayed. This is an optional way to isolate specific points in the image.

### EYEDROPPER AND COLOR SAMPLER TOOL

**Window: Palettes:**

This is one of the key tools for measuring. The Eyedropper has two measuring options: (1) the Eyedropper is used for random image sampling. The mouse is placed over the image. (2) The Color Sampler is used to place up to four fixed points on an image. Either option is used in conjunction with Curves or Levels to identify highlight (white), shadow (black), or midtone (gray) areas. Double clicking on this tool in the Toolbox brings up a dialog box for the Eyedropper sample size. The default *Point Sample*, samples only one pixel in a given area. This means you may end up with a single, non-representative pixel being read, measured, and used for calculations. The preferred setting is 3 by 3 average, which increases the sample size and minimizes erroneous readings.

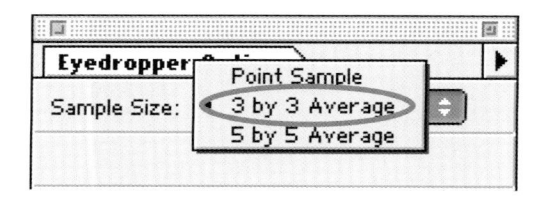

### INFO PALETTE **Window: Palettes:**

This essential palette is a digital densitometer (see Glossary). It displays the X and Y pixel coordinates of the cursor and the Color Sampler points as well as the values for 7 color spaces. To use this tool for black-and-white images, set it for grayscale and RGB color spaces. The palette will display the image's dot percentages and RGB values (Levels) when the cursor or the Color Sampler points are placed over a given image area. The palette will display before and after values when making changes in the Curves and Levels dialog boxes.

### EYEDROPPER

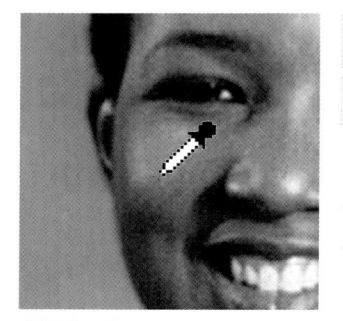

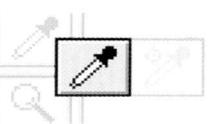

Double click on the Eyedropper Tool icon to access the Eyedropper Options dialog box in the Options Palette.

### COLOR SAMPLER TOOL

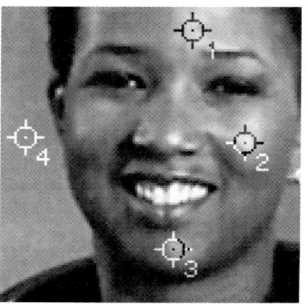

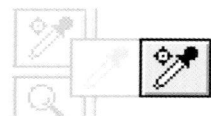

Double click on the Color Sampler Tool icon to access the Color Sampler Options dialog box in the Options Palette.

This example illustrates what the four fixed point icons of the Color Sampler look like.

**Remove Sampler Points**

Here are two options to remove the Color Sampler point. Make sure the Eyedropper Tool is active.

- Drag them off the image.
- Hold down the **Opt /Alt** key. This will cause the measuring icon to change to scissors. Click on the Sampler icon to remove it.

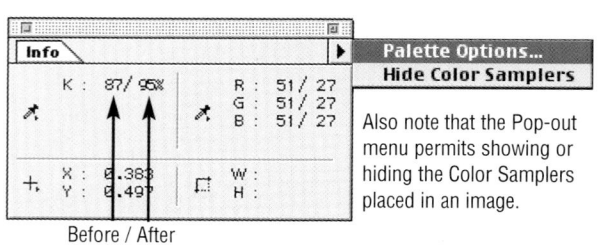

Before / After

Also note that the Pop-out menu permits showing or hiding the Color Samplers placed in an image.

Notice that once a change has been made to an image, but is not yet finalized, the Info palette will show splits for values before and after the change.

46

## INFO PALETTE OPTIONS (cont.)

The color space or spaces displayed by this palette can be accessed and changed through the Pop-out Palette Options menu. It is also possible to change the Mouse Coordinates Ruler Units.

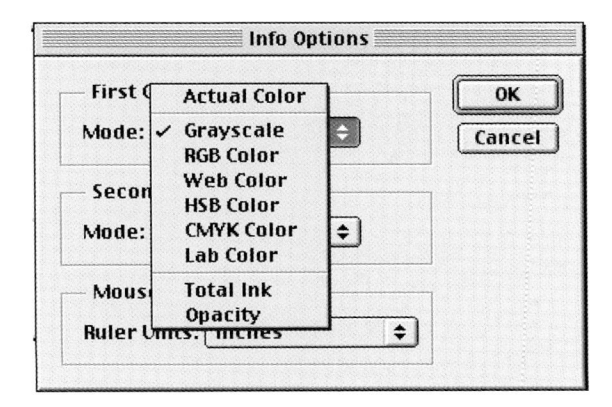

Another option to alter the color space settings for the Info Palette is to depress one or both of the Eyedropper icons within the Info Palette.

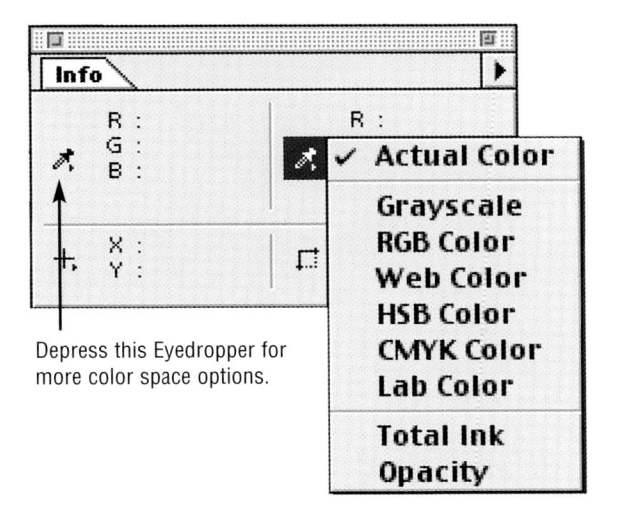

Depress this Eyedropper for more color space options.

## SETTING UP THE INFO PALETTE OPTIONS

The color space or spaces displayed by this palette for black-and-white images should be set to grayscale and RGB color.

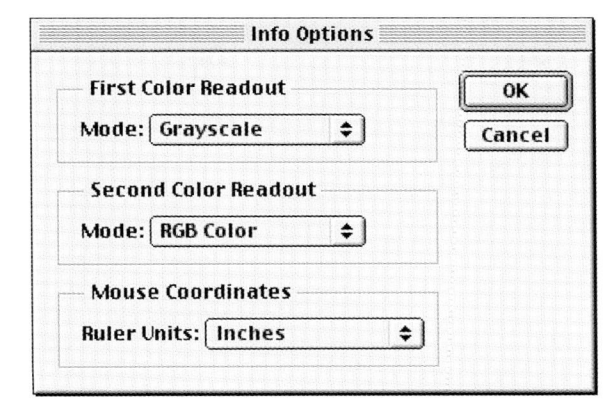

### COLORS PALETTE  Window: Palettes:

This tool permits sampling of any area within an image in digital CMYK, RGB, or grayscale dot values. The Colors Palette is found under the Window menu. It is used by clicking on an image area with the Eyedropper Tool. The selected value is displayed in either the foreground or background color box in the palette. This value in the Colors Palette dialog box will stay displayed until another area is clicked.

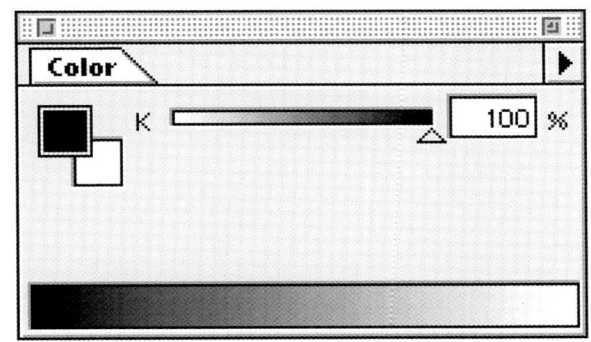

# REPRODUCING GRAYSCALE IMAGES

## MEASURING TOOLS

### SAMPLER POINTS & THE INFO PALETTE

Whenever a Sampler point is placed on an image, the Info Palette displays the values associated with the point.

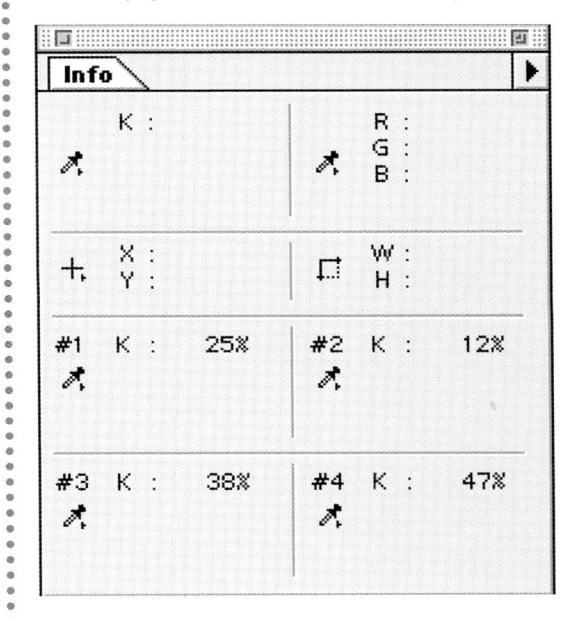

### COLOR PALETTE TIP

Use the Color Palette as fifth point when all of the four Sampler points are placed on an image.

47

# REPRODUCING GRAYSCALE IMAGES

## LEVELS

### SET WHITE/BLACK TARGET COLOR PICKER

This tool is used in conjunction with Curves or Levels to establish (or dial-in) the target highlight and shadow values of the image. (RGB values may also be used.) To enter the Color Picker from Curves or Levels, double click the Set White or Set Black icon. Then, establish the highlight or shadow dot values. Be sure to place zeroes in the C, M, and Y boxes and click **OK**. A different Color Picker may also be accessed by clicking on the Foreground or Background box in the Tools palette. This picker looks the same as the Set White and Black pickers. However, it is not possible to set highlight and shadow points from the tool palette picker. Highlight and shadow points can **only** be set through their respective pickers in the Curves or Levels dialog box.

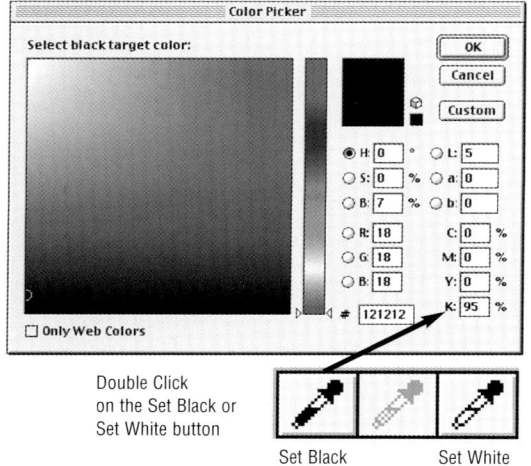

Double Click on the Set Black or Set White button

Set Black    Set White

### IMPORTANT!

When establishing highlight and shadow values, use the K (black) channel only. Be sure to enter zero values in the C, M, and Y Channels.

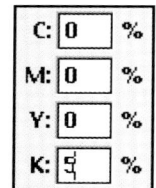

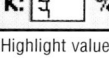

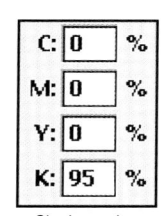

Highlight value    Shadow value

## LEVELS  Image: Adjust

This tool shows a Histogram that identifies the image characteristics by RGB levels (which range from 0 to 255). It has two sliding adjustment bars that allow you to change the input and output values. We have divided this tool into three adjustment classifications: manual, semi-automatic, and automatic.

- With the **Manual** method, you sample areas with the Eyedropper Tool, read the values in the Info palette, and then adjust any or all of the five arrow sliders to make changes to meet reproduction requirements. This method requires a lot of expertise and can be time consuming. If you choose to use the Gamma (midtone) slider in the Levels dialog box, this adjustment is always done manually. Its use is covered in the How To section of this book.

- The **Semi-Automatic** method uses the Set White and Set Black tools. You manually pick target highlight and shadow areas. This tool also allows you to visually locate the areas having the lightest or darkest pixels. You do this by holding down the **Opt/Alt** key as you slide the right or left arrow below the input histogram back and forth. (The Preview option must be deselected and LUT Animation must be selected in the General Preferences for this effect to work.)

- The **Automatic** method requires that the white target and black target points be set in their respective Color Pickers. When you click on the Auto button, the program picks the white and black points in the image. While this method works, extraneous data in the photo such as borders or large dark or light areas can make it necessary to change the clip values to get the best results (see the sidebar, Clip Values, page 51).

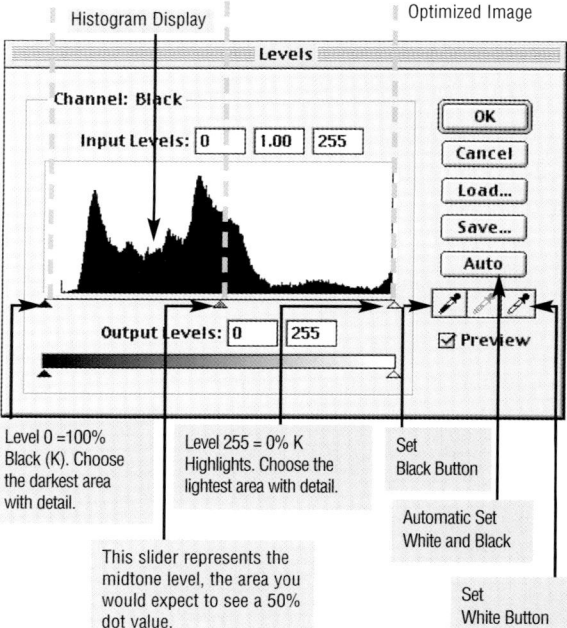

**Load and Save** - These options are available for many of the adjustment tools. A particular setting can be saved, then loaded, and used on another image. This feature is helpful for repeating adjustments on images requiring similar changes thus speeding production.

Histogram Display    Optimized Image

Level 0 =100% Black (K). Choose the darkest area with detail.

Level 255 = 0% K Highlights. Choose the lightest area with detail.

Set Black Button

Automatic Set White and Black

This slider represents the midtone level, the area you would expect to see a 50% dot value.

Set White Button

**Manually adjusting Input Levels:** This upper scale adjustment is used to change the current image input values to increase contrast. It does this by increasing the total number of light or dark pixels in the image.

For example, use a 16-step posterized ramp and move the Input Levels slider from level 0 to level 68.

The gradient ramp now shows that there has been a dramatic increase in the number of the darkest pixels in the image. All pixels from level 68 and down have been assigned the maximum darkness value. By increasing the total number of dark and light pixels in an image, the contrast is increased. Notice also that the number of shade steps in the ramp has been reduced from 16 to 12. In a halftone image, increasing the contrast too far reduces the number of shades of gray and results in a posterized image.

After clicking **OK**, look at the images histogram and notice the increase in number of darkest pixels and the redistribution of the other steps.

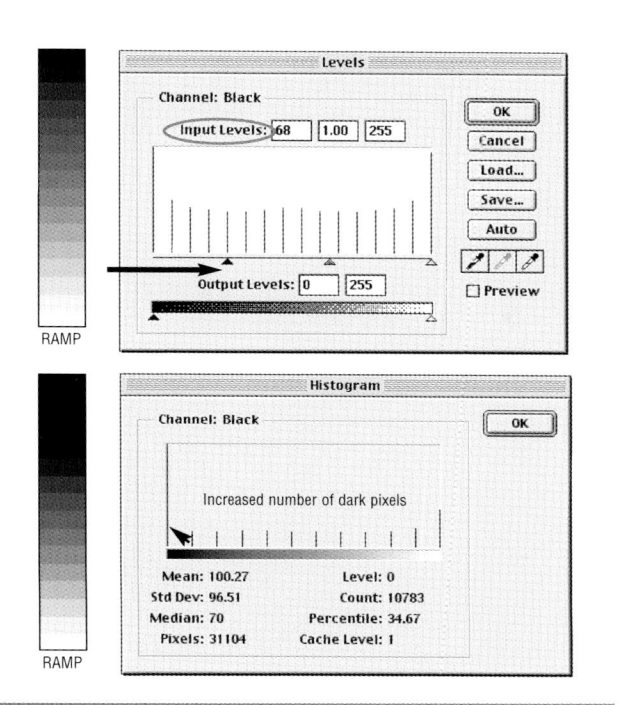

---

**Manually adjusting Output Levels:** The bottom scale is used to adjust or limit the lightest and darkest values in an image. For example, if the bottom left arrow slider is moved from 0 to 12, the image will not allow any values below 5% to be printed (level 12 is equal to a 95% dot value).

The example to the right was created using a 16-step posterized ramp. The left Input Levels slider is moved from level 0 to level 68 and the output has been limited to level 68.

Now the pixels from level 68 and down have been remapped to the darkest value allowed, but the darkest value allowed has been limited by the output limit slider to level 68. The resulting ramp shows less contrast. When used on a halftone image, the output slider should be used to limit the resulting image's darkest and lightest output values (i.e., to a 95% shadow dot and a 5% highlight dot). While this tool can be used to lower contrast in an image, it is most useful for limiting output values to a specific range.

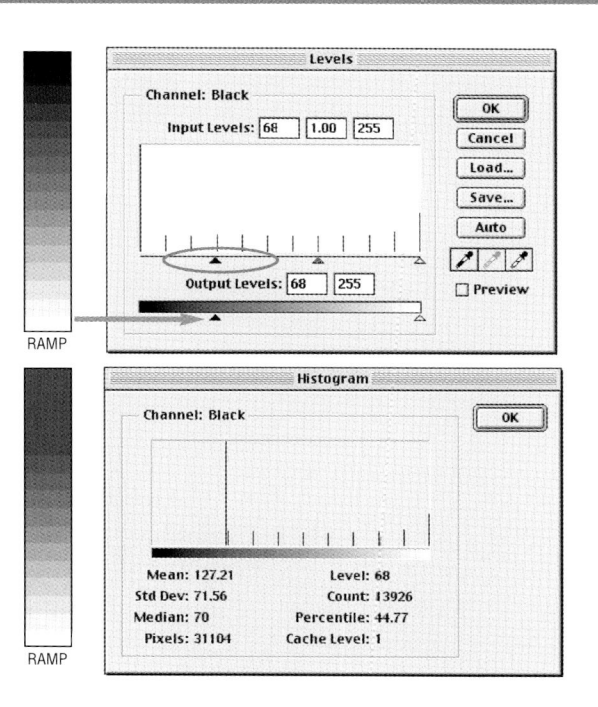

# REPRODUCING GRAYSCALE IMAGES

## LEVELS

### MAKE YOUR OWN RAMPS

This allows you to experiment with the Levels tool to get the feel of how to control it.
1. Make a new file, 6" wide x 1" high.
2. Select grayscale and a resolution of 72 DPI.
3. Set to the foreground and background colors to their default. The Foreground = 100% black and the Background color= 0% white.
4. Use the Gradient Tool from the tool box to create a ramp like the one you see to the left.
5. Select Image: Map, Posterize from the menu and posterize it to have 16 levels (use 11 if you want even 10% increments, 21 if you want 5% increments).
6. Now you have a ramp on which to try different adjustments with the Levels tool. Observe how different adjustments change the look of the ramp. This information can then be related to how this tool works with scanned images.

### MIDTONE (GAMMA) ADJUSTMENT

The Levels tool has a midtone adjustment slider that ranges in value from .10 to 9.99 with the 1.0 value being an equal distance between the light and dark slider. A larger number increases the light tones in the image, and a smaller one decreases the light tones in the image. The Levels tool is limited since only three points of the reproduction are selectively adjustable: highlight, shadow, and midtones. While this is often sufficient, the Curves tool allows more than 3 points of the image's tones to be selectively adjusted.

### EASY ENTRY FEATURE: DIAL-IN VALUE BOXES

Many dialog boxes can now accept values that are input directly into individual settings boxes rather than having to drag sliders to change values.

**49**

# REPRODUCING GRAYSCALE IMAGES

## CURVES

### EXTREME EFFECTS OF MOVING CURVE ENDPOINTS

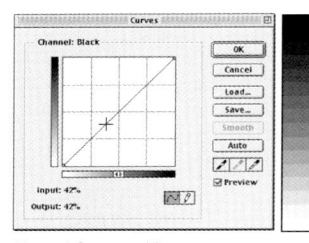

Normal Curve and image

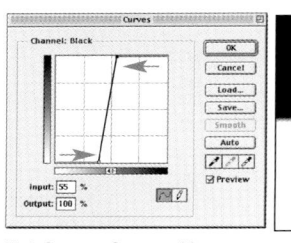

High Contrast Curve and image

If the endpoints of the curve are moved as close to the vertical axis as possible, the resulting image is posterized (it gains the extreme contrast of a line art-type image).

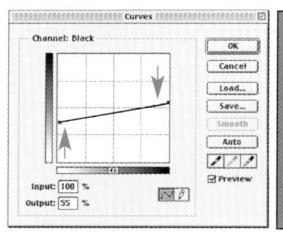

Low Contrast Curve and image

When the two endpoints of the curve are moved closer to the horizontal axis, the result is a flat image. Adjusting the curve in this manner decreases contrast.

## CURVES  Image: Adjust

The Curves dialog box, as its name suggests, allows adjustment of the image's tonal reproduction characteristics by adjusting a curve. Curves is the most precise tool in Photoshop to adjust image contrast. It is possible to adjust specific areas of the tone such as midtone values, 1/4 tone values, 3/4 tone values, or multiple points along the curve. These terms are the traditional terminology used in the prepress field, making Curves the easiest tool to use when communicating specific Dot or % values for different types of paper and printing presses. Highlight (white) and shadow (black) settings are chosen in Curves via their respective Color Pickers.

The highlight and shadow adjustments with this tool, just like the Levels tool, can be divided into three classifications: manual, semi-automatic, and automatic.

- In **Manual** mode, sample an area with the Eyedropper Tool, read the value in the Color palette or Info palette, and then drag the end points of the curve manually to make changes to meet target tone reproduction requirements. This method requires a lot of expertise and can be time-consuming.

- The **Semi-Automatic** mode involves using the Set White and Set Black controls to define target values, and then manually selecting the target highlight and shadow areas. This tool also allows you to visually locate the area you have selected on the curve. This area is indicated by an open circle that appears on the curve. To get the circle, hold the mouse button down while the pointer is over the selected area on the image. (This is the method described in the How To section.)

- The **Automatic** method requires that the target White and Black point be set in the appropriate Color Picker. Clicking on the Auto button allows the program to pick the white and black points. (See the Auto Range options sidebar on page 51.)

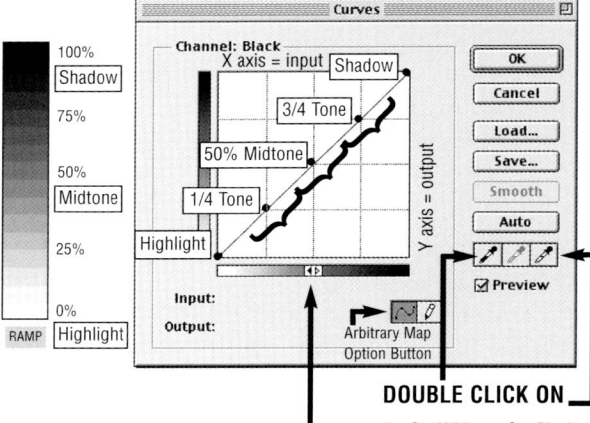

**Note:** that clicking here reverses the scale from working in screen % values to RGB levels.

**DOUBLE CLICK ON** the Set White or Set Black button to select the Color Picker for that tool's settings.

### Manually adjusting the end points of the curve

**Input:** Plotted on the X axis, this adjustment heightens contrast by increasing the total number of light or dark pixels in the image.

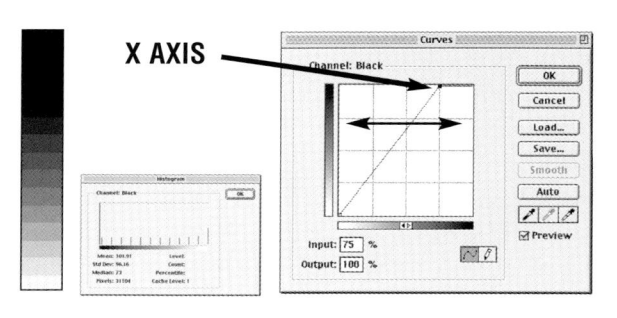

**X AXIS**

**Output:** The Y axis is used to set or limit the lightest and darkest values in an image. If the input and output values are set to 75%, the image will not have any values above 75%.

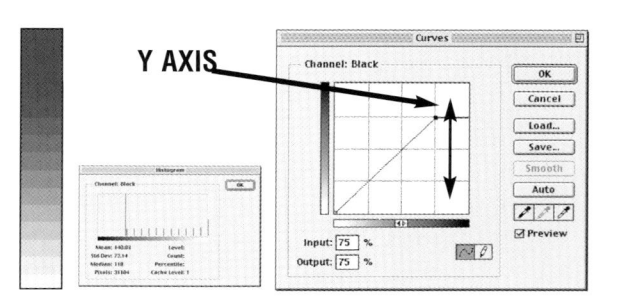

**Y AXIS**

## Adjusting the midtones

There is no automatic adjustment for midtone values between the endpoints of the curve. To adjust a midtone area on the curve, move the cursor up to intersect a part of the line which forms the curve and click to place a point at that spot on the curve. You can then drag the point up or down to increase or decrease values in the image that are along the curve. When making adjustments with one control point, the Curves tool works much like the Levels Gamma adjustment. The unique adjustment feature of the Curves tool is that it allows more than a single midtone control point. In fact, up to 14 additional points (besides the highlight and shadow anchors) can be placed along the curve allowing specific areas of the tone to be changed without strongly affecting other areas. To prevent other tone areas from changing value, anchor those points on the curve.

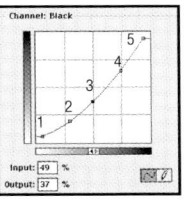

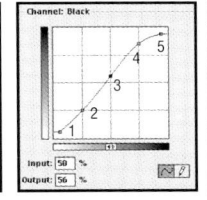

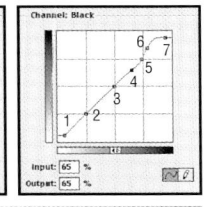

## The Curves tool display

When working in Curves, be sure that you have selected the % mode (unless you prefer levels) so that your adjustment looks like the first one on the right. You do this by clicking on the double arrow in the gradation bar. When in % mode, dragging a point down lightens an image. When working in Levels on the curve, dragging a point down darkens an image. You must drag the mouse in the image or have the cursor over an area in the curve to get the input and output values to display.

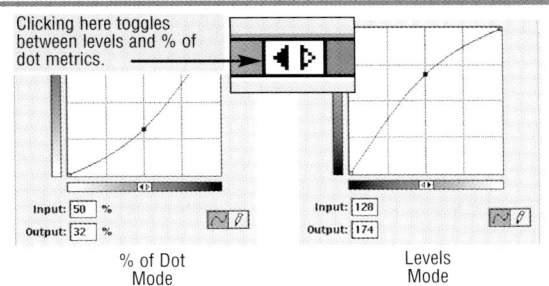

### ARBITRARY MAP

Arbitrary Map is part of the Curves tool. To activate it, click on the pencil button at the bottom of the Curves dialog box. The cursor will change to a pencil when you draw inside the graph. The Arbitrary map tool can be used to make discontinuous changes to the curve. The **Shift** key can be used to constrain the lines drawn when the tool is clicked to define a specific start and end point along the curve. This tool can be particularly helpful when cleaning up scanned line art or when remapping a small number of pixels in a detailed area of an image.

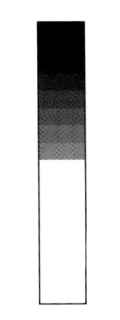

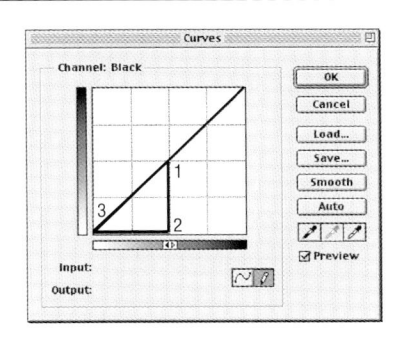

## Manually adjusting midtones on the curve

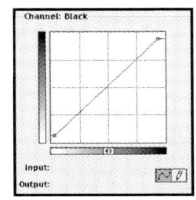

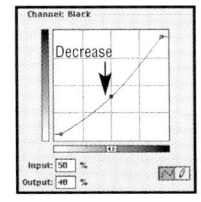

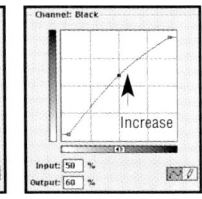

The Input and Output boxes in the Curves dialog box become available and show the Dot % or Levels values when you have clicked on a particular point on the Curve. When these boxes are active it is possible to type in exact values or use the arrow keys to adjust the Curve in small increments.

There are two visual tip offs to help determine if you are working in the Dot % or Levels mode. (1) The Input and Output Values read Dots % or Levels values and (2) the orientation of the Gray bars.

This is the change to the ramp on page 49 that was made by holding the Shift key and clicking on points 1, 2, and 3.

# REPRODUCING GRAYSCALE IMAGES

## CURVES

### THE AUTO BUTTON AND AUTO RANGE OPTIONS

This feature is used in conjunction with the Curves or Levels tool and requires that the proper White Point and Black Point values be setup prior to using this tool. Hold down the **Opt/Alt** key and click on the Auto button in either Curves or Levels. The Auto Range option dialog box is displayed with the default clipping values of 0.5%. This setting throws out the top and bottom 5% of the pixels used by the Auto tool equation before it calculates where to set White and Black Points in an image.

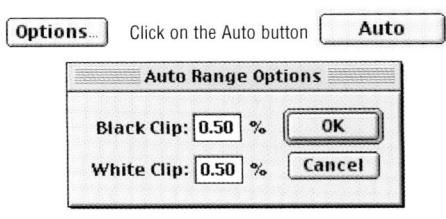

You might want to raise the **Clip Value** if there are large white or black areas in the image that you do not want to have used as part of the automatic calculation of the highlight and shadow points in the image. The clip values range from 0.0 to 9.99%. This is the largest number of pixels at each end of the calculation range that can be removed from the calculation is about 10%.

### BRIGHTNESS/CONTRAST

Brightness/Contrast is one of three basic image adjustment tools available in Adobe Photoshop. This tool works especially well for making adjustments to line work. However, in a comparison between Levels, Curves, and Brightness/Contrast for continuous-tone image adjustment, Brightness/Contrast provides the least amount of control because specific points of the image cannot be adjusted independently. So do not use it for grayscale images!

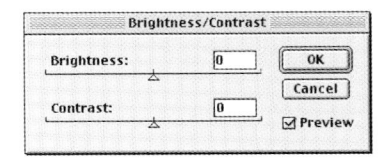

51

# REPRODUCING GRAYSCALE IMAGES

## HISTOGRAMS

### HOW MANY GRAY LEVELS?

Quality black-and-white reproduction for print requires that the scanner be capable of capturing 256 levels of gray despite the fact that many images will not have all 256 levels.

### THE HISTOGRAM IN THE LEVELS CONTROL

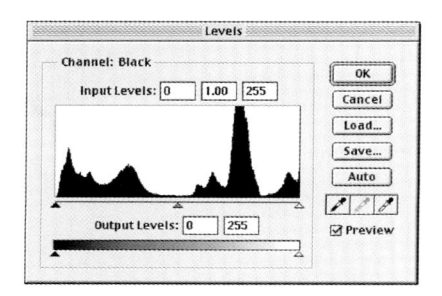

Notice, when using the Levels tool, a smaller version of the Histogram is provided to aid in adjusting the image values.

## HISTOGRAM Image

The Histogram plots the number of pixels that are in a given level of the image. A level is the same as the RGB (Red, Green, and Blue) value displayed in the Info box for a given color. In the case of grayscale images, the RGB levels are equal because gray is defined as neutral (not cast or tinted with a hue). Additive color theory tells us that the RGB values must be equal to create a neutral value. The levels range from 0-255.

### Using the Histogram

The Histogram provides a visual representation of the image and permits a better understanding of the visual distribution of tones within the image. The Mean is an average of brightness values in a particular image. An image with a Mean value of around 128 usually identifies an image with an average distribution of tones. Images that have a Mean value range of 170 to 255 are light in character. Images that have a Mean value range of 85 to 0 are dark. Each of these image categories (light, average, and dark) follow the guidelines for image adjustments. These adjustments are discussed in the section More About Midtones on page 68. The Histogram can be used to: categorize the image, determine the number of levels in the image, analyze the amount of data in each level, and view the result of adjustments to the image. The examples to the right illustrate the Histogram and how different types of scans or adjustments display in the histogram.

Placing the pointer at any single level in the Histogram displays information about that point. If there is no value at a selected level, then no data exists at that point.

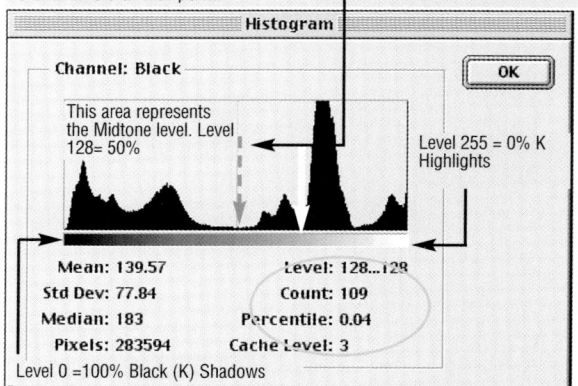

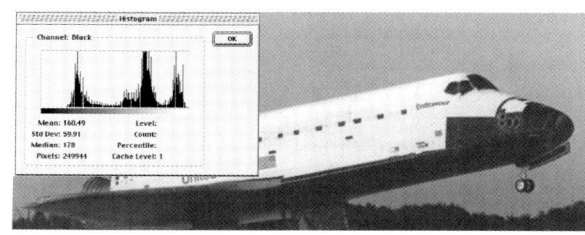

Histogram for a light scan. This scan was produced on an 8-bit scanner. Notice the densely packed tones on the right side. This represent the light tones.

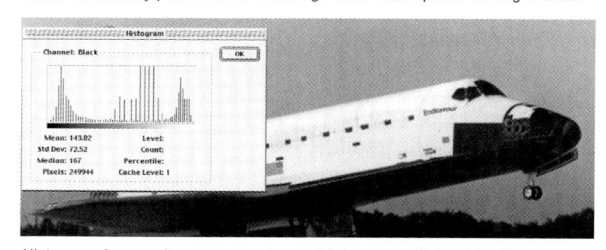

Histogram from an image scanned on a 4-bit scanner. Only 64 levels are available for adjustment.

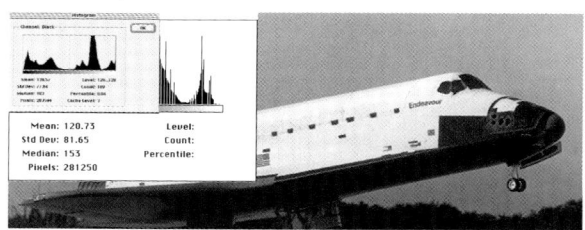

Histogram after the White Point, the Black Point and the midtones are adjusted. The tones have distributed themselves more evenly.

## PAGE SETUP  File

The Page Setup dialog box has two important options that can be used with black-and-white images: the Halftone Screen Data and the Transfer Function. Use these if you need to override the halftone screen functions of your page layout program or if you want to compensate an individual halftone for a specific type of dot gain. To export this information, the file must be saved in EPS format.

**Transfer Functions**

The Adobe Photoshop manual indicates that the Transfer Function was "designed to compensate for dot gain due to a mis-calibrated imagesetter." It qualifies the statement by stating that it is better to calibrate an imagesetter with specialized software recommended by the imagesetter manufacturer. We also use the Transfer Function to compensate for dot gain that occurs due to different ink absorption rates of coated and uncoated papers and to varied printing characteristics of specific types of printing presses. For example, a 50% dot on film might print like a 60% dot on coated paper (10% dot gain), and the same film might print like an 80% dot on newsprint (30% dot gain). If an image is being used for different purposes (i.e., a newspaper ad on newsprint and a high quality magazine ad on coated paper), the image will display different types of dot gain on each material. The specific curves can be created, saved, and loaded to be used again. It would be possible to set up curves specific to different vendors' needs without changing the original image. For more information on dot gain, see Appendix B page 122.

**Halftone Screen data**

The desired line screen and the type of halftone dot can be selected from the Halftone Screen dialog box. This information which can be saved only in EPS format will override the settings in page layout programs. This is useful if there is a need to use different screen rulings in the same document.

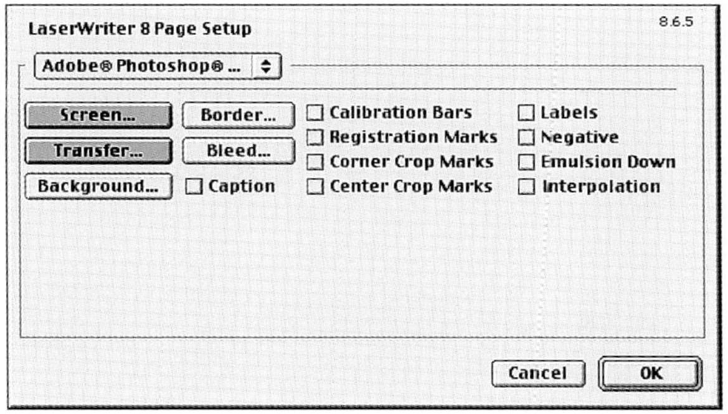

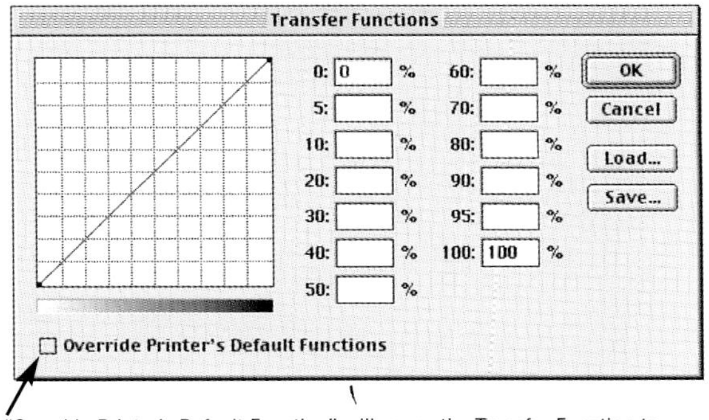

"Override Printer's Default Function" will cause the Transfer Function to override any other calibration software that is being used to calibrate the imagesetter. If it is not checked, the results of the transfer curve are additive to any calibration that is already being applied to the imagesetter.

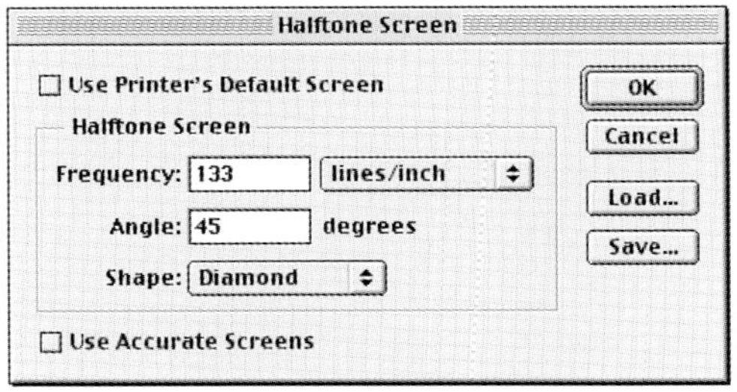

# REPRODUCING GRAYSCALE IMAGES
## PAGE SETUP

### IMAGESETTER MIS-CALIBRATION

Imagesetter mis-calibration occurs when the size of an uncompensated (no transfer function used) dot on the final film does not match the values indicated by the densitometer in the Info palette. An example would be if the Info palette indicated there should be a 50% dot and the film actually has a 69% dot. To determine the correct compensation value to plug into the 50% Transfer Function box, find the difference between 50% and 69% and subtract that difference from the original value. This value (31) is then placed in the 50% transfer curve box. That value will now compensate for the 19% dot gain. Continue this process with other dot percentages along the curve. Note: It is a good idea to verify that your film is being output on a calibrated imagesetter.

### PRINTING TIP

Halftone dot % values can be remapped to another value to compensate for how a particular press or paper reacts and produces dot gain. It is important to work closely with the printer to determine the values they would like applied to a given image. A test strip can be run by producing rectangular areas with screens that vary in value from 5% to 95%. The printer can measure these values and then measure the dot percentages that are actually printed on the paper. The difference between the two values allows a transfer curve to be built and saved for specific situations.

A good set of basic transfer functions saved would include :

| | |
|---|---|
| Web Press | Sheet-fed |
| Coated | Uncoated |
| Newsprint | LaserWriter |

More can be added as needed.

### SAVING A NEW DEFAULT:

To save a new default Halftone Line screen or Transfer Function, hold down the **Opt/Alt** key and click the –>Default button. To reset to the original setting, hold down the **Opt/Alt** key, and press <–Default.

With the **Opt/Alt** key held down, the Load and Save buttons change as shown to the right.

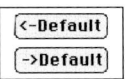

# REPRODUCING GRAYSCALE IMAGES

## SHARPENING

### WHEN UNSHARPENING ISN'T

The term Unsharp Masking (USM) comes from a conventional camera color separation technique that uses a piece of frosted mylar to make a photographic mask through which the separation is exposed. The result of this process is a separation with an increase in contrast in the reproduction giving it the illusion of sharpness. This term *Unsharp Masking* has been carried over to scanners and desktop computer software.

### RULES OF THUMB FOR SHARPNESS

MEDIA
- Generally, original images such as 35mm and 4" x 5" originals require more sharpness than 2 1/4" x 2 1/4" transparencies. A 2 1/4" x 2 1/4" requires less sharpness since its thinner emulsion allows the image to be sharper from the start.
- Most second generation originals (dupes) are less sharp and require added sharpness.
- Reflection prints require less sharpness because the dyes in the prints are enhanced.

CONTENT
- Images with areas of great contrast differences require less added sharpness. Some examples are: different density areas adjacent to each other, dark lines against a light area such as telephone wires against a bright sky, window frames, and screen patterns.
- Images with fuzzy content require more added sharpness.
- Some images should be left unsharp, i.e., soft bridal shots or other artistic effects.

SIZE
- The greater the enlargement, the more sharpness is required.
- The smaller the enlargement or the greater the reduction, the less sharpness is needed.
- A 8.5" x 11" 300 dpi scan can take more sharpening than an 8.5 " x 5.5" 300 dpi scan.

## SHARPEN, SHARPEN EDGES, SHARPEN MORE, AND UNSHARP MASK

These filters provide different ways of making an image appear sharper by increasing the contrast between adjacent pixels. The Unsharp Mask command is the only filter with user controllable settings. Sharpen, Sharpen Edges, and Sharpen More can also be used but are not recommended since they are not adjustable. The Unsharp filtering effect increases contrast in the reproduction and makes it appear sharper. Basically, it fools the eye into believing it is seeing greater detail by creating additional contrast and enhancing the differences between the light and dark transitions in an image.

### UNSHARP MASK `Filter: Sharpen`

The Sharpen, Sharpen More, and Unsharp Mask filters produce sharpening effects that increase the contrast in adjacent pixels in a selection. The strongest and most controllable filter in this tool set is the Unsharp Mask (USM) filter.

Three parameters can be adjusted: **Amount, Radius,** and **Threshold.**

- **Amount** (USM relative value) ranges from 1% to 500%. Higher numbers produce stronger sharpening effects. Typically 150%-200% achieves good results.

- **Radius** values control the number of pixels around an image's edges that have sharpness applied. These values range from 0.1 to 99.99 pixels. If a high value is specified for the radius, more pixels around the edge pixels will be amplified. A typical setting of 1 to 2 pixels creates good contrast.

- **Threshold** acts as a mask that protects pixels from having USM applied. Values range between 0 and 255. The larger the value, the more an image area is protected from having USM applied. The value used to apply USM to the entire image is 0.

*Tip* - The Threshold value is a good tool to protect lighter tones. This is often useful for keeping some skin tone areas soft while sharpening the rest of the image. The example to the right shows values that can be used for creating this effect.

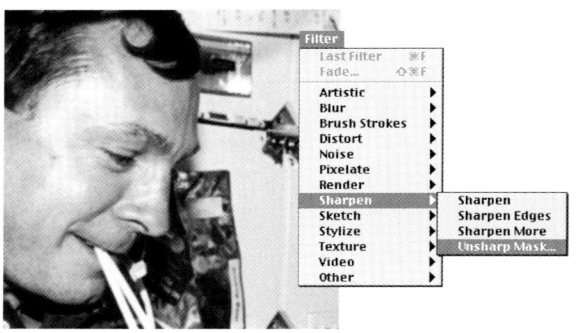

Image before Unsharp Mask

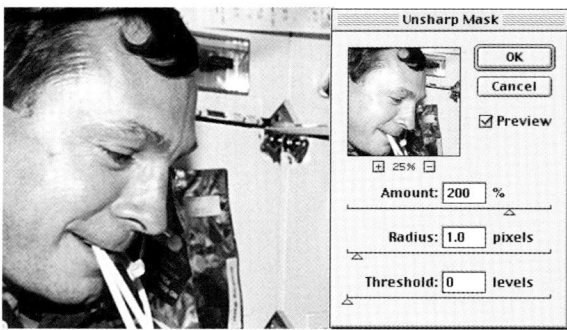

Image after Unsharp Mask 200, 1, 0

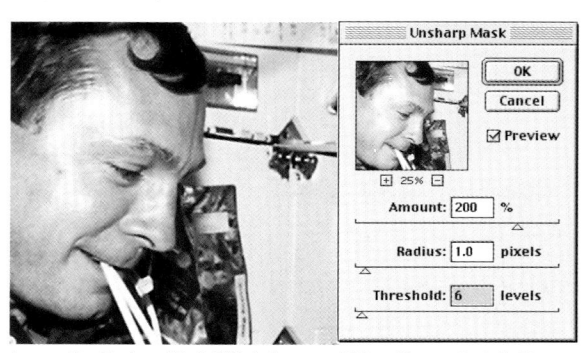

Image after Unsharp Mask 200, 1, 6

This setting protects lighter (highlight) image tones

54

# REPRODUCING GRAYSCALE IMAGES
## DEGRADING FILTERS

## DEGRADING FILTERS - BLUR>GAUSSIAN BLUR, NOISE>DUST & SCRATCHES

There are a number of situations when an image needs to be blurred, made fuzzy, or generally degraded. These filters provide a way to accomplish that. Of all of the Blur and Noise filters, Gaussian Blur and Dust & Scratches have the most controllable settings. That is why we use them. The other filters do not have as much latitude and cannot be controlled as easily.

### GAUSSIAN BLUR  Filter: Blur

The Blur, Blur More, and Gaussian Blur filters produce image softening effects that decrease the sharpness in adjacent pixels within a Selection or on an entire image. The strongest and most controllable filter in this tool set is the Gaussian Blur filter. Gaussian Blur uses increments in tenths of a pixel to blur an image. The higher the value, the more the image is blurred or degraded.

**Gaussian Blur can be used to:**

1. Smooth an Image.

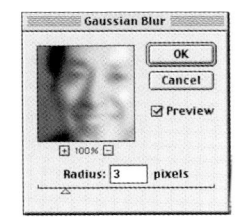

2. Soften a Masks edge.

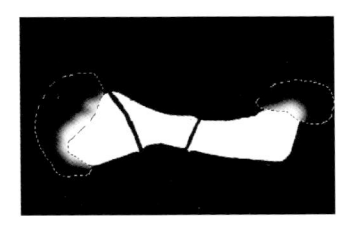

3. Special Effects.

### DUST & SCRATCHES  Filter: Noise

The Dust & Scratches filter produces another type of image softening effect that is designed to remove dirt, dust, and scratches in continuous tone image data. This filter works within a Selection or on an entire image. This tool offers two refined controls for adjusting image: **Radius** and **Threshold**

- **Radius** values control the number of pixels applied to the image for this filter effect. These values range from 1 to 16 in increments of 1 pixel. If a high value is specified for the radius, more pixels around the edge pixels will be amplified to degrade the image. A typical setting of 3 to 4 pixels will reduce dust and dirt.

- **Threshold** acts as a mask that protects pixels from having the Dust & Scratches filter applied. Values range between 0 and 255. The larger the value, the more protection is applied to the image. A good starting point for a Threshold setting is between 6 to 12.

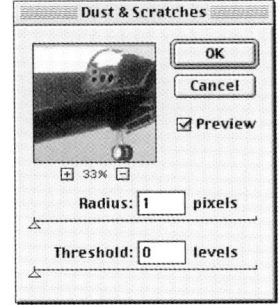

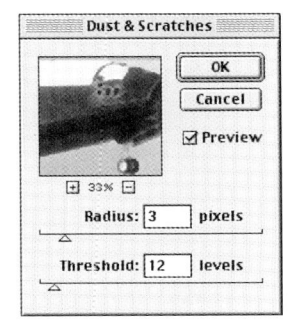

For more about Dust & Scratches, see page 112.

55

# REPRODUCING GRAYSCALE IMAGES

## LINE IMAGE TOOLS

Line work, Line art, Line shots, and Line images are different names for the same type of raster images. Line work images typically reproduce without halftone screens in the printing process and have only two tonal values, black and white. There are two primary tools for adjusting line images and two secondary tools.

The primary tools include (1) *Threshold* and (2) *Brightness* and *Contrast*. The secondary tools are *Posterize* and Mode change to *Bitmap*.

There are two scenarios for working the line images: (1) The image is scanned as a one-bit-per-pixel image (bit mapped) or (2) the image is scanned as an eight-bit-per-pixel image. See the sidebar on this page.

### WORKING WITH ONE-BIT-PER-PIXEL LINE IMAGES

It is usually difficult to adjust or alter a one-bit line image in Photoshop for two reasons: (1) all of the tonal data in the file has been reduced to a black and white tone and (2) there are no meaningful tools available in the Photoshop bitmapped mode.

To adjust a previously created line image, use **Image>Mode**. This converts the line image into grayscale. This strategy makes Levels, Curves, Threshold, and Brightness and Contrast available.

### WORKING WITH EIGHT-BIT-PER-PIXEL LINE IMAGES

The best method for working with line images is to start from a grayscale image. This allows maintaining all the tones that will be adjusted to create a high quality line image. Once the grayscale image is captured then tools like Curves, Levels, Threshold, Brightness and Contrast, Posterize, and the 50% Threshold option can be used to make the image high contrast. The reason for using a grayscale file and the tools is to maintain and refine the details of the line image.

### THRESHOLD  Image Adjust:

Usually, Threshold is the first choice for creating high contrast line images, but Brightness and Contrast can provide the same results with not much more work.

**Original Continuous tone (CT) image**

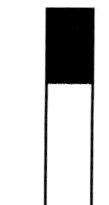

**CT image with 128 Threshold**

**CT image with 68 Threshold**

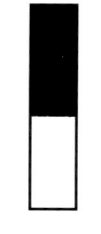

**CT image with 196 Threshold**

The problem with this method is that while these tools technically work, they do not have any significant effect on changing the line thickness of an image.

## BRIGHTNESS & CONTRAST `Image Adjust:`

This tool has two sliders. The rule of thumb is to adjust the Contrast to +100, and use the Brightness to target and then refine the break between white and black image areas.

**Original Continuous tone image**

**CT image with +0, + 100 B&C**

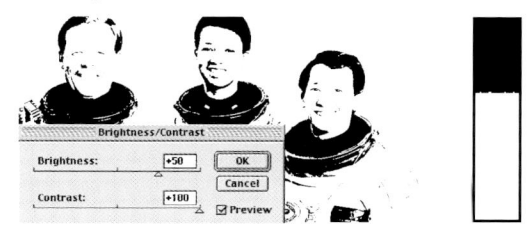

**CT image with +50, + 100 B&C**

**CT image with -50, + 100 B&C**

## POSTERIZE `Image Adjust:`

This secondary tool is only useful for images that are perfectly scanned with equal amounts (2 Levels) of black and white.

**Original Continuous tone image**

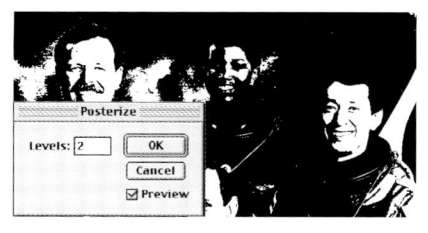

This example illustrates how little control Posterize has. Images must be perfect to use Posterize. If images do not have perfect tones, then the line image results will be less than satisfactory.

## BITMAP `Image Mode:`

This secondary tool produces bitmap results exactly like Posterize did. Typically the Bitmap mode options are on images that have been previously adjusted with tools like Threshold or Brightness & Contrast.

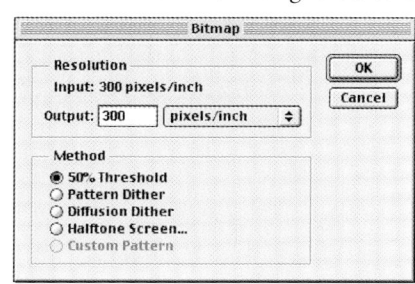

# REPRODUCING GRAYSCALE IMAGES
## LINE IMAGES TOOLS

### INTERMEDIATE LINE IMAGE TIP

Curves is sometimes used to adjust line images.

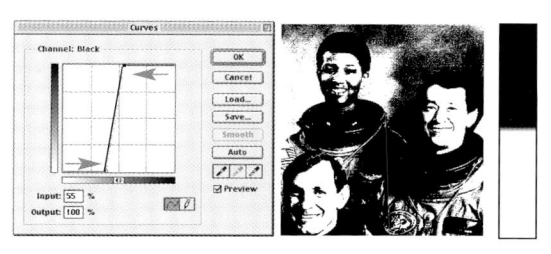

If the endpoints of the curve are moved as close to the vertical axis as possible, the resulting image is posterized (it gains the extreme contrast of a line art-type image).

57

# METHODOLOGY
## TO REPRODUCE GRAYSCALE IMAGES

In this section of the book, you will get an overview of the key concepts and techniques used in adjusting black-and-white images for reproduction.

## STRATEGY

1. Examine the original.
2. Capture image data — Scanner or Camera.
3. Identify the image category and tones.
4. Measure and adjust highlights.
5. Measure and adjust shadows.
6. Measure and adjust midtones.
7. Apply Unsharp Mask.
8. Save file for output or export.
9. Review image for rescanning or corrections.

## SAVE THE ORIGINAL SCAN, SAVE THE SETTINGS!

Providing you have enough space on your system, save the original scans and the settings so that after you produce the first proofs, you can go back and make corrections as far back in the process as you would like without starting from scratch.

## THE REPRODUCTION PROCESS

A typical process for an image destined for publication in a brochure is to take the continuous-tone original, scan it for conversion to digital data, display the data via a workstation and a monitor, optimize the image, convert the digital data to halftone film dots, then print it on paper. The goal during the conversion process is to learn how to optimize each phase of the operation to produce predictable quality results. When this happens, the final result will be a good reproduction.

### 1. Examine the continuous-tone original

The first step in the process is to examine the original that is to be reproduced. It should be correctly exposed, have fine grain, and have good overall sharpness and contrast. If an image is lacking in any of these areas, additional corrections will need to be made to minimize any negative characteristics. Once you learn how to correct good quality originals, the same techniques can be used to improve bad images. But, some images may require using masking techniques and greater adjustments to achieve optimum results.

### 2. Capture image data

#### Scanning the original

The next stage of the process is scanning. This converts continuous-tone data from photographic prints, slides, or original art into digital data. For halftone reproduction, this data should be captured as a single grayscale channel, 3 RGB channels, or 4 CMYK channels. It should not be captured as *Halftone data*. This is often misunderstood. The halftone capture mode available on many desktop scanners is meant for programs that cannot use grayscale data.

The bit depth or number of levels of information that can be gathered by a scanner determines how smoothly a continuous-tone image will reproduce. The maximum number of levels for achieving good results in the PostScript™ output language is 256. To get 256 levels, a scanner must have an 8-bit-per-pixel bit depth in grayscale and a 24-bit depth for color scanning. See appendix A: *Resolution* for more details. These digital levels range from level 255 (0% dot) to 0 (100% dot), white to black respectively.

#### Using a Digital Camera for Capture

Typically, digital cameras capture RGB image data. Convert it to grayscale with the *Mode* change or use one of the images three RGB channels.

The bit depth or number of levels of information that can be gathered by a the camera is critical to how smoothly a continuous-tone image will reproduce. To capture 256 levels, the camera must have the ability to capture at least a bit depth of 8 bit per pixels for grayscale and a 24-bit depth for RGB color images. See appendix A: *Resolution* for more details. These digital levels of a camera image ranges from level 255 (0% dot) to 0 (100% dot), white to black respectively.

### 3. Identify the image category

After an image is scanned or captured with a camera, it is helpful to use Photoshop's Histogram feature to display a variety of information about the image. By viewing the histogram, it is possible to tell if the scanner or camera gathered enough levels of data and if the data falls in the proper range. The mean value of the histogram can help determine if the scanned image is in the light, dark, or average image categories.

### 4.& 5. Establish highlights and shadows

To capture and reproduce the critical details in an image, the highlight (lightest) and shadow (darkest) tone areas must be set to specific target values for individual reproduction requirements.

In an image being prepared for printing on offset stock (not newsprint), where the original contains a complete range of tones encompassing both highlight and shadow detail, the digital data should range between levels 240–250 (2–6%) for the lightest areas and between levels 15–5 (95–98%) for the darkest areas.

These guidelines are also useful for images going to non-print media such as the World Wide Web. Just use the Levels target values for white and black points.

If you are going to print or to the web, *Normalizing* brings an image in line with these target values. The target values necessary to properly reproduce an image will vary depending on a variety of factors, including the type of paper stock, the specific printing press, and the halftone line screen. When learning about normalized images, it is best to discuss the proper target values with your print shop. For on-line imaging, use the above Levels target values. Basic guidelines for target values for images going to print are found in appendix B: Calibration.

To normalize an image, the continuous-tone image must be measured either with a densitometer or by comparing it to a known dot % value that would most closely reproduce that continuous-tone shade. This process establishes the relationship of the density (amount of light or dark) of the original image to the digital values, to the halftone, and to the values printed on paper in the reproduction.

Densitometers are instruments that can measure and display density and % dot values for images. Density is a measure of a reflective original's ability to absorb or reflect light or a transparency's ability to block or transmit light. Densitometers can measure transmissive, reflective, or digital media. Densitometers are available in stand-alone desktop and hand-held models; they can be incorporated into cameras, scanners, and computers.
Adobe Photoshop has a built-in digital densitometer. This is the floating Info Palette. It can provide measurements in dot % values or RGB levels.

6. **Adjust the midtones**

   After the end points of an image are chosen, measured, and adjusted, the midtones must be adjusted to achieve the proper separation of tones. The correct amount of midtone adjustment will provide good contrast in the reproduction. Photoshop is optimized for average images and these type of images usually require little adjustment to their midtones. Light images will require an increase in midtones and dark images will require a decrease in midtones.

   If you are not an experienced user and have not done a lot of testing, it is important that you have your monitor calibrated. The monitor is an important tool in making accurate judgments on midtone adjustments. Review pages 10-14 for more about monitor calibration.

7. **Sharpen the image**

   Typically, one of the last adjustments is to add back the sharpness that was lost as a result of the input scanning process. To do this, an Unsharp Mask filter is used. Don't let its name fool you. Of all the sharpening features available in Photoshop, Unsharp Mask is the most controllable and is modeled after high-end scanner tools. Some scanners can sharpen on input. Test your scanner using different settings to determine if it produces acceptable results.

8. **Save the image**

   After sharpening, all that is left is to save the image in the correct format and to output an initial round of proofs.

9. **Review for corrections**

   When you get the proofs back, compare the results to the original. If further adjustments are necessary, go back and make them and produce another round of proofs. After some experience, you will understand where to go in the process to make adjustments.

# METHODOLOGY
## TO REPRODUCE GRAYSCALE IMAGES

### "D" IS FOR DENSITY

Density is the ability of an object to absorb light. As density increases, less light is reflected

### EXPERT INFORMATION - DIFFERENT COUNTING SCALES USED WHEN REPRODUCING IMAGES

**Density values for various media:**

Transparency Media
Transparent media is measured in density values that range between 0.0 D to over 4.0 D.
Typical transparency highlights are 0.25 D (+ or - 0.1 D).
Typical transparency shadows are 3.0 D (+ or - 0.25 D).

Reflective Media
Reflective media density values range between 0.0 D to 2.2 D.
Typical highlights are 0.05 D (+ or - 0.06 D).
Typical shadows are 1.8 D (+ or - 0.40 D).

Halftone Media
Halftone film media is measured in density from 0.00 dmin to 4.0 dmax. and dot % values of 0 -100 in 1% increments.
Typical halftone film highlights dot % values are 0-10%.
Typical halftone film shadows dot % values are 90-100%.

Digital Media - Levels
Digital files are measured in levels that range from 255 to 0 levels in 1 level increments.
Typical digital level values for highlights areas are 255-245 levels.
Typical digital level values for shadows areas are 0-10 levels.

# HOW TO:
## IDENTIFY IMAGE CHARACTERISTICS

**WARNING! WARNING! WARNING!** ⚠

If your monitor is not calibrated, you will have to work entirely by using the number display in the Info Palette. Failure to calibrate your monitor may result in undesired results. In other words: what you see on screen is not what you get on output. If you would like to learn how to calibrate your monitor for black-and-white work, refer to pages 9 through 11.

## EVALUATING AN IMAGE

Printing presses cannot easily print continuous-tone images. To overcome that limitation, we create an optical illusion with halftone dots. A screen pattern is used to break the image's continuous tones into various sized dots that give the illusion of shades of gray.

The first step in converting a continuous-tone image to a halftone is to identify the image areas and determine the halftone target values for the reproduction. When the target values are chosen correctly, the reproduction will emulate the original.

### SIMULATED PHOTOGRAPH

Specular Highlights -
0% dot allowed in reflections and areas that go to white and hold no detail

Highlight -
Target Value 5%
Lightest area with detail

Midtones -
Target Value 50%

Shadow -
Target Value 95%
Darkest area

**Next**, scan the image directly into Photoshop with a scanner plug-in for the specific scanner. See your scanner guide for specific instructions.

After the image is scanned, the results of the scan can be viewed with the Histogram. For example, the Histogram for this image shows a Mean value of 105. This value helps to identify this image as one that is near an average-looking image. Also notice that the Histogram is densely packed, indicating that the scanner was indeed gathering 256 levels of data. If it had scanned in 64 levels of gray, three out of every 4 levels would be missing in the histogram.

To view the histogram, select Histogram from the Image menu.

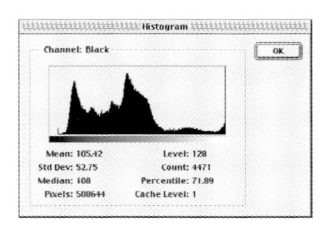

Histogram of image scan with 256-level grayscale scanner

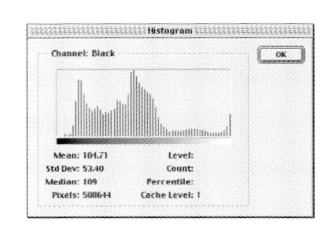

Histogram of image scan with 64-level grayscale scanner

The problem with reproducing images is that each image has a unique highlight, midtone, and shadow settings. This is what makes image reproduction and scanning difficult. A critical skill for achieving good results is to learn how to evaluate and determine an image's highlight and shadow areas. It is also important to be able to visually identify Light looking (Highkey), Average, or Dark looking (Lowkey) or some where in between.

# HOW TO:
## IDENTIFY IMAGE CHARACTERISTICS

**HIGHKEY IMAGE**

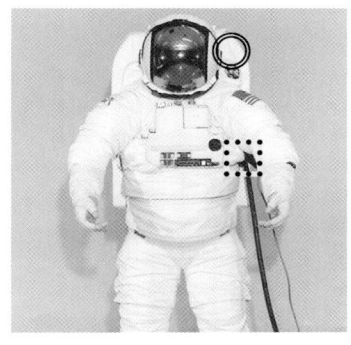

This is an extremely light-looking or Highkey image. It has a majority of light tones.

**AVERAGE IMAGE**

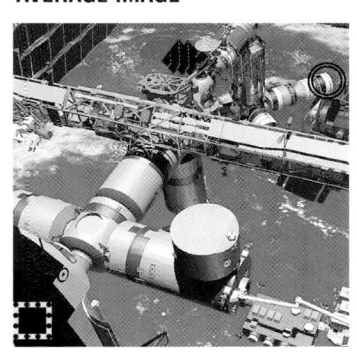

This is an average-looking image. It has equal amounts of light and dark tones.

**LOWKEY IMAGE**

This an extremely dark-looking or Lowkey image. It has predominately dark tones.

○ This icon represents an image's highlight area with a slight amount of image detail.

▫ This icon represents an image's shadow area with the blackest image details.

**IN BETWEEN A HIGHKEY & AVERAGE IMAGE**

This image is visually between an extremely light-looking image and an average-looking image.

**IN BETWEEN AVERAGE & LOWKEY IMAGE**

This image is visually between an average looking image and an extremely dark-looking image image.

**AVERAGE IMAGE WITH NO WELL-DEFINED HIGHLIGHT AREA**

This is an average looking image, but it does not have an easily defined white highlight area.

This page is a small sample of light, average, and dark image categories. What these images have in common is that 5 out of 6 of them have highlight and shadow areas. Approximately 80% of images headed for reproduction will have well-defined and measurable highlight and shadow areas.

**61**

# HOW TO:
## ADJUST HIGHLIGHTS AND SHADOWS

Adjusting the image to reflect the proper highlight and shadow range is a critical step in achieving a good quality black-and-white image. This process frames the image so that the tonal range can be adjusted to give the best results in reproduction. This is necessary because of the physical limitations of the printing process. For example, an offset printing press cannot hold the detail in images under certain conditions that are specific to each press. If the highlights are too light, they may not print. If they are too dark, the image may lack contrast. Follow the steps on the next two pages to learn how the highlight and shadow points of an image can be properly identified and adjusted.

### WHICH IS MORE CRITICAL TO THE REPRODUCTION: HIGHLIGHT OR SHADOW?

When the highlight dots are off by a few percent, the eye perceives a significant amount of change. If a 5% dot is off by 3%, it causes a dramatic change to the highlight, either by loss of highlight detail or by loss of contrast. Shadow placement, though critical, has a larger tolerance. When shadows are off by a few percent, it is harder for the eye to notice because it is so dark. If a 95% shadow dot is off by 3%, it is not as noticeable.

### THRESHOLDING & VIDEO SUPPORT

Thresholding is a technique to more easily determine highlights and shadows using Levels. It is done by holding down the **Opt/Alt** key then clicking and dragging the white arrow sliders. Some video cards do not support this technique nor does Adjustment Layers.

## SET HIGHLIGHTS AND SHADOWS

Open a grayscale image file. For this example, it is faster and easier to work on images with a resolution of 72 pixels per inch - see image resampling on page 103. Display the **Info Palette** and the **Color Palette** by selecting them from the **Windows** menu.

### Preset target values

1. In the first step on page 60, the appropriate target highlight (white point) and shadow (black point) were chosen.

   The highlight value is 5% and the shadow value is 95%. Compensating for dot gain for specific printing processes is addressed in the Calibration section.

Input dot 10%
Target: 5% Highlight Dot

Input Dot 100%
Target: 95% Shadow Dot

Determining the proper range of values for the best reproduction is mostly a matter of experience. These values are a good place to start as long as the image actually has highlight and shadow areas.

### Tool set-up

2. Use Levels to find and set the highlight and shadow points of the grayscale image.

   Open the Levels dialog box by selecting **Image** and then **Adjust** from the menu bar. Double click on the Set White Point (highlight) button. This brings up the Color Picker for the Select White Target Color control. Set the C, M, and Y values to 0 and set the K (black) value to 5%. Click **OK**.

3. Next, double click on the Set Black Point (shadow) button in the Levels dialog box.

   In the Select Black Target Color control, set the C, M, and Y values to 0 and set the K (black) value to 95%.

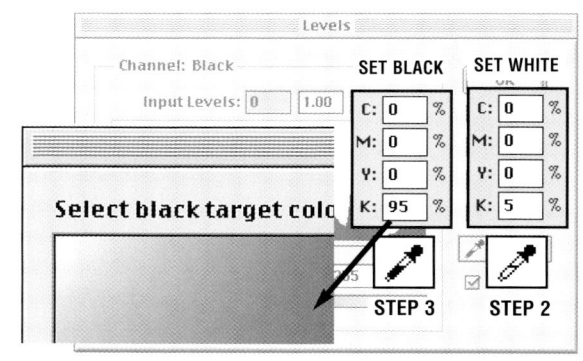

These dialog boxes are NOT the same as the **Color Picker** dialog box which can be selected from the Tool Box. The Set White and Set Black settings are saved to their own locations. The values will remain set from session to session until new values are entered.

### Locating the highlight and shadow

4. Determine where the White Point or highlight is going to be placed in the image.

   The Levels tool can help. Click and drag the right hand (white) Input Levels arrow. Hold down the **Opt/Alt** key. Slide the arrow to the left and then back right. Make sure you have Video LUT Animation checked in the Preferences dialog box and that Preview is not checked. The areas that turn white first are the highlight areas. Return the slider to the full right position. This is a good method for quickly identifying the lightest or darkest areas in the image.

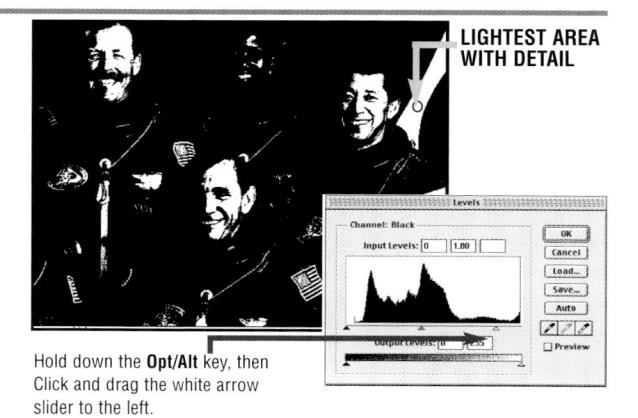

LIGHTEST AREA WITH DETAIL

Hold down the **Opt/Alt** key, then Click and drag the white arrow slider to the left.

## UNSHARP MASKING (USM)

This brings us to the final image adjustment to be made prior to saving the file for output: sharpening. When using a scanner, it is often necessary to add sharpness lost during the original scanning process. High-end scanners and some desktop scanners allow the user to add sharpness as the image is being processed. If your scanner supports enhancing sharpness, deactivate this feature for this tutorial. Refer to page 54 for more details about the Unsharp Mask (USM) adjustment range.

1. With the correct image window active, select Filter: Sharpen: Unsharp Mask from the menu bar.

2. Enter: Amount: 150%; Radius: 1 pixel; Threshold: 0. Click **OK**.

3. To toggle between the before and after effect of the sharpening, use the Edit: Undo/Redo command.

Determining the correct amount of sharpness is a subjective decision. If the effect is taken so far that it creates distinct white or black lines in the contrast transition areas of an image, you have over sharpened. Note that the amount of sharpness shown on screen is often softened by the actual printing process, so experiment with various settings.

Image after Highlight, Shadows, and Midtones are adjusted

Image after USM
Amount: 100, Radius: 1, Threshold: 0

Image after USM
Amount: 150, Radius: 1, Threshold: 0

Image after USM
Amount: 200, Radius: 1, Threshold: 0

Image after USM
Amount: 200, Radius: 2, Threshold: 0

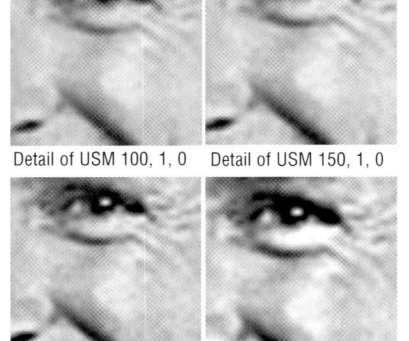

Detail of USM 100, 1, 0    Detail of USM 150, 1, 0

Detail of USM 200, 1, 0    Detail of USM 200, 2, 0

# HOW TO:
## SHARPEN THE IMAGE

When reproducing images, sharpness "puts the icing on the cake." The strategy is to first adjust the image's highlights, shadows, and midtones to get the best image reproduction, then apply sharpness. If necessary, you can go back and make minor image adjustments after sharpness is applied.

### LETTING THE SCANNER SHARPEN

An often asked question is, "Should I let my scanner and scanner software make image adjustments or should I do them in Adobe Photoshop?" If you understand how your scanner is performing adjustments such as sharpness and you are satisfied by its performance, by all means, let the scanner do the adjustments. In a production environment the less user intervention, the better. It is more likely, however, that you will want to use Photoshop at first until you fully understand how the adjustments work. You will then be able to use that experience to evaluate how well the scanner's automatic adjustments are working and you will understand how to change them manually, if necessary.

# HOW TO:
## SAVE THE FILE

### FILE FORMAT EXTENSIONS FOR WINDOWS

For better Cross Platform Compatibility, set up the **Append File Extension** in the General Preferences.

This makes upper or lower case three-character file extensions available for the end of file names to indicate file formats.

| | |
|---|---|
| Photoshop Native file format | PSD |
| Amiga IFF | IFF |
| BMP | BMP |
| Photoshop EPS | EPS |
| Photoshop DCS 2.0 (for Spot Color) | EPS |
| Flashpix | FPX |
| Joint Photographic Experts Group (JPEG) | JPG |
| PCX | PCX |
| Photoshop PDF | PDF |
| Pict File | PCT |
| Pict Resource | RSR |
| Pixar | PXR |
| Raw | RAW |
| Scitex CT | SCT |
| Targa | TGA |
| Tagged Image File (TIFF) | TIF |
| Integrated Color Management | ICM |
| Compuserve GIF | GIF |

## SAVE FORMATS

The primary Save options for black-and-white images created in Adobe Photoshop are TIFF (Tagged Image File Format) and EPS (Encapsulated PostScript).

- **TIFF** files contain bitmapped data only and should be used if the image will be cropped by the page layout program by a rectangle, circle, or odd-shaped box, or if the image will be colored in the page layout program. The image will use the default halftone line screen settings of the page layout program for output. This file format produced smaller files than EPS format and allows the use of LZW (lossless) compression which can save space.

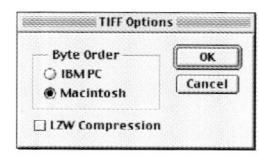

- **JPEG** (Joint Photographic Experts Group) compression is a destructive (lossy) form of file compression that actually throws away data to save space. It is usually used for for images headed to the Web and to compress images for storage.

  In Photoshop, the settings range from excellent to fair. The excellent or good settings produce acceptable results and can be used when disk space and file size becomes an important consideration. If you save and re-save images with JPEG, the file can become degraded. If resaving is necessary, the rule of thumb is to use high-quality and low-compression ratios each time. Technically speaking, the image information is being degraded, but using the high quality option does not degrade the file so much it becomes unuseable. Running some tests will identify the number of times it is possible to resave a file.

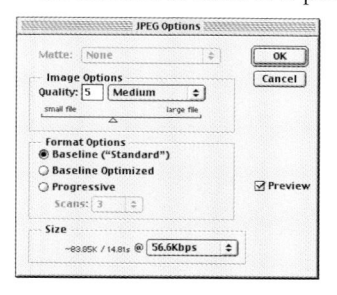

- The EPS format in Photoshop (Photoshop EPS) is a metafile format that contains pixel data and vector data. Vector data allows the user to save the transfer function data, line screen data, clipping path (silhouette) and transparent whites (if the mode has been changed to bitmapped), as part of the file. Line screen and screen angle data saved in this format will override the data in a page layout program.

  EPS format supports Mac and TIFF (IBM) bitmap preview options and can encode the file in either binary (which is half the size and takes half the time to download) or ASCII.

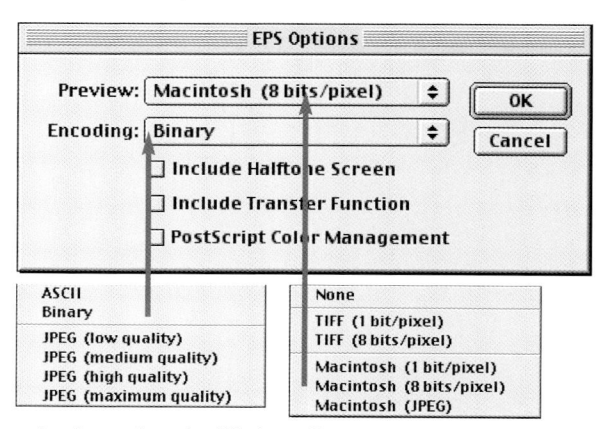

- Preview options for Windows files are TIFF and None.
- Preview options for Macintosh files are Macintosh 1-bit and 8-bit-per-pixel.
- Use Binary encoding for EPS.
- JPEG compression is based on your particular quality and compression requirements.

### TRANSPARENT WHITES

When a bitmapped file (a file either scanned as line art or converted to a bitmap through the Mode menu) is saved, the EPS dialog box gives you the option to save the image so that the white areas in the image will be completely transparent.

- The **Photoshop** file format is the default file format for newly created images, it is the fastest option for saving files and supports all of the Photoshop image modes.

## SAVING FILES WITH LAYERS

The Photoshop format is the only file structure that supports Layers. This means the Photoshop file format will not work with most page layout programs, except Adobe's InDesign. To use a Photoshop file in a page layout program, the final corrected or retouched Photoshop file needs to be flattened. Use the Layers Menu or the Pop-out Menu in the Layers Palette.

## WHEN TO USE: SAVE, SAVE AS, AND SAVE A COPY

### Save

The purpose of Save is to update the file as you are working. The most convenient way to apply this option is with the keyboard shortcut Cmd/Cntrl S. The rule of thumb is to use a Save after each step of an image processing adjustment or after each stage of an imaging project. This is the best way to ensure you do not lose any work that has been done.

Note: even if you have made a mistake and saved a bad correction it is still possible to recover from that by using the History Palette. Be sure not to close the file. See page 18 for more about Histories.

### Save As

The purpose of Save As is to give the end-user the opportunity to create an exact duplicate or copy of a file at that specific time by changing the file name. This is a great recovery strategy. Our advice to use a naming system that is convenient, and logical, such as the File name with a "v" and a number for version.

For example, Rocketv1, Rocketv2, etc. The benefits of being able to return to a critical stage of a project out weight the extra space that multiple versions take up on your computer's hard disk.

### Save A Copy...

This option is also found under the File menu. It offers another choice for you to save versions of a file at various stages of the job without replacing the image you are currently working with on screen. It places the file in a folder of your own choosing on the computer's hard disk.

The Save A Copy option also permits you to discard Channel data and Flatten images (that are in the Photoshop file format) and save them as other file formats. Save As does not allow you do this.

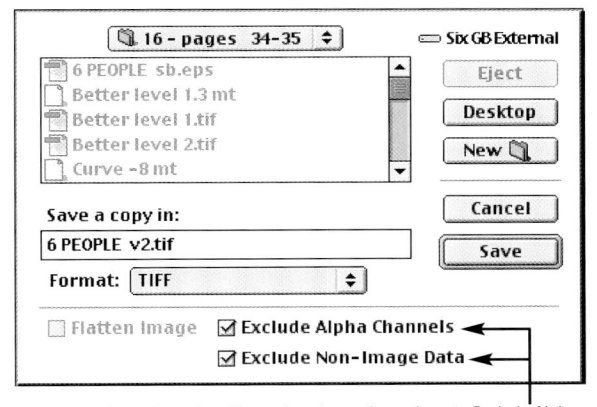

The Save A Copy dialog box illustration shows the options to Exclude Alpha Channels and Non-Image Data and all the available file formats even when an image is a Layer.

# HOW TO:
## SAVE THE FILE

### PICT FORMAT

This format should be avoided if at all possible for PostScript™ imaging process. It is unreliable, corrupts easily, and often causes errors when it is sent to a PostScript™ output device.

**67**

# MORE ABOUT MIDTONES

This section discusses the Curves tool and its ability to make a variety of changes that enhance the quality of an image.

### CURVES TIP
Note the diagonal line in the Curves dialog box. As the mouse button is held down over the image, a little round ball appears to visually highlight the area that is being probed. This, along with watching the Info Palette, will help to locate specific areas of an image on the curve. You can then alter those areas by clicking on the curve in that area and placing a control point. Remember, unless that area is masked, changing that control point will change all the other areas of the image that also have that value.

### HOUDINI ACT!
To remove unwanted points on a Curve, just drag them outside of the Curves dialog box and they vanish.

### WHAT IS CONTRAST?
Contrast is the difference between white and black. When an image exhibits a great difference between the white and black areas, this is known as having high contrast. In an extreme sense, the best contrast is in line work where there are only two tones: white and black. On the other end of the spectrum, the worst contrast is a constant level of gray. It can be light or dark gray, but only one level. Understanding these concepts and how they plot on a graph provides us the tools to determine how to create contrast for halftone images using Photoshop.

**The basic moves** *(Ensure the highlights and shadows are properly adjusted first)*
Here are some guidelines for making midtone corrections in images. These corrections are made to optimize the image and compensate for the effects of tone compression that occur when an image is converted from continuous-tone data to digital data and then printed.

### Light images (+) midtone
To create contrast in light images, increase the midtone values along the curve at the 50% value. A good starting place is 5%-10 % points from the original position. The only way to trust the results and gain experience is to make and save several incremental changes, produce film and proofs, and compare them to the original and the monitor display.

*After the highlights and shadows are set.*

*After increase in midtones.*

### Dark images (-) midtone
To create contrast in dark images, decrease the midtones. Start with a reduction in midtones between 5%-10% from the 50% input value indicated in the curves dialog box. Make and save several incremental changes and then produce film and proofs and compare them to the monitor display.

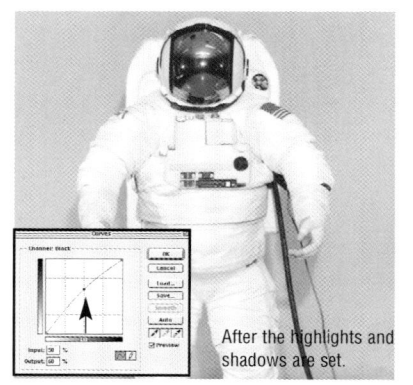

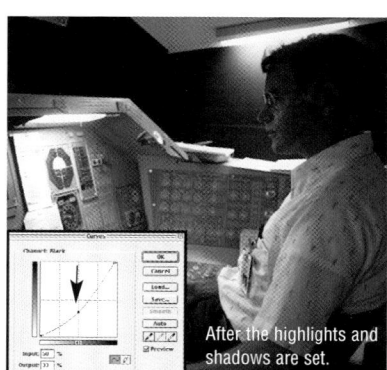

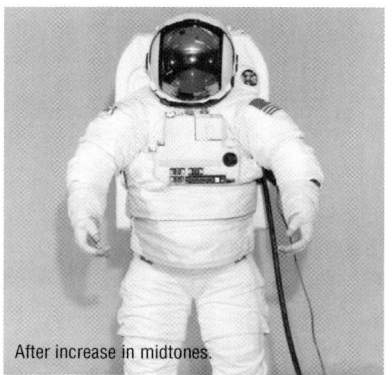

*After the highlights and shadows are set.*

*After decrease in midtones.*

### Saving settings
After any adjustment is made in Levels or Curves, it is possible to save the parameters of those dialog boxes. This is an easy way to recall the endpoint settings when changing between Levels and Curves. Several sets of different combinations of endpoints can be made and then loaded into the curve prior to making a midtone adjustment. Settings for midtone adjustment can also be saved. Experimenting with and defining your own set of curves will increase your productivity when reproducing multiple halftones.

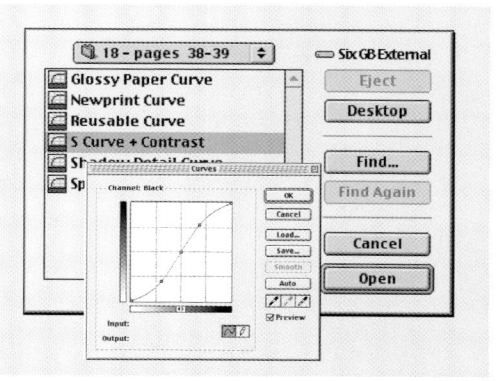

## THE MULTI-POINT METHOD FOR MORE DETAILED CONTROL

The multi-point method allows specific midtone points to be changed. Others midtone points that are anchored in place and shift only a small amount. Precise control is a delicate balance. If it goes too far in one direction or the other, a trade-off within the reproduction takes place.

### Better control with a light image

Increasing the 1/4 tones and the midtones with the multi-point method gives you better contrast in the light-looking image without adversely effecting the 3/4 tone and the shadow areas. The example on the right shows how to use 5 points to create better contrast on a light-looking image.

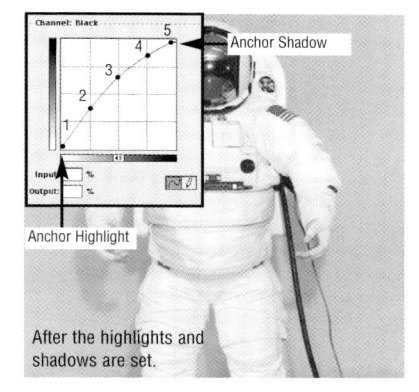

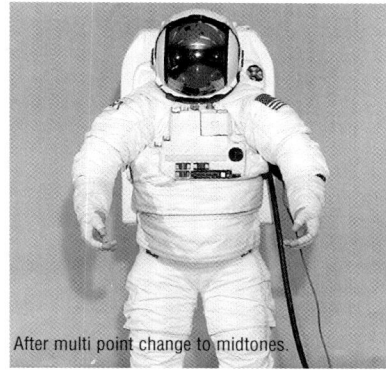

### Better control with a dark image

A dark image, on the other hand, requires a decrease in the 3/4 tones and the midtones to get a better balance between detail and contrast. Remember to anchor the highlight and shadow points on the curve before making curve adjustments.

### Better control for average images

An average image can have greater contrast through the use of an "S" curve. This type of curve takes both ends of the tone and separates them, creating more contrast. Be careful not to go too far or the resulting image might appear posterized.

Note: Images on pages 68 and 69 do not yet have USM applied.

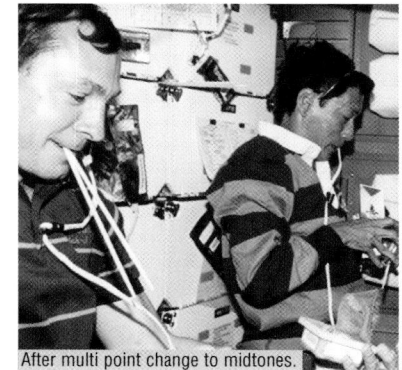

# MORE ABOUT MIDTONES

### MIDTONE GUIDELINES

The use of one point or multiple points to adjust midtones is dependent on each image's content. The following guidelines outline when to use which method.

**One control point**
This method works well in situations where images are globally light or dark. Use this method with a dark image where 1/4 tone details are not present or important. In this situation, midtones (1/4 tones-3/4 tones) are reduced globally to bring out the important shadow details.

**Multiple points**
Use multiple points to bring out details in specific image areas that would otherwise lose them if a global change was made. A multi–point method will permit specific tones to be adjusted while maintaining detail in other areas of the image.

An example of this would be a dark image where important 1/4 tone detail needs to be maintained. In this situation, the 3/4 tone and midtone would be reduced to bring out shadow detail and the 1/4 tone would be anchored in place or increased to differentiate highlight detail.

### EXCHANGEABLE CURVES

Curves saved in the Transfer Curves dialog box are fully exchangeable with those saved in the standard Curves dialog box. Try the Save and Load functions of both dialog boxes.

### HOW MANY POINTS ARE ENOUGH?

Though it is possible to have up to 16 points to control the reproduction, once 4 or 5 points are understood and adjusted, more points are rarely needed except when creating extraordinary contrast or for special image-correction needs.

# HOW TO:
## MAKE CORRECTIONS

### GET ORGANIZED!

The most successful imaging operations all have one thing in common – every detail of a job's production is organized. When you first start producing black-and-white images, it is important to keep track of your original scan and the saved settings you used to create the final product. The key is to establish a system of folders and file names for storing image files and related information like Curves or Levels parameters (used through Load and Save).

For example, an image management system might consist of 4 folders. One for the original scan, another for final adjusted images, a third folder for the image adjustment information of Curves and Levels settings and a fourth to hold the three previous folders. The saved settings can then be used with the original scan as a starting point if additional adjustments need to be made to the corrected image.

**Note**: You can't save USM settings. Try incorporating them into the file name e.g.,*Scan of President 1,100,0*.

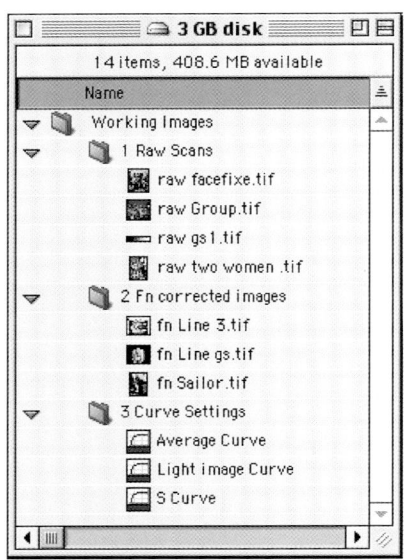

The illustration above shows scanned files organized in three folders.

## TROUBLESHOOTING BLACK-AND-WHITE HALFTONES

When making corrections based on proofs in a black-and-white image reproduction system, there is a sequence of events that needs to occur to ensure consistent results. This is only possible if a system is in calibration. With a calibrated system, the user can be comfortable knowing there is visual and numerical agreement between each of the system's components. It is then possible to make specific changes, based on proofs, that refine the image reproduction process. The following are typical symptoms and remedies that occur when reproducing black-and-white images.

**SYMPTOM:** Shadow areas look too dark and lack detail.

**SYMPTOM:** The whitest highlight areas have detail but appear "flat," lacking contrast.

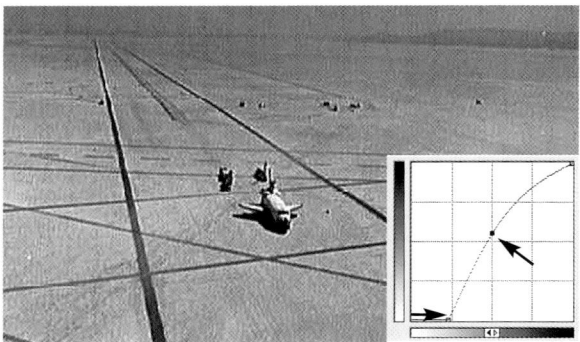

**REMEDY:** First check the reproduction's output values. Measure the midtone and shadow points. If the shadow values are in agreement with the expected target values, then correct the reproduction by adjusting the midtone and 3/4 tone shadow areas. Use the Curves tool. Decrease the 3/4 tones in 4% or 5% increments until the image does not look too dark. In this particular image a dramatic midtone adjustment (over 25%) was required (see the inset Curve dialog box). Sometimes re-scanning is necessary if detail is not available in the image.

**REMEDY:** Adjust the highlight and midtone areas to create better contrast. There is no well-define highlight area, so normal highlight target values will not be effective. If they were used, it would make the reproduction too contrasty. To get the correct highlight setting takes trial and error combined with skill to manually alter the highlight until you achieve the correct looking contrast (we took and educated guess and reduced the highlight 25%). Once the highlight is set, increase the midtones to create good contrast. This will bring out highlight and midtone detail.

**SYMPTOM:** Highlight areas lack detail.

**REMEDY:** This image appears to have improperly set highlights, they measure 0% dots or 255 levels. The only effective way to fix this image is to rescan it. Since it came from the NASA web site all that can be done is to place a 5% dot value in the highlight areas to artificially create highlight image tones. Our final results are not dramatically different from the original.

**SYMPTOM:** Image reproduces too light and is lacking good contrast.

**REMEDY:** This image needs the midtone increased. Before making that adjustment, make sure the highlight and shadow points are set correctly. We used 5% in the highlight and 95% in the shadow. This will ensure the image has good highlight and shadow contrast. The highlight placement is critical and should be set between 1% and 5%. The real problem with this image is poor midtone placement. By increasing the midtone, the image can achieve better highlight to midtone contrast.

# HOW TO:
## MAKE CORRECTIONS

### TIPS FOR EVALUATING ORIGINALS AND PROOFS

1. Place the Proof and original side by side in a neutral and balanced lighted area. Have the Photoshop file that produced the proof on you monitor.
2. Look at and compare specific image areas of the proof to the original. Compare highlights, midtones, and shadows.
3. Use the Photoshop Info Palette to guide your corrections by measuring the halftone values used in each image area.
4. After you have corrected the image, do a Save As. Then re-open the image and compare it to the corrected image.
5. Create a new Proof if you think the correction is OK.

# HOW TO:
## MAKE CORRECTIONS

### WHAT IS POSTERIZATION?

Posterization is an effect that reduces the number of shades of gray in an image between the lightest and darkest tones. Posterization can be introduced by moving the Curve too dramatically. This will cause the image's tones to look unnatural and torn apart. In extreme cases, Posterization will ruin an image reproduction.

Original Image

The example above is an extreme example of a Posterized Image.

**SYMPTOM:** Highlight and Shadow areas look and measure OK, but the reproduction lacks overall contrast.

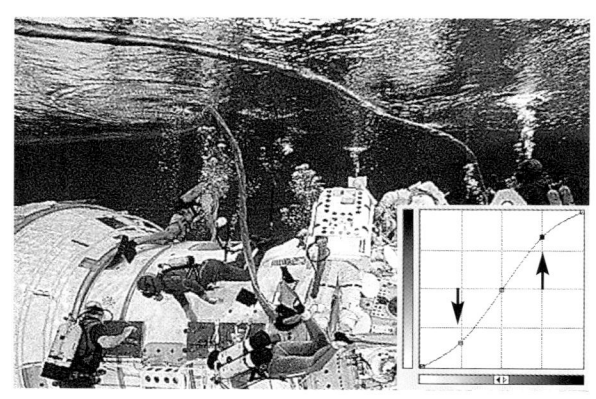

**REMEDY:** After measuring the image, we found the highlights and shadows are set correctly and that increasing or decreasing the midtone makes the image reproduce too light or dark, respectively. This image needs more contrast because it is a poorly exposed photograph, (hey, it was shot underwater). This is a situation where an "S" curve is used to increase the midtone contrast. The degree of change to the curve is based on how flat the original is. Be careful in this situation, moving the curve too far can introduce Posterization that will degrade the image.

**SYMPTOM:** This image is lacking contrast.

### CORRECTION A

### CORRECTION B

**REMEDY:** This is a poorly scanned photograph. The highlights and shadows are not set correctly. After setting the highlight and shadow points, the midtones are too dark. The remedy is to reduce the midtone by 10.

- *Correction A* has only the highlight and shadow points adjusted.
- *Correction B* has the highlight shadow and midtone points adjusted.

72

# HOW TO:
## MAKE CORRECTIONS

**SYMPTOM:** Image lacks sharpness.

**REMEDY:** Increase the USM. Use the Amount value starting with a percent between 150% and 200% for a 300 dpi image. Leave the pixel Radius at 1 and Threshold at 0.

This example above had 300 USM applied with the pixel Radius at 1 and Threshold at 0.

This over-sharpened example had 300 USM applied two times, with the pixel Radius at 1 and Threshold at 0.

**SYMPTOM:** This image appears well exposed but the faces are too dark.

### RETOUCHED IMAGE

**REMEDY:** This image needs to be retouched. Adjusting Curves or Levels might bring out the details in the faces, but other tones in the image might suffer by becoming too light looking. The Snapshot option was used in this example to lighten the faces.

For masking information see pages 26 through 41.
For retouching information see pages 76 through 79.

### SHARPNESS TIP:

It is usually necessary to increase USM. The guideline in Photoshop is to use the Amount value and start at 150%. Leave the pixel Radius at 1 and Threshold at 0. Learning to fine tune the amount of USM requires experimentation. Fine tuning is accomplished by applying different amounts of USM to images. After making film and proofs, re-print the image to determine the amount of USM that will provide the correct amount of sharpness.

### USM THRESHOLD TIP:

Threshold in the USM filter works like a mask to protect highlight areas. Threshold is a good to tool for protecting grainy highlight image areas. Experiment to find the right values. If the Threshold is set too high, highlight image detail can become blurred.

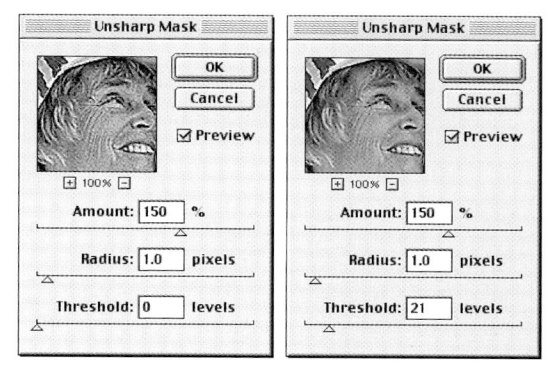

In the examples above, we used a 0 Threshold (the USM dialog box on the left) and a 21 Threshold (the USM dialog box on the right).

# REPRODUCING GRAYSCALE IMAGES

## REVIEW

The Reproducing Grayscale Images section is about the predominate Photoshop image processing tools, Photoshop imaging methods, and image reproduction strategies for reproducing grayscale images.

- **Preadjust Tools**

  The measuring tools such as the Eyedropper, Info Palette, and image processing highlight and shadow eyedropper options have to be set up so images can be predictably viewed, measured, and adjusted.

- **Use Levels and Curves**

  Levels and Curves are the main image processing tools for reproducing grayscale images. Both tools allow you to control highlights, shadows, and midtones. However, Curves is clearly a more sophisticated and therefore more powerful tool than Levels. The difference is that Levels has only three points of control and Curves has up to sixteen points of control.

- **Use the USM Filter**

  After the images tones are adjusted, we suggest sharpening the image with the *Filter>Unsharp Mask*. This is the most controllable filter for sharpening.

- **Suggested Working Order**

  While it is important to understand the tools for image reproduction, we suggest the following order of work activities which will create consistent, quality results.

  1. Examine the original
  2. Capture image data — Scanner or Camera.
  3. Identify the image category and tones.
  4. Measure and adjust highlights.
  5. Measure and adjust shadows.
  6. Measure and adjust midtones.
  7. Apply Unsharp Mask.
  8. Save file for output or export.
  9. Review image for rescanning or corrections.

  See page 58 and 59.

- **Tips**

  At the end of this section, we offer more intermediate information about how to adjust midtones and how to make correction to an image.

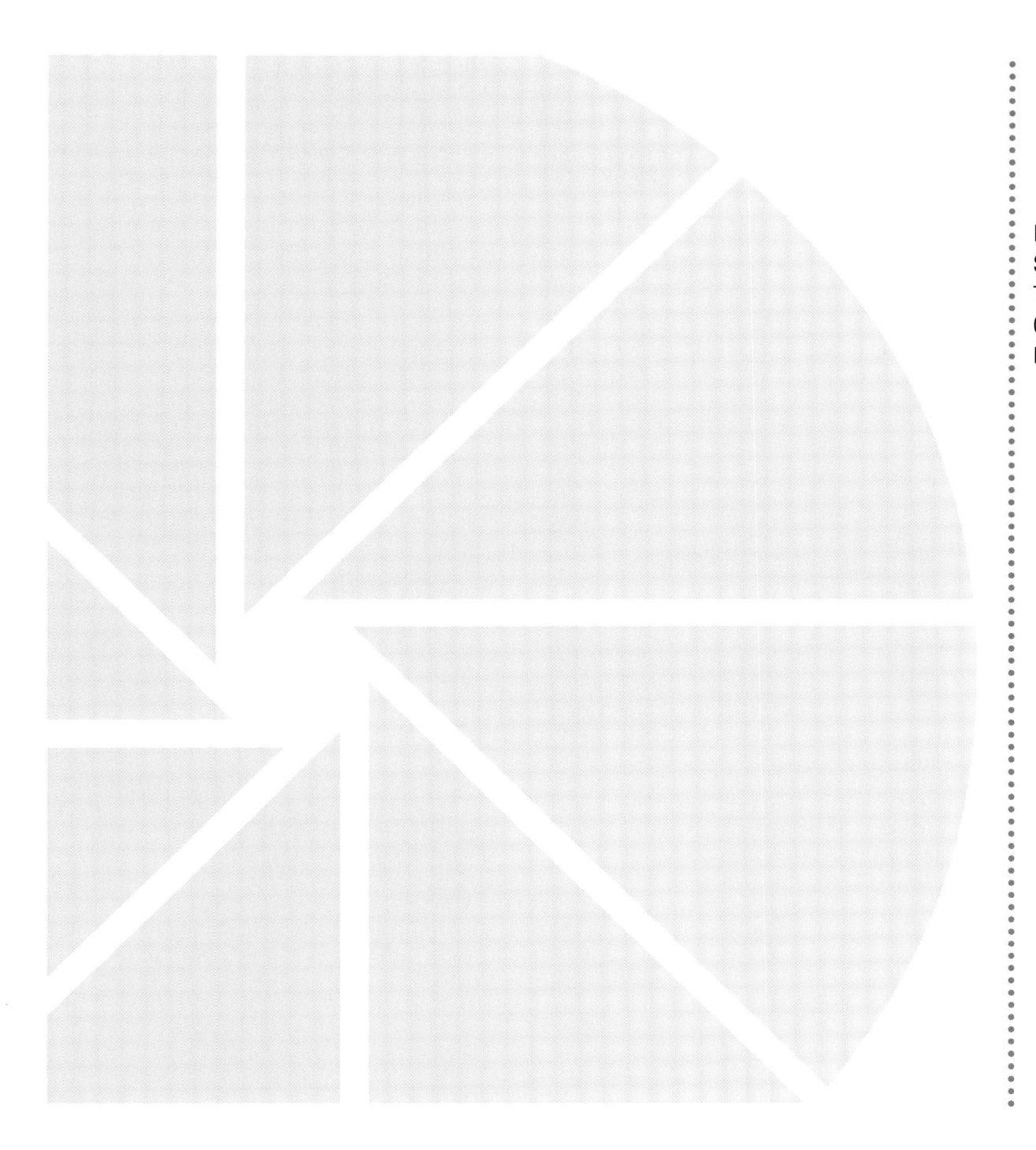

# RETOUCHING BASICS

Retouching Strategies ...........................76
Snapshot vs Selections.........................77
Toning Tools ........................................78
Cloning ................................................79
Review.................................................80

# RETOUCHING BASICS

## RETOUCHING STRATEGIES

**RETOUCHING STRATEGIES AT-A-GLANCE**

1. Use Snapshots.
2. Use Selections with Curves.
3. Use Dodge and Burn.
4. Use the Rubber Stamp for cloning.

**RUBBER STAMP TOOL TIP**

We have found that the Rubber Stamp Tool is often misused to apply tone corrections to images. The Rubber Stamp Tool will work sometimes, but cloning a large image area to blend tones becomes a time-consuming process. This is why we suggest using (1) Snapshot, (2) Selections, and (3) Dodge and Burn before using (4) the Rubber Stamp. This permits you to get the tones of the image correct before cloning. Use the Rubber Stamp Tool for blending edges and removing other imperfections that might look unnatural.

We also know there is no absolute formula for applying the Rubber Stamp Tool. So our advice is to use it for fixing small image areas with blemishes or imperfections in the original photograph. Also we use it for areas such as dirt that was scanned into the image or for removing freckles and hot spots on glasses.

## WHERE TO BEGIN TO RETOUCH AN IMAGE?

While Photoshop is full of great tools for retouching images, start by getting the image contrast right before using any selective correction techniques. This saves countless hours of repetitive retouching. The How to Section (pages 44-73) explains how to optimize grayscale image contrast. After an image has achieved its optimum contrast, we suggest using certain tools before others to retouch images. We know there is no absolute order for retouching but, here is our prioritized list of grayscale retouching tools and techniques:

1. Take a Snapshot of the image after Levels, Curves, or Filters have been applied to it.
2. Create a mask with a Selection and use the black and white image processing tools such as Curves or Levels.
3. Use the Toning Tools with the Dodge and Burn options.
4. Use the Rubber Stamp Tool for cloning.

**THE EXAMPLE BELOW SHOWS HOW TO WORK WITH SNAPSHOTS AND HOW TO RETOUCH AN IMAGE.**

The image below has poor exposure on the fleshtone areas. In this situation, the image's contrast has been optimized to bring out the important image details everywhere except the face.

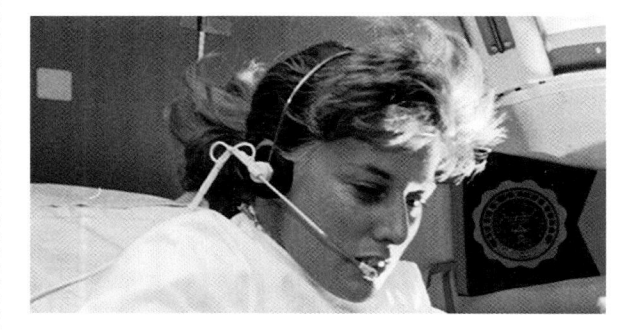

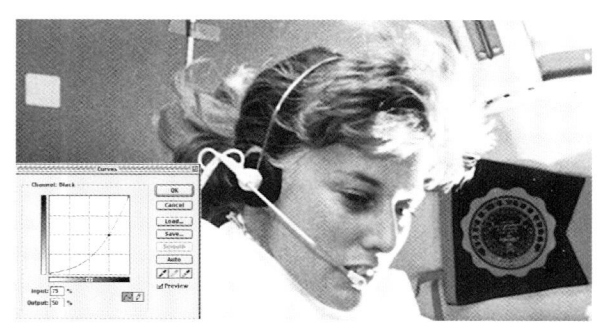

After the Snapshot is taken, the History Palette is setup so there is the original image's Snapshot and the New Snapshot. The Source of the New Snapshot is clicked on and the History brush is used to paint the correction. *See the next pages sidebar about Snapshots.*

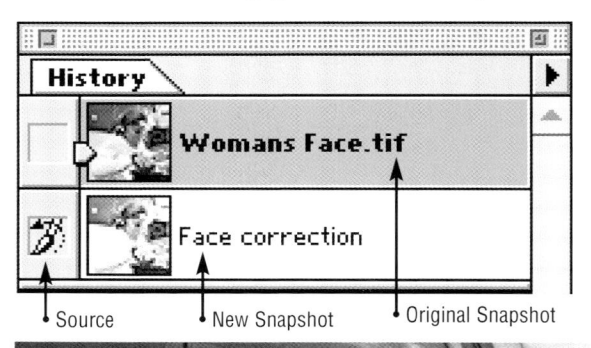

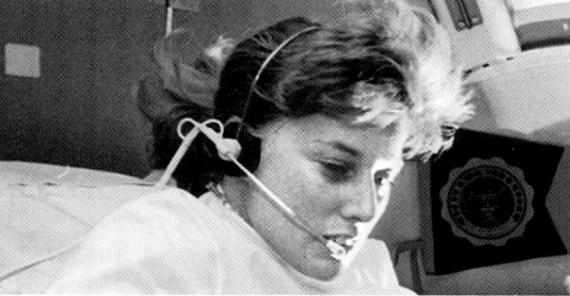

The image above shows the effect of the Curves adjustment to bring out the details in the face. This adjustment ruins the rest of the image's contrast and detail.

The image above shows the effect of the correction that was painted from the New Snapshot. This adjustment brings out the details in the face. All of the other important image details are unchanged.

76

## THE EXAMPLE BELOW SHOWS HOW TO WORK WITH SELECTIONS TO RETOUCH AN IMAGE.

Just like the pervious example, the image's contrast has been optimized to bring out the important image details everywhere except the face.

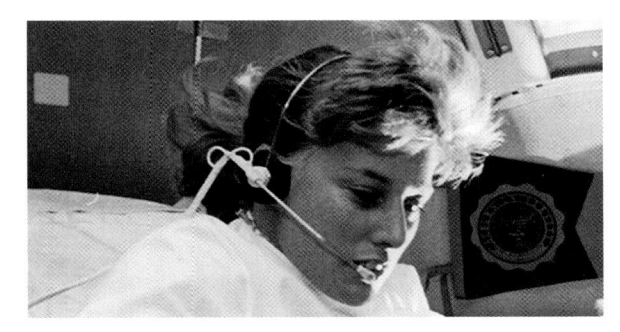

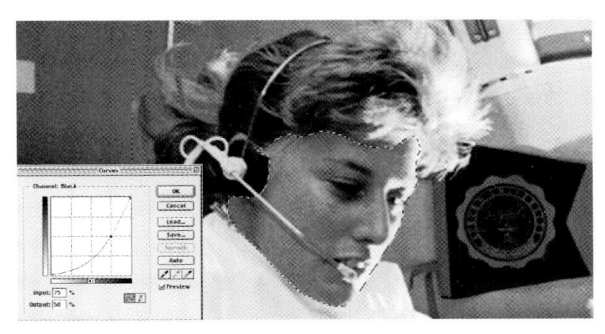

The image above shows the Selected face area and the Curves correction applied.

- To create this Selection, we started out by using the Magic Wand.
- Then Quick Mask was used with small brushes to refine the edges around the face and hair image areas.
- Curves was used on the final Selection to correct the face area.

## SNAPSHOTS VERSES SELECTIONS

Both the Snapshot and Selection methods work for retouching. Choosing one method over the other is sometimes a matter of having experience with a particular tool. One of the compelling reasons we suggest using Snapshots before trying a Selection can be seen in the final retouching of our examples.

- Using the Snapshot was easier to retouch the areas around the hair by using different size brushes with various opacity settings. And if a mistake was made such as going too far with the correction, it was easy to click on the Source of the original Snapshot and paint back to the original.
- Using a Selection took more time to create an accurate mask. We also recognize, that in some situations, it is necessary to create a Selection. In this example, the face mask required tone transitions from the face into the hair areas. Since Quick Mask required using painting skills as did the Snapshot, it reinforces that, in this case, the Snapshot was the best choice. The final results are similar but, one of the main differences is that the correction was not seen until the mask was created. Note the circled image areas below.

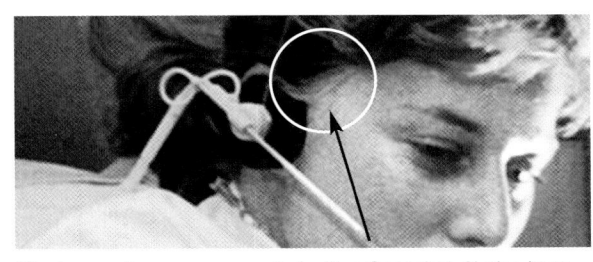

The image above was corrected with a Snapshot. Notice how the hair areas close to the face has natural transitions.

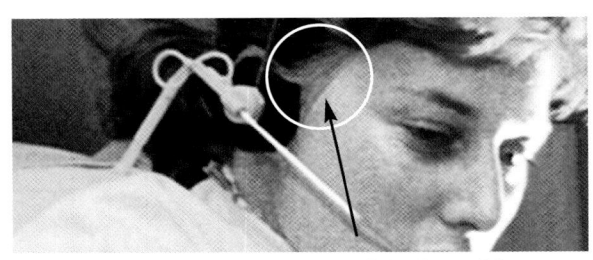

The image above was corrected with a Selection and Curves. Notice how the hair areas close to the face is too light.

# RETOUCHING BASICS
## SNAPSHOT VS SELECTIONS

### HOW TO CREATE A SNAPSHOT AT-A-GLANCE

1. Correct or alter the image overall.
2. Use the Pop-out menu on the History Palette to take a Snapshot. Undo (Optional).
3. Select the Source of the newly created Snapshot.
4. Click on the Top Snapshot on the right side area.
5. Select the History Brush from the Tools Palette and correct the image.

### IS ONE METHOD BETTER THAN ANOTHER?

Both Snapshots and Selections work extremely well. Our advice is to use both methods in conjunction with each other.

For example, in the image corrected with Selections and Curves, why not use a Snapshot with the correct brush size and different opacities to quickly repair the areas close to the face and the hair that are too light.

# RETOUCHING BASICS

## TONING TOOLS

### DODGE & BURN TOOL

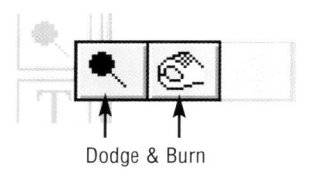

Dodge & Burn

### TONING TOOLS GUIDELINES

When correcting extreme highlight or shadow areas, we find the Toning Tools to be too powerful and are best for expert Photoshop operations.

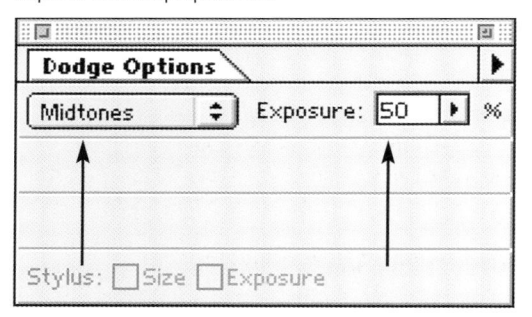

When working in any image areas, start with the midtone option and an Exposure of 50%. Test and then vary different Exposure levels to achieve the desired results.

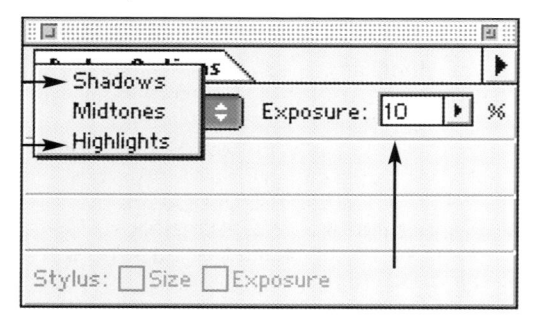

Use low exposure values between 5% and 10% when using the highlight and shadow area Toning Tools.

## DODGE & BURN

The Toning Tools have evolved from the photographic darkroom techniques of using a hand-held mask between the image being projected from a light source and the photographic print paper. The mask holds back or lets light through to a specific image area to make the print lighter (dodged) or darker (burned). The Dodge & Burn Tool offers dodging and burning highlight, midtone, or shadow areas with different amounts of exposure.

The Dodge & Burn Tools are useful for fixing or cleaning up specific image areas (highlights, midtones, and shadows) by allowing adjustments to specific areas with different size brushes and various exposures. The Sponge Tool (that is grayed out in the sidebar) is for color images and is not available with grayscale images.

### USING DODGE & BURN

After the image is open, we suggest using the Sampler Tool. Place the Sampler point strategically on the image and make sure the Info Palette is available. In this example, the Dodge Tool was used to lighten the image.

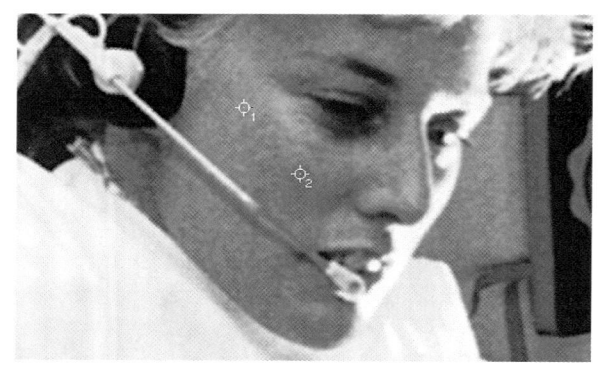

During the Dodging or Burning process use the Undo/Redo (**Cmd/Cntrl** Z) to toggle between the original file and the corrected file. This allows using the Eyedropper Sampler Points in the Info Palette to verify before and after retouched density values.

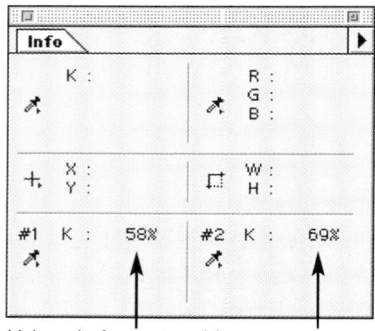

**ORIGINAL**

Values before retouching

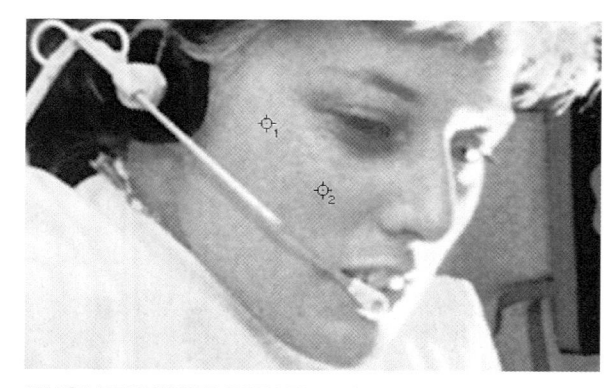

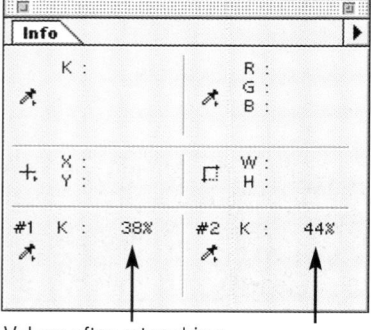

**IMAGE RETOUCHED WITH THE DODGE TOOL**

Values after retouching

78

## CLONING WITH THE RUBBER STAMP TOOL

The Rubber Stamp Tool is useful for repairing or cleaning up dirt, scratches, tears, etc. from specific image areas. This tool also allows copying one portion of an image with brushes to another area of an image. This is usually called cloning.

In this example the photograph was torn at one corner. Then it was taped on the back in close proximity to its original position and was scanned.

**1. Choose the Rubber Stamp Tool with an appropriate brush size.**

Move the brush near the area to be cloned. In this example, we started retouching at the top and to the left of the tear.

The circle in the example above represents the brush size.

**2. Set the Source for Cloning.**

Once the brush is in the right location, depress the **Opt/Alt** key to pick up the Source for the Rubber Stamp Tool.

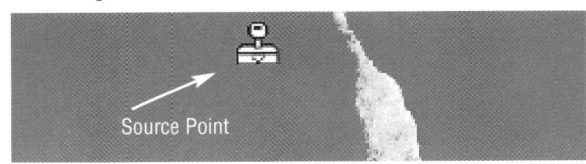

When the **Opt/Alt** key is depressed, the brush icon will change to the Rubber Stamp Icon. When the brush icon changes to the Rubber Stamp Icon, click the mouse to pickup the Source area.

**3. Move the brush to the Destination.**

After picking up the Source point, release the mouse button and the **Opt/Alt** key. Then move the mouse to a new destination.

In this example, we moved the brush over the tear and depressed the mouse. This paints image data from the Source (that was picked up in step 3) to the new Destination. As the mouse moves, so does the Source point.

The cross hair represents the Source point. The cross hair can be seen in the image when painting from the Source to the Destination with the Rubber Stamp Tool.

When the Rubber Stamp Tool is set to *Aligned* (this is the default setting), the cross hair will change position and follow the mouse's movements.

**4. Paint with the Rubber Stamp Tool.**

Using the Rubber Stamp Tool is an on-going process. This makes it necessary to frequently alter the Source and Destination areas as cloning is done to various density areas in the image. The example below is the final cloned image.

Note: After the cloning was done in this exercise, a soft-edged Selection was created over the tear area. Then a Gaussian Blur of 3 pixels was applied inside the Selection.

# RETOUCHING BASICS
## CLONING

### RUBBER STAMP TOOL

### CLONING AT-A-GLANCE

1. Choose the Rubber Stamp Tool with an appropriate size brush.
2. Set the Source for Cloning. Depress the **Opt/Alt** key and click with the mouse.
3. Move the brush to the Destination. Depress the mouse button to paint from the Source to the Destination.
4. Paint with the Rubber Stamp Tool.
- Be careful when using the Rubber Stamp Tool, it could cause unusual patterns in the images

### DODGE & BURN AND CLONING TIPS

- To learn cloning methods, take some time to experiment and practice with the mechanics of selecting a Source and Painting to a Destination with the Rubber Stamp Tool. We suggest experimenting with a large brush. This makes it easier to see the results of testing the Rubber Stamp Tool.
- Use Long Brush Strokes. This allows using undo to see the effect of Dodging & Burning and of cloning.
- Use the History Palette.
  (1) Set the History options so there are a large number of States available. This makes it easier to back track and correct improper brush strokes.
  (2) Make sure there is an original Snapshot, so if some of the retouching is inaccurate, it is possible to recover by painting back to the original.

**79**

# RETOUCHING BASICS

## REVIEW

**RETOUCHING STRATEGIES AT-A-GLANCE**

1. Use Snapshots.
2. Use Selections with Curves.
3. Use Dodge and Burn.
4. Use the Rubber Stamp for cloning.

The Retouching Strategies section offers direction about where and when to begin retouching an image.

While we know there is no defined order for retouching images, we provide a prioritized list of where to begin. See the sidebar on this page and page 76.

We also show examples of how to retouch the same image three different ways using, (1) Snapshots and Curves, (2) Selections and Curves, and (3) Dodge and Burn.

- **Using Snapshots vs Selections**

    In a number of situations, using Snapshots with Curves can be faster and just as effective as using Selections with Curves to retouch an image.

    We also know there is not one method that is best. Both the Snapshot and Selection techniques can work well. Our advice is to learn how to use both methods so they compliment each other as you work in Photoshop.

- **The Toning Tools offer Dodge and Burn options**

    We suggest using this tool in very simple retouching situations because it has two drawbacks. The first drawback concerns contrast. Dodge and Burn does not offer as much control over image contrast as methods that use Curves. The second drawback concerns the complexity of Dodge and Burn options. Dodge and Burn has powerful options with limited latitude that take time, patience, and skill to learn. It is much easier to use other tools such as the Snapshot that offers more flexibility to control image contrast and more latitude for retouching.

- **The Rubber Stamp Tool**

    The Rubber Stamp Tool is often misused to apply tone corrections. We suggest using this tool for cloning and not for making tone corrections.

# LAYERS

Layers Basics ........................................... 82
Managing Layers ..................................... 85
Layer Mask .............................................. 86
Adjustment Layer .................................... 88
Text and Layers ....................................... 89
Shadows on Images ................................ 90
Review ..................................................... 92

# LAYERS

## LAYERS BASICS

### THE MOVE TOOL

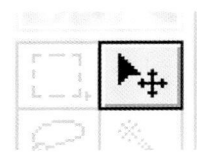

The Move Tool is used to create Layers by dragging-n-dropping images and to reposition images on Layers.

The Layers Palette is accessed from the Window Menu.

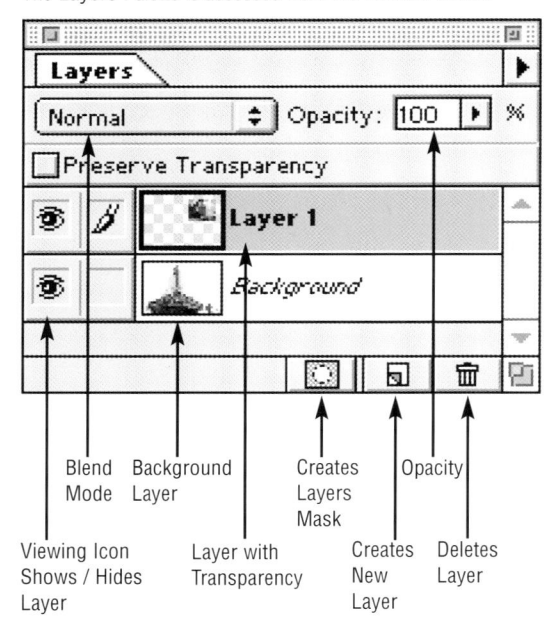

Blend Mode
Background Layer
Creates Layers Mask
Opacity

Viewing Icon Shows / Hides Layer
Layer with Transparency
Creates New Layer
Deletes Layer

**Tip:** Working with Layers can sometimes be overwhelming because it has so many options and features in the Layers Palette. If you become overwhelmed, remember to work as simply as possible. Follow our guidelines.

Layers can be thought of as a way to stack images—one image on top of another in a file. One of the main purposes of Layers is to create composite images. Each Layer has its own blending modes, opacity capabilities, and masking options. To learn the behavior of the Layers Palette is like the rest of Photoshop tools, practice and experimentation create successful results.

### TYPES OF LAYERS

There are two types of Layers that can be used for compositing images in the Layers Palette.

1. **Background Layer.**

    When an image is opened for the first time in Photoshop, it becomes a Background Layer. Technically speaking, it is named *The Background Layer* and the name is in Italic Type.

    - A Background Layer sets the size (physical dimensions) and resolution of the file for any subsequent Layers that are placed on top of it.
    - A Background Layer does not have Transparency.
    - A Background Layer can be repositioned with the Move Tool. This changes the Background Layer to become a Transparent Layer.
    - To change a Background Layer so it has Transparency, change the italic name to plain text. This is done by double clicking on the actual Background Layer. This action takes you to the Make Layer dialog box with plain text. The options are to use the default name which is Layer 0 or to create your own descriptive name.

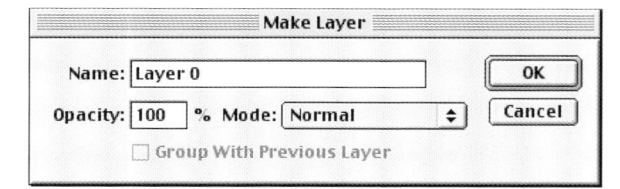

2. **Layers with Transparency.**

    Layers with Transparency may have their opacity adjusted so you can view other Layers beneath it.

    - Layers with Transparency can be positioned on top or underneath other Layers and repositioned.
    - Transparent Layers are supported only by the Photoshop file format.
    - Use Flatten to remove the Transparency from a Layer. This makes it a Background Layer.

The example above shows the results of using the Move Tool to drag an image on a single Layer. The Transparent background is displayed with a checkerboard pattern.

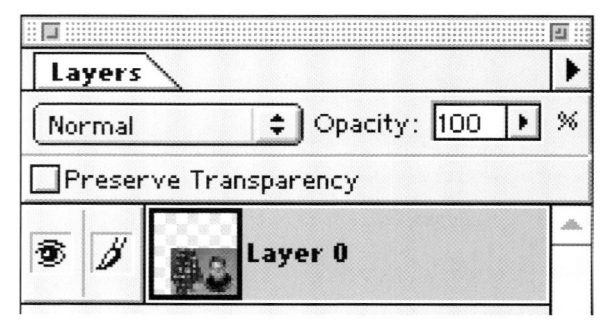

The example above shows the Layers 0 Icon in the Layers Palette.

## THERE ARE FOUR BASIC WAYS TO CREATE LAYERS

1. Drag-n-Drop one image onto another image with the Move Tool.

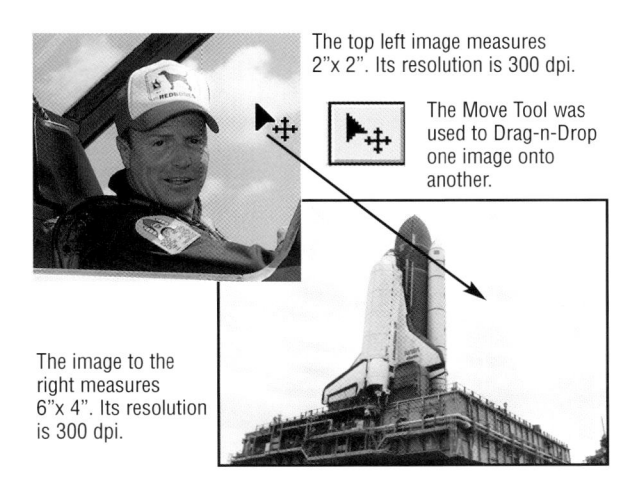

The top left image measures 2"x 2". Its resolution is 300 dpi.

The Move Tool was used to Drag-n-Drop one image onto another.

The image to the right measures 6"x 4". Its resolution is 300 dpi.

The above example shows the results of using the Move Tool to Drag-n-Drop one image onto another and then position it. It becomes a composited image with two Layers.

2. Copy an image to the clipboard and then paste it into that image or onto another image.

To copy a complete image to the computer's clipboard, use Select All **Cmd/Cntrl A** and then use *Edit>Copy* **Cmd/Cntrl C**.

Use Paste **Cmd/Cntrl V** to create a new Layer. This is not the most efficient method to create Layers if you are using large images (over four megabytes).

3. Use the Duplicate Layer feature or icon by Dragging-n-Dropping it on an existing layer.

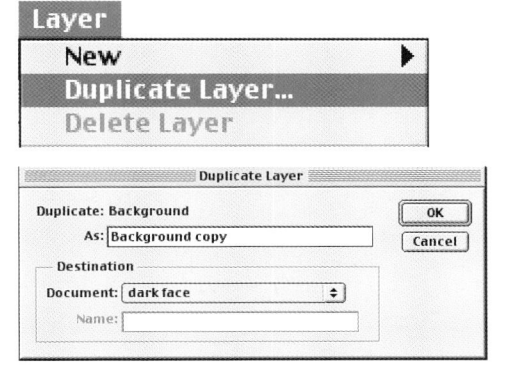

The Duplicate Layer dialog box allows either naming the new Layer for your existing document or creating a new file.

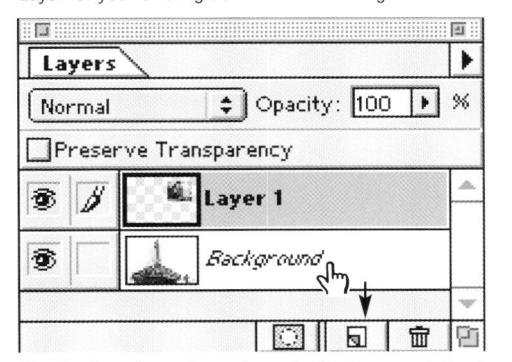

The Duplicate Layer Icon allows duplicating an existing Layer.

4. Click on the the Duplicate Layer icon to create a blank Layer.

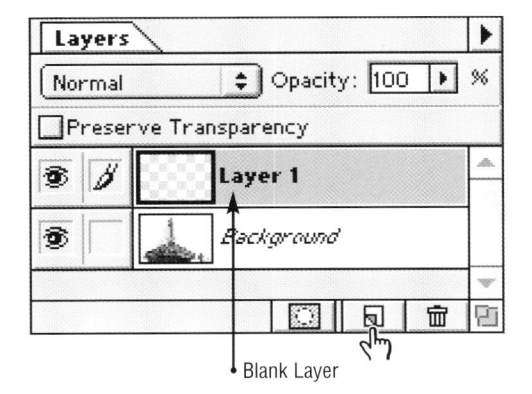

Blank Layer

# LAYERS
## LAYERS BASICS

### FOUR WAYS TO CREATE LAYERS AT-A-GLANCE

1. Drag-n-drop-one image onto another image.
2. Use Copy and Paste.
3. Use the Duplicate Layer feature or Layers Palette Icon.
4. Click on the Duplicate Layer icon.

### LAYERS, FILE SIZE, AND FILE FORMAT

- In Photoshop, it is possible to create up to 99 Layers in one image. In some cases, if you are working with large files that have many Layers, the CPU speed and the amount of RAM might limit the number of Layers that can be created.

- Layers are the only option for working with transparency in Photoshop, and Layers is only supported by the Photoshop file format. Expect with InDesign, this means that if the image is being used in a page layout application or on the web, you must Flatten the image so it can be converted from the Photoshop file format to TIF, EPS, JPEG, or to GIF.

83

# LAYERS

## LAYERS BASICS

### POSITIONING LAYERS

To change a Layers position, go to the Layers Palette. For Transparency, there needs to be at least two Layers. Use the mouse to click on a Layer and drag that Layer to another position in the Layers Palette. In our example below, one Layer is moved up so it would be on top of another Layer. When moving Layers, the Layers Palette displays a thick black line. This thick black line indicates the Layer that is being moved will reside on top of the Layer that is below the thick black line. The illustration below shows what happens when a Layer is repositioned on top of another Layer.

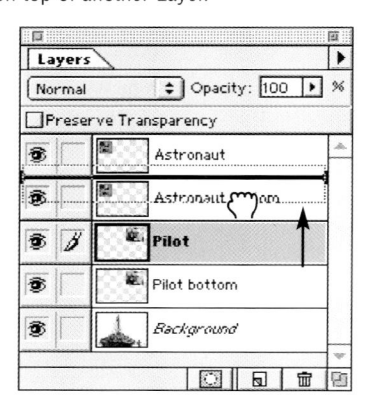

The illustration below shows the effect of moving a Layer up one Layer.

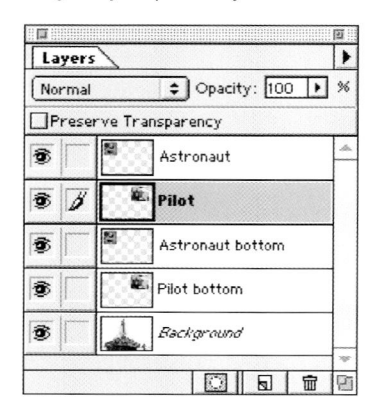

## TARGETING LAYERS

To Target a Layer is to make a particular Layer active so it can be worked on. Here are two ways to Target a Layer.

1. Use the mouse to click on a Layer in the Layers Palette.

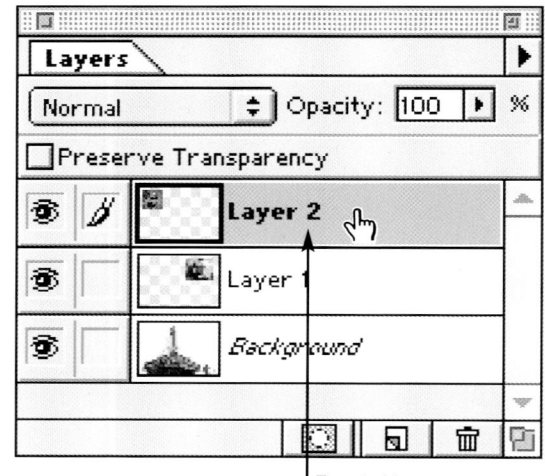

•Targeted Layer

2. Choose the Move Tool. Hold down the Opt, Cmd, keys on the Mac and Alt, Cntrl, keys on Windows.

   Watch your screen when holding down the two keys and you will see a double arrow icon. Use the mouse to click on the image area. The image area that is clicked on becomes the Targeted Layer in the Layers Palette.

•Layers Targeting Icon use **Opt/Alt** + **Cmd/Cntrl**, click.

## VIEWING LAYERS

The Eyeball icons on the left side of the Layers Palette are used to view all Layers. If the Eyeball icon is turned on, then the Layer viewed.

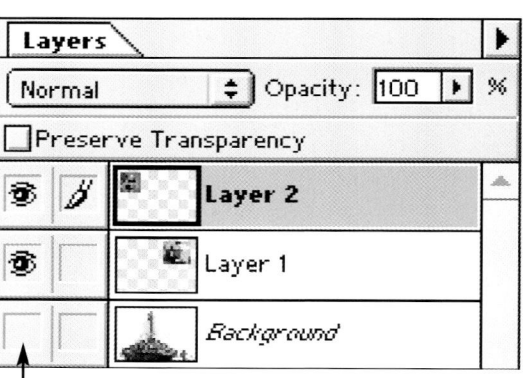

The example above shows the Layer Eyeball Icon turned off.

The example above shows the effect of turning off the Background Layer Eyeball icon. In this example only Layers 1 and 2 are visible.

# LAYERS
## MANAGING LAYERS

### DELETING LAYERS

There are three ways to delete a Layer.

**1. Move the Layer to the Layers Palette Trash.**

Use the mouse to pick up and move the Layer.

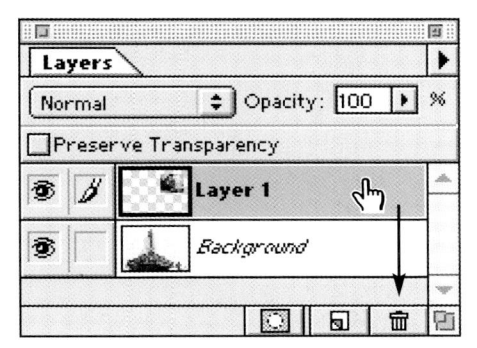

**2. Use the delete option**

Target the Layer to be deleted. Then use the Layers Palette Pop-out menu delete option.

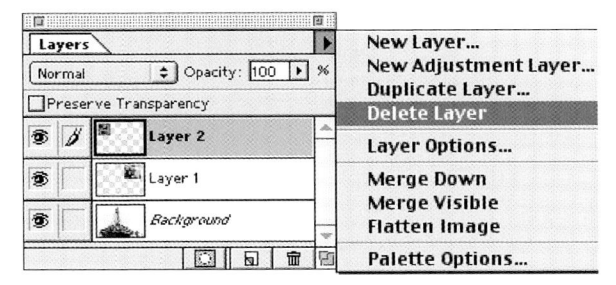

**3. Use the Layers menu delete option.**

Target the Layer to be deleted. Then use the Layers Menu Delete Layer option.

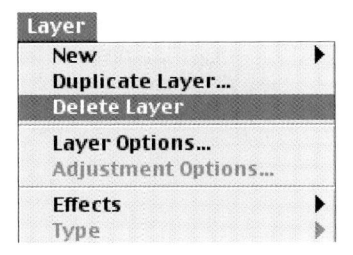

### MERGING DOWN LAYERS

Layers can be merged into one Layer. This helps keep the files size manageable. Use the Layers Palette Pop-out menu or **Cmd/Cntrl** E. This will combine the Targeted Layer with the Layer directly below it.

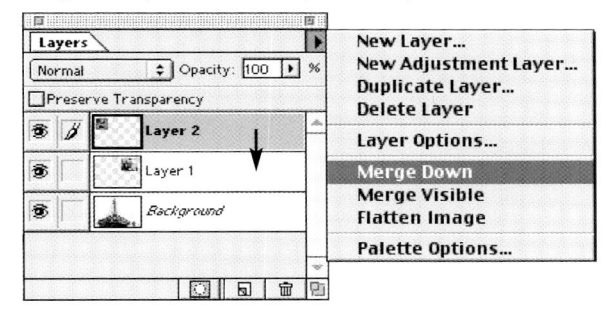

### MERGING VISIBLE LAYERS

The Merge Visible option permits hiding Layers that you do not want to remove. This is useful for removing unwanted or extra Layers in the file. To use the Merge Visible option, click on the Layer's Eyeballs to turn off and hide Layers. Then select Merge Visible from the Layers Palette Pop-out menu. When the Merge Visible operation is complete, click the Layers Eyeballs onto show the Layers.

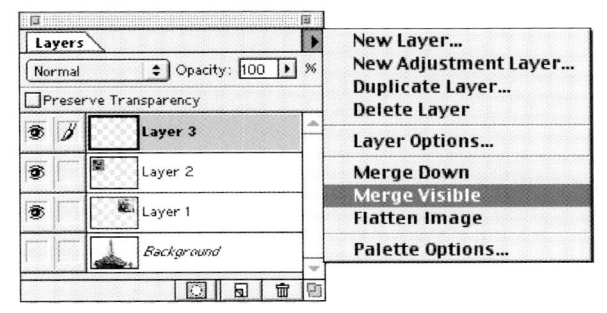

### FLATTENING LAYERS

There are two direct ways to Flatten a Layer.

1. In the Layers Palette, use the Layers Palette Pop-out menu Flatten option.

2. Use the Layers menu Flatten option. See examples in the sidebar.

1. Layers Palette Pop-out menu.

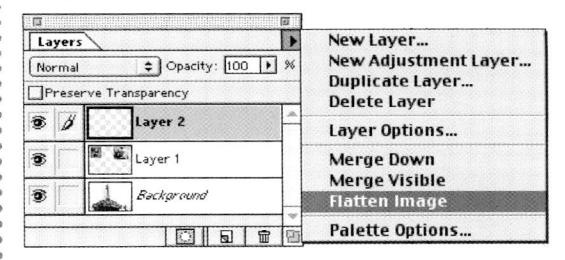

2 Layers menu.

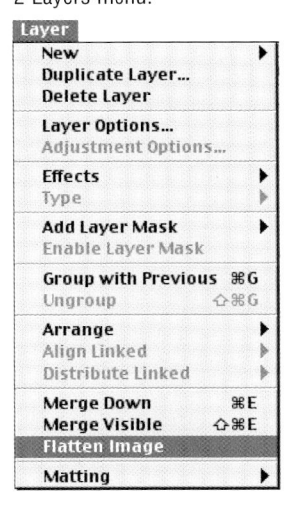

85

# LAYERS
## LAYER MASK

### LAYER VS LAYER MASK

One way to tell if you are working on a Layer or a Layer Mask is to examine the Layer's Palette.

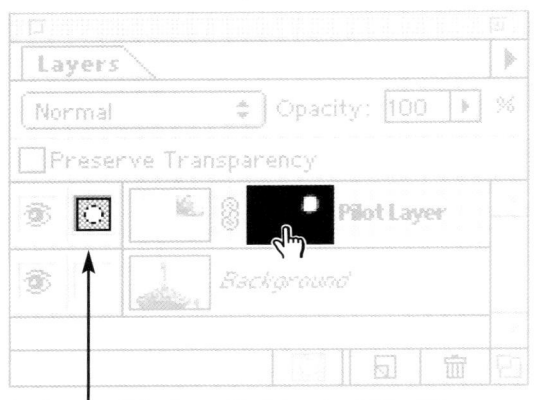

Look to see if the Layer Mask icon is visible. If the Channel icon is visible, then the Layer Mask is available.

Look to see if the Layers icon (the paint brush) is visible. If the brush icon is visible then the Layer is available.

A Layer Mask is a flexible way to create advanced masking effects on images without destroying the actual image information. Clearly a Layer Mask is a creative tool, but we also think of them as part of the recovery strategy. The Layer Mask allows you to paint on it with various shades of black or white to affect an image. If you do not like the results then you can paint or fill the Layer Mask with white to start over without destroying the image. A Layer Mask is actually a Channel and can be viewed in the Channels Palette. Here is one way to work with a Layer Mask.

**1. Have two images open.**

Make sure the Layers Palette is open. In this example, we used two images, image 1 (the shuttle) and image 2 (the pilot).

Image 1 to the left measures 6"x 4". Its resolution is 300 dpi.

Image 2 on the left measures 2"x 2". Its resolution is 300 dpi.

**2. Drag image 2 on top of image 1.**

Use the Move Tool from the Tool Palette. This will create a new Layer (Layer 1) that is the Targeted Layer. Position image 2, the Pilot, on the right side of the Shuttle image.

The above example shows two Layered images.

**3. Create a Layer Mask.**

In the Layers Palette, go to the lower left icon. Select the Mask Icon to add a Layer Mask to the Pilot Layer.

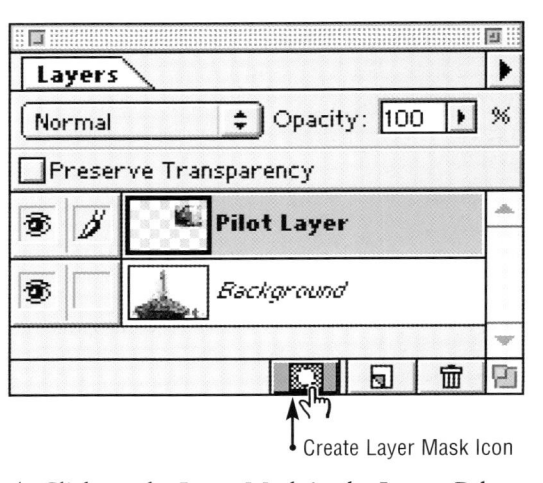

• Create Layer Mask Icon

**4. Click on the Layer Mask in the Layers Palette.**

This will highlight the Layer Mask with a black boarder effect. You are now working on the Layer Mask for Layer 1 the Pilot Layer.

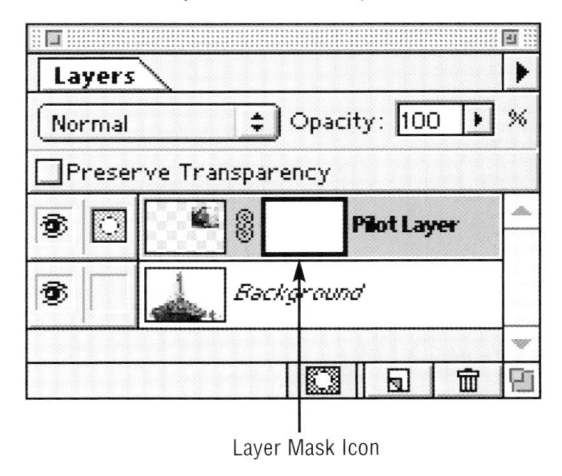

Layer Mask Icon

5. **Use a soft-edged brush to paint the edges of the Layer Mask.**

    The goal is to create a soft-edged effect around the border of the Pilot image.

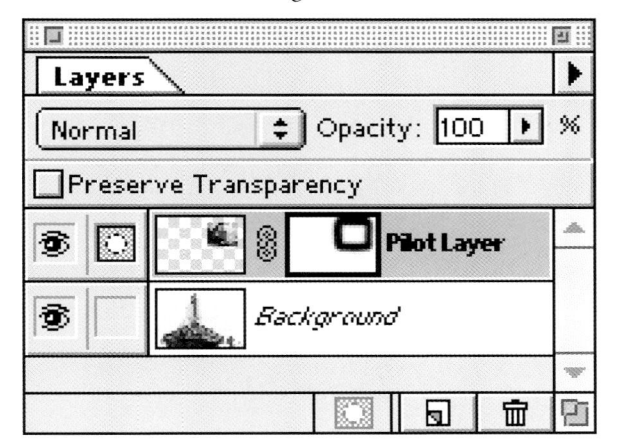

The above example shows the Layers Palette with the Layer Mask. In this example, we used the Eraser Tool because it has four different brush options. To make this technique work more effectively, it is necessary to experiment with different brush sizes and types (soft-and hard-edged).

- When using the Eraser Tool, consider using the key board shortcuts D to default the Foreground and Background colors and X to reverse them when painting white and black areas on the Layer Mask.
- To make the sides of the Pilot image blend better; use the Eraser Tool with different size brushes to paint the edges of the Pilot image within the Layer Mask.

The image above is the final result of painting with a soft-edged brush on a Layer Mask.

## REMOVING A LAYER MASK

To remove a Layer Mask but not the Layer, drag the Layer Mask to the Layers Palette Trash can. This action will take you to a dialog box that says, *Apply mask to layer before removing?* Select *Discard* to remove the mask.

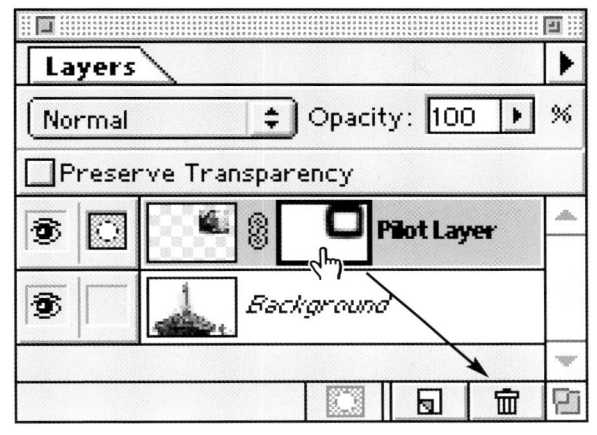

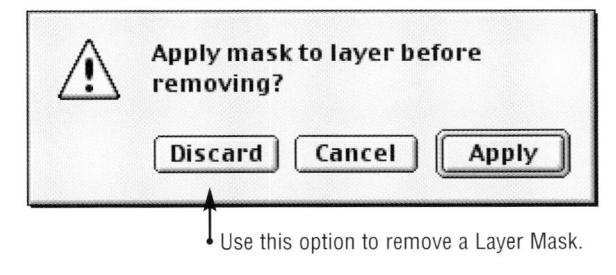

Use this option to remove a Layer Mask.

### LAYER MASK TIP:

A way to think about a Layer Mask is that the white areas let the light or active image area be seen. The black Layer Mask areas (similar to a Channel Mask) protect the image from being affected.

# LAYERS
## LAYER MASK

### HOW TO VIEW A LAYER MASK

- Depress the **Opt/Alt** key and click on the Layer Mask Icon in the Layers Palette. This will display the Mask on the computer screen.
- To display the image, but still be working in the Layer Mask, click on the Layer Mask again while the **Opt/Alt** key is still depressed.

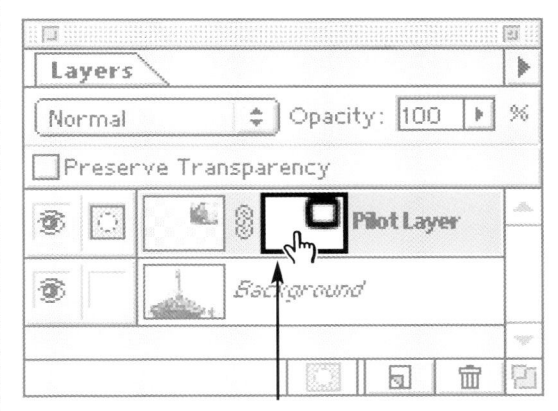

Depress the **Opt/Alt** key and click on the Layer Mask.

The image above shows what the Layer Mask looks like.

87

# LAYERS

## ADJUSTMENT LAYER

### SELECTIVE CORRECTIONS WITH ADJUSTMENT LAYER

One way to work with the Adjustment Layers is to make selective corrections with Selections. The Adjustment Layer still applies the correction to other Layers below it, but the correction will only be within the Selected area.

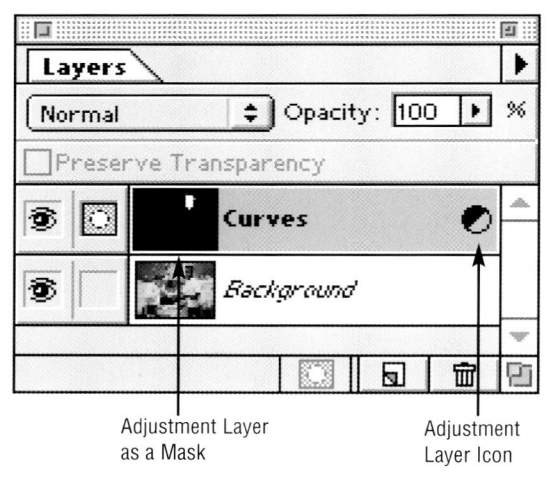

Adjustment Layer as a Mask

Adjustment Layer Icon

In the example above, note the mask on the Curves Layer. This represents the Adjustment Layer and the Selection.

The Adjustment Layer feature offers six options for applying and saving image processing to adjustments to grayscale images. They include Levels, Curves, Brightness & Contrast, Invert, Threshold, and Posterize. The two most useful image processing options for correcting grayscale images within this feature are Levels and Curves. Levels and Curves features work almost the same exact way with or without the Adjustment Layer (except for Thresholding). See the sidebar on page 62 about Thresholding & Video Support

The Adjustment Layer is the best method to non-destructively correct an image. Each image processing tool such as Levels or Curves becomes a Layer with its particular settings. The advantage of using the Adjustment Layer is that you do not have to commit to a final adjustment until the image is flattened and saved. This means it is possible to apply any image processing adjustments to an image and return at any time to those exact Levels or Curves settings and make further correction adjustments as long as the Layer is available.

The Adjustment Layer affects any Layered images below the Layer. The only drawback with this image correction strategy is that the image and its Layer can only be saved in the Photoshop format.

### TWO WAYS TO CREATE AN ADJUSTMENT LAYER

1. Use the Layers menu and select:
   *New>Adjustment Layer*.

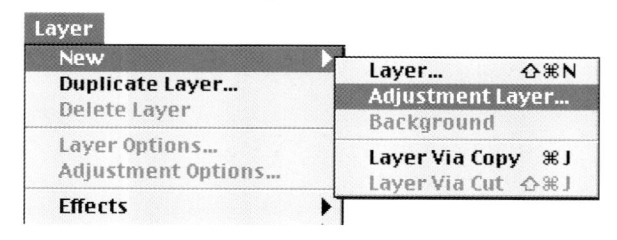

2. Use the Layers Palette Pop-out menu and select:
   *New Adjustment Layer*.

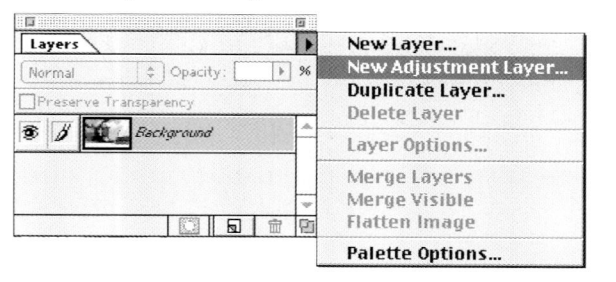

**The Adjustment Layer dialog box.**

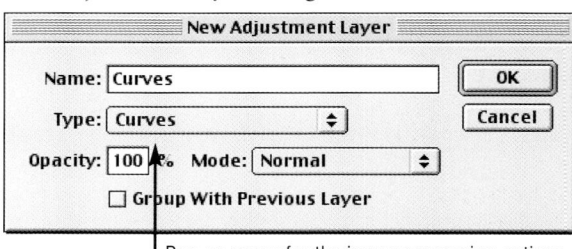

Pop-up menu for the image processing options.

Once you are in the Adjustment Layer dialog box there is a Pop-up menu for the image processing options.

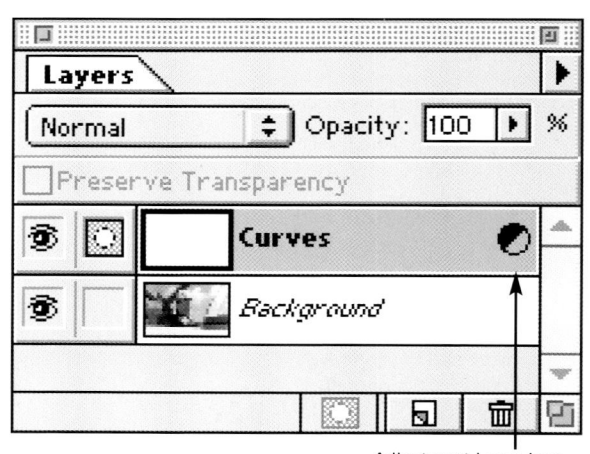

Adjustment Layer Icon

The example above shows an Adjustment Layer in the Layers Palette. Note in the Curves Layer in the Layers Palette. It has a Split Circle icon. This identifies the Adjustment Layer.

**Be aware!** that Adjustment Layers that have Curves or Levels adjustments affect any Layers below it. If Curves or Levels have been used to adjust image contrast of one Layer, then that particular correction will be applied to other Layers that are below it.

## TYPE LAYER

Text in Photoshop has been dramatically improved since the introduction of version 5.0.2. When text is created it generates a Type Layer. This Layer is slightly different from a typical image Layer or an Adjustment Layer. The difference is the Text Layer uses text outline technology (PostScript) to create high quality and editable text in a Layer. This is really cool. Below are steps that introduce the Type Tool and Type Layers.

1. To create a Type Layer click on the Text Tool in the Tool Palette.

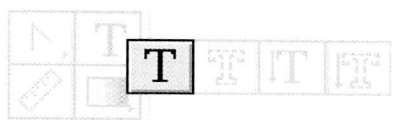

The pointer on the mouse will change to an I-beam pointer when the cursor is place over an image. The small line through the I-beam marks the position of the type baseline.

2. Click in the image area to set the insertion point for the text.
3. Choose the preview option to display the type in the image.
4. Select the type options such as type size and font, etc.
5. Change the tone value of the text by clicking on the the color box. Next, use the Color Picker, and then click OK.
6. Keyboard type in the bottom area of this dialog box.

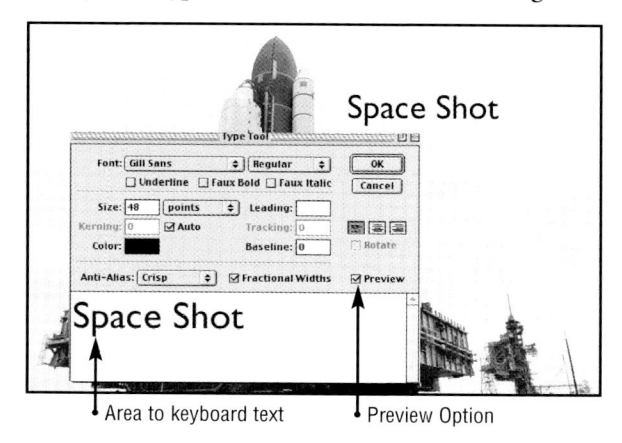

• Area to keyboard text  • Preview Option

The above illustration shows the Type Tool dialog box with the Preview option on so text is displayed in the image.

After the Type dialog box has been OKed, a new Layer is created. The Type Layer represents text that uses outline technology. The Type Layer is identified with the letter T on the right side of the Layers Palette.

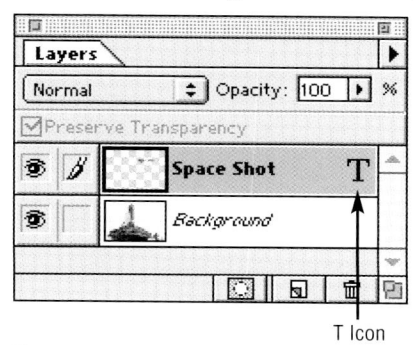

T Icon
Text can be edited easily when the letter T is available on the right side of a Type Layer. Double click on the Layer to enter the type dialog box.

### Render Layer

Outline text is typically rendered as pixels. Use the Menu options, *Layers>Type>Render Layer*.

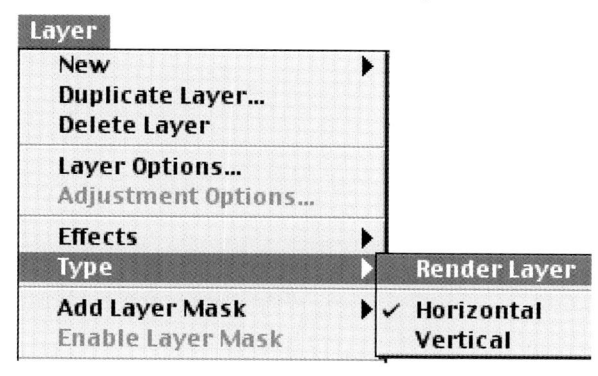

Before Rendering type as pixels, be sure to create a backup image that has outline text using Save As or Save a Copy.

# LAYERS
## TEXT AND LAYERS

### OUTLINE TYPE

Drawing and page-layout programs such as Macromedia Freehand, Adobe Illustrator, PageMaker, or QuarkXpress create outlined type. Outlined text consists of mathematically defined shapes that can be scaled to any size without losing its smooth edges. When Photoshop opens a text image that contains outlines, it rasterizes it into pixels or bitmap type.

### BITMAP TYPE

Image-editing programs such as Photoshop use pixels that create bitmap type. The sharpness and edges of bitmap type depends on the type size and the resolution of the image. Typically, pixel based type shows jagged edges.

A rule-of-thumb for printing applications is if you are using pixel based type, the file must be a high-resolution image (over 800 dpi) for the edges to be smooth.

### MISSING "T" IN LAYERS

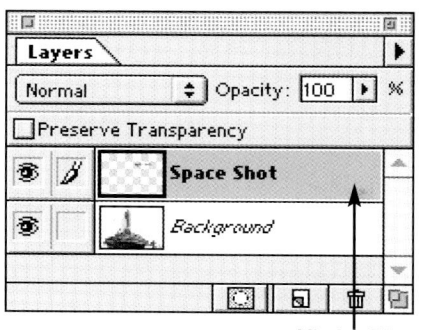

Missing T Icon
The above Type Layer has been rendered as pixels. Note that the letter T on the right side is not available. This removes the high quality type outline technology.

89

# LAYERS

## SHADOWS ON IMAGES

**ORIGINAL IMAGE**

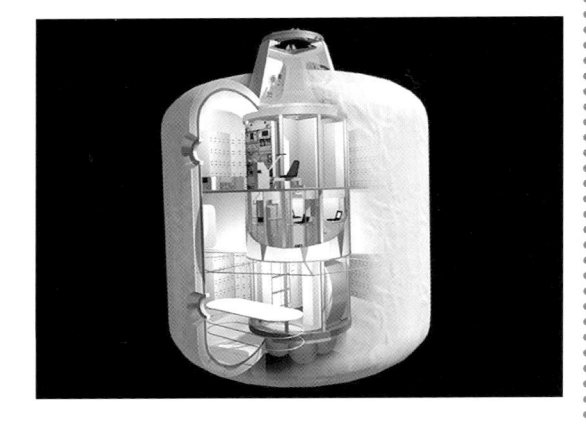

**VIEW THE LAYERS AND CHANNELS PALETTES**

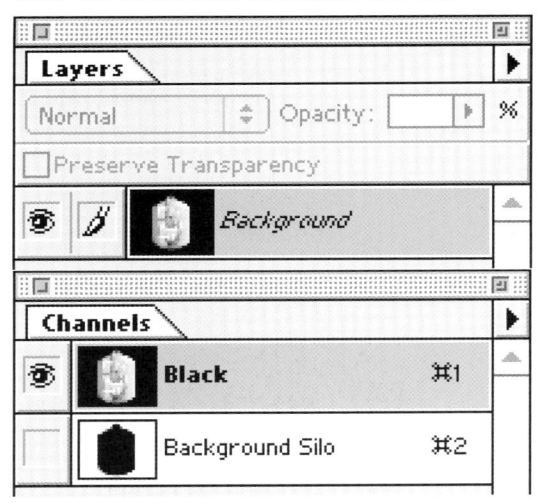

The illustrations above show how the Layers and Channels Palettes look before the drop shadow exercise was started. Note the previously created Channel.

Creating drop shadows is a popular Photoshop option. If you have never made drop shadows, the next two pages provide the basics for using Layers and the associated tools to create drop shadows.

In this example, we are starting with an image that has a previously created Channel. A Selection was used to knock out the background of our example image. The image becomes silhouetted.

1. **Create a new Layer with Transparency.**

   - An easy way to create a Layer with Transparency is to double click on the Background Layer and change the Layers name to Top Image Layer.

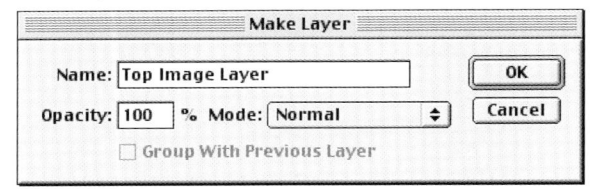

2. **Load the Selection from the Channel and use *Edit>Clear* to make the Selected area Transparent.**

   - Since the Selection's active area is the image's background, fill the Selection with the Clear from the Edit menu.
   - This will make the background of the image become Transparent.

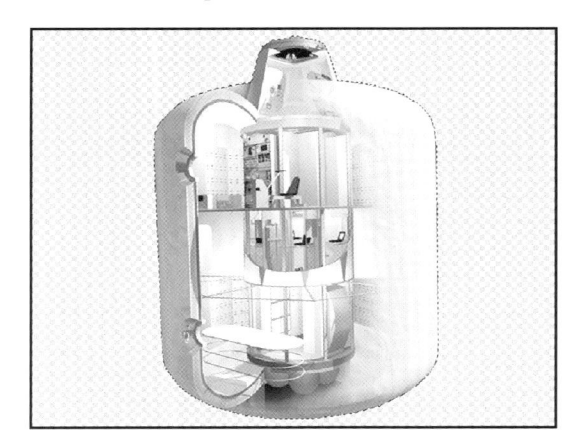

The illustration above shows the image with a Transparent background area.

3. **Duplicate the Layer.**

   Drag-n-drop the Layer to the Duplicate Layer icon.

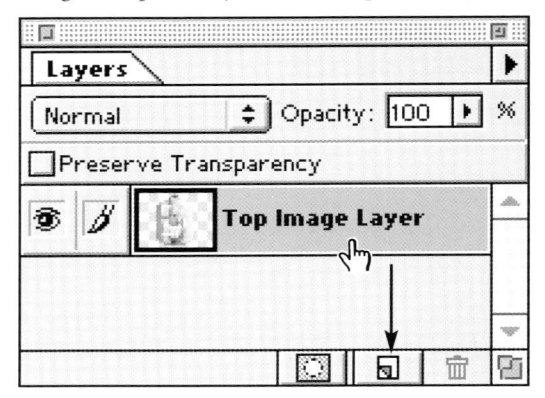

4. **Rename the Layer.**

   Double click on the Layer and use the name *Shadow Layer*.

5. **Use the Move Tool to reposition the Shadow Layer to the bottom on the Layers Palette.**

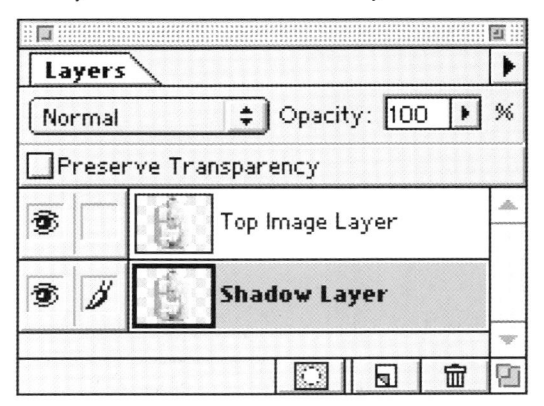

The above illustration shows the arrangement of the Top Image Layer and the Shadow Layer.

In this exercise we know there are number of ways to reposition and name Layers. We choose to use this order because it seems logical to us.

90

6. **Create the Drop Shadow.**
- Make sure the Shadow Layer is the Targeted Layer.
- Load a Selection from this Layer. Hold down the Cmd/Cntrl key and click on the Shadow Layer.
- To view only the Shadow Layer, click on the Eyeball of the Top Image Layer. This will turn off the top Layers view.
- Fill the Selection with Black. Use *Edit>Fill* and choose the Foreground Color that is black. After the image in Shadow Layer is filled with Black, Deselect the Selection.

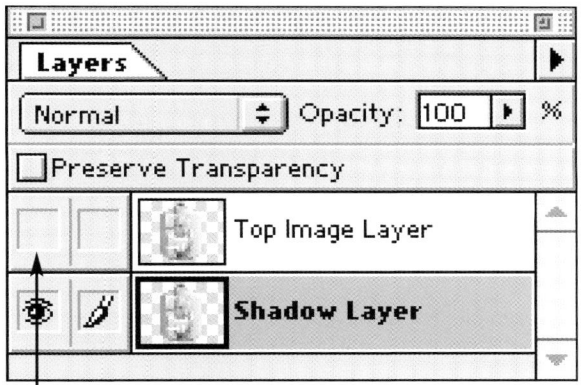

Layers Eyeball Icon turned off.

7. **Use the Move Tool to move the Shadow Layer slightly to the right and down.**

   This will create the basic drop shadow.

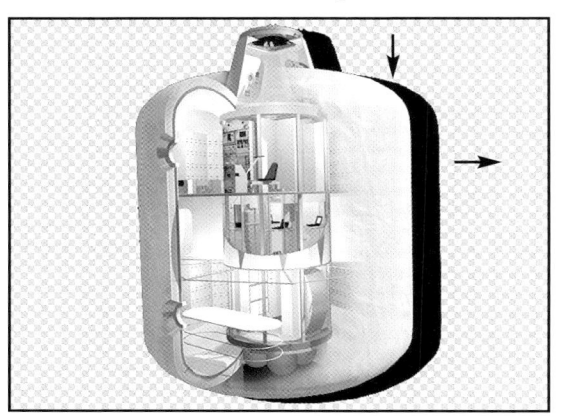

8. **Use Gaussian Blur. Apply it to create a soft-edged shadow on the Shadow Layer.**

   The amount of blur depends on the effect that is required. We used a Gaussian Blur of 15 pixels.

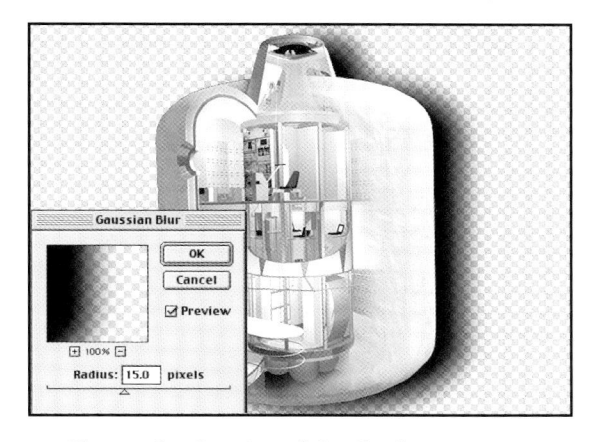

9. **Change the Opacity of the Shadow Layer to 50%.**

   Select the 5 key or keyboard in 50 into the Layers Palette Opacity option.

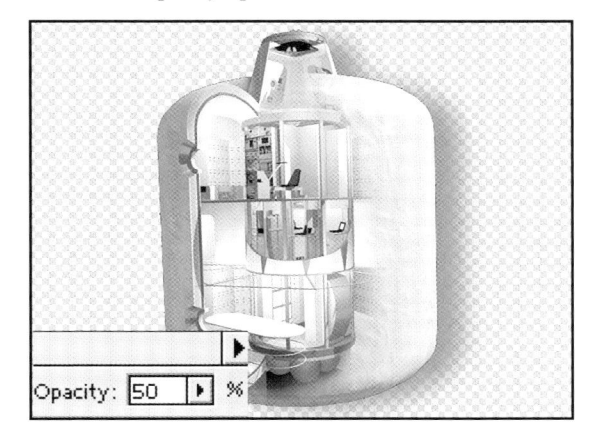

10. **Flatten the Image.**

    Use the Layers menu or the Layers Palette Pop-out menu.

# LAYERS
## SHADOWS ON IMAGES

### DROP SHADOWS AT-A-GLANCE

1. Create a new Layer with Transparency.
2. Load the Channel as a Selection and use *Edit>Clear*.
3. Duplicate the Layer.
4. Name the Shadow Layer.
5. Place the Shadow Layer at the bottom of the Layers Palette.
6. Create the Drop Shadow.
7. Move the Shadow Layer to the right and down.
8. Use Gaussian Blur to soften the shadow.
9. Change the opacity of the Shadow Layer.
10. Flatten the Image.

### LAYER EFFECTS FOR DROP SHADOWS

Drop Shadows can be created by using the *Layers>Effects* menu options.

Our advice is to learn how to create Drop Shadows manually with Layers, then learn how to automate making drop shadows with *Layers>Effects*.

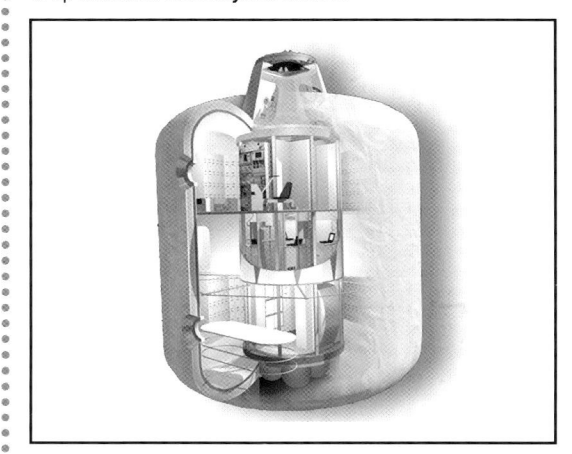

The image above is the final Flattened image with a shadow.

# LAYERS
## REVIEW

The Layers section is about the fundamentals of using Layers.

The most obvious use of Layers involves placing one image on top of another for compositing.

- **There are four basic types of Layers**

    (1) **Background Layer**

    In Photoshop, the Background Layer is identified by Italic type. Background Layers sets the size and resolution of any Layers that are placed on top of it.

    (2) **Layers with Transparency**

    Layers with Transparency can have their opacity changed, can be repositioned on an image and are only supported with the Photoshop file format.

    (3) **Adjustment Layer**

    The Adjustment Layer allows non-destructive corrections and image. This tool has six options for applying and saving image processing adjustment to images. It creates a Layer with the re-adjustable settings of the image processing tool as long as the Adjustment Layer is available.

    (4) **Text Layer**

    High quality outline text can be created as a Layer in Photoshop. This makes it possible to edit the Layer until the file has to be prepared and Flattened for output.

- **Create a Layer**

    The most popular way to create a Layer is to use the Move Tool. Drag-n-Drop is a feature of the Photoshop Move Tool. Drag-n-Drop one image onto another to create a Layer.

    Another way to create a Layer is to copy an image to the computer's clipboard and then paste it from the clipboard onto another image. Every time you paste a grayscale image on to another image, you create a Layer.

When using Layers, there are a number of techniques that need to be mastered, they include:

- **Targeting Layers**

    This makes a specific Layer available. The most common way to Target a Layer is to use the Move Tool to click on a specific Layer in the Layers Palette.

- **Viewing Layers**

    The Eyeball Icons in the Layers Palette are used for viewing layers. When the Eyeball Icon is on, the Layer can be seen. If Eyeball Icon is off, the Layer cannot be seen.

- **Deleting Layers**

    There are three ways to delete Layers.

    (1) Use the Move Tool and in the Layers Palette, drag the Layer to the Layers Palette Trash.

    (2) Target the Layer in the Layers Palette and use the Layers Palette Pop-out Menus Delete option.

    (3) Target the Layer in the Layers Palette and use the Layers Menus Delete option.

- **Merging Layers**

    To help in managing Layers, they can be merged.

- **Flattening**

    Flattening Layers is necessary to prepare the final file so it can be save in an output file format such as TIFF or EPS. Photoshop is the only file format that supports Layers.

- **Layer Mask**

    Layer Mask is part of the Layers Palette that allow you to create a mask over each layer. A Layer Mask is a Channel that you can add or subtract white, black, or shades of gray from. When adding or subtracting from the Mask, the appearance of the image in the Layer is changed. If you were to remove the Layer Mask, the image would be returned to it original state.

# PHOTOSHOP TIPS

Color to Grayscale Options......................94
Ghosting ..................................................97
Creating Extraordinary Contrast .............98
No More Moirés!.....................................99
Cropping ...............................................100
Scaling ..................................................102
Actions Basics ......................................104
Actions-Batch Processing ....................106
Creating a Mirror Image .......................108
Extending Backgrounds........................110
Dust Busting .........................................112
Line Images ..........................................113

# PHOTOSHOP TIPS
## COLOR TO GRAYSCALE

### WHICH COLOR TO GRAYSCALE METHOD IS BEST?
Each technique has its benefits and they all will work. Typically, it depends on the situation and what the client requires from the color image to be converted to grayscale.

### SETTING FOR VIEWING CHANNELS IN BLACK AND WHITE

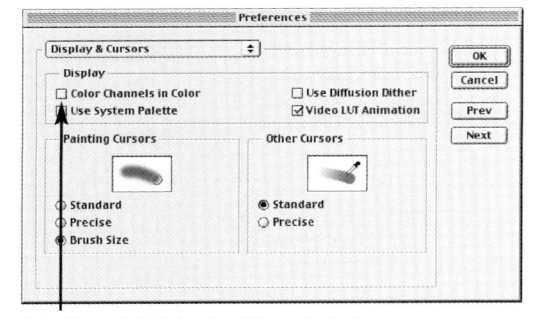

Color Channels in Color should be unchecked.

### COLOR IMAGES TO GRAYSCALE
A source image is not often available in grayscale. Photoshop provides a number of ways to convert images from color to grayscale.

### COLOR TO GRAYSCALE VIA THE MODE CHANGE
The standard way to convert an RGB image to grayscale in Photoshop is straightforward:

1. **Open the color image file, then go to:** Image>*Mode*>*Grayscale*.

2. **Click on OK.**

   A dialog box will ask if it is OK to discard color information. After this image becomes a grayscale image, it is necessary to set white, black, and midtones using any of the previous techniques.

### COLOR TO GRAYSCALE - PICK A COLOR CHANNEL
You can also convert RGB color images to grayscale by deleting two of the three color channels that make up the image. In some cases, this method will produce better results. The distribution of tones within each color channel is based on the image's overall color content. Depending on the image's color make up, one channel might have better contrast than the others, or it might have better contrast than the converted grayscale image.

1. **Set Display & Cursors Preferences.**

   To inspect individual channels in black and white, make sure the Color Channels in Color check box is NOT checked in the General Preferences dialog box.

2. **View individual Channels.**

   Use **Cmd/Cntrl** 1, **Cmd/Cntrl** 2, and **Cmd/Cntrl** 3 to view each channel. **Cmd/Cntrl** Ø permits viewing of the composite color Channel.

3. **Identify the best Channel.**

   Then select grayscale from the Mode menu. The program will keep the selected channel and discard the other two Channels.

**CMD/CNTRL Ø**

**CMD/CNTRL 1**
Grayscale Channel

**CMD/CNTRL 1**
Red Channel

**CMD/CNTRL 2**
Green Channel

**CMD/CNTRL 3**
Blue Channel

## LAB COLOR L CHANNEL TO GRAYSCALE

Open an RGB image, convert it to LAB with the *Image>Mode>LAB*.

- Use the Channels Palette or the keyboard shortcut **Cmd/Cntrl** 1 to display the L Channel.
- Use *Image>Mode>Grayscale* to convert to grayscale.

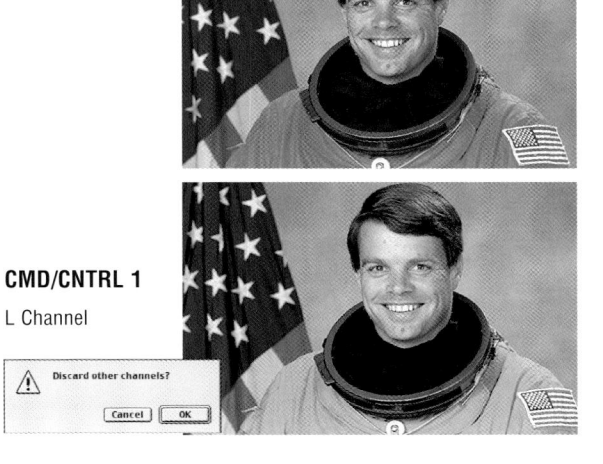

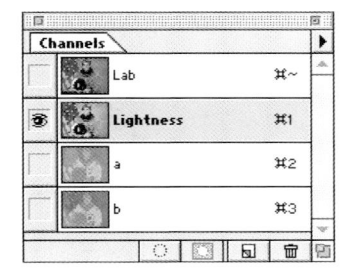

**CMD/CNTRL 1**
L Channel

# PHOTOSHOP TIPS
## COLOR TO GRAYSCALE

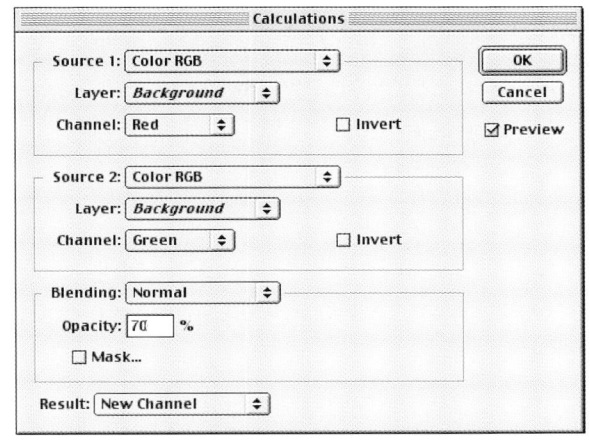

### RGB TO LAB
Change the Mode to go from RGB to LAB.

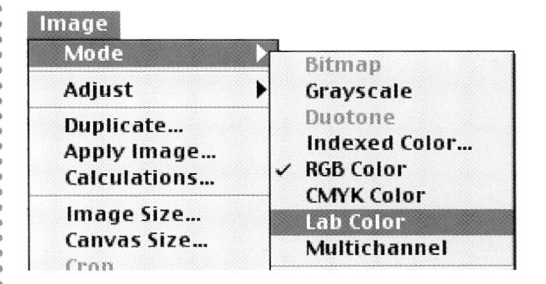

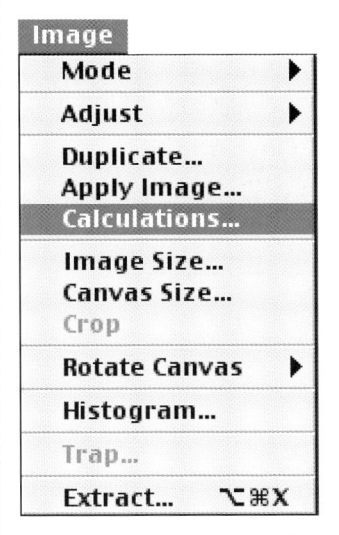

## CALCULATIONS - THE BEST OF TWO CHANNELS

Using Calculations under the *Image>Calculations* menu is an advanced way of creating a grayscale image from a color file. The Calculations option makes it possible to blend two channels together to take the best from both to create a new image. For example, consider that one Channel is lacking in certain image details that are available in another Channel. Calculations allows blending or adding a percent (0% to 100%) of another Channels information to the original Channel. The end result would be a grayscale image with more detail.

- Experiment using the *Normal* Blend setting command found in the Calculations *Blending* sub menu.
- Try using different color image channels that add extra detail and *Opacity*. Check on the preview button to see the results on screen. This technique can be especially helpful with problem images or bad scans.
- Use the *Result* option at the bottom of the dialog box to create a New Channel.

Use the Image Menu to access Calculations.

95

# PHOTOSHOP TIPS
## COLOR TO GRAYSCALE

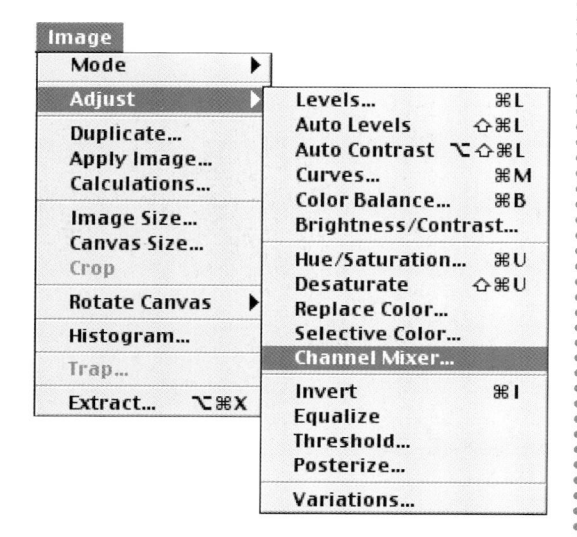

### USE CHANNEL MIXER

Channel Mixer provides an infinite number of options to change the distribution of tones within each color channel and blend them into grayscale images.

- Check the Monochrome option.
- Leave the Constant value set to 0.

Here are three variations on this tool.

Channel Mixer Source

Channel Red   +100
Channel Green  + 0
Channel Blue   + 0

Monochrome checked on

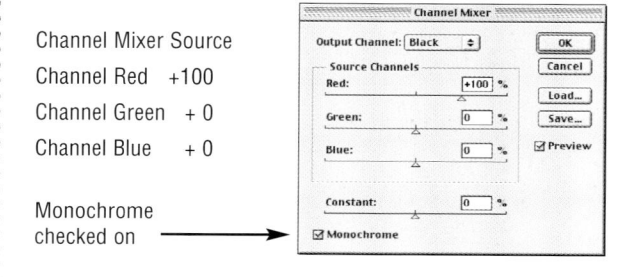

Channel Mixer Source

Channel Red    + 0
Channel Green +100
Channel Blue   + 0

Monochrome checked on

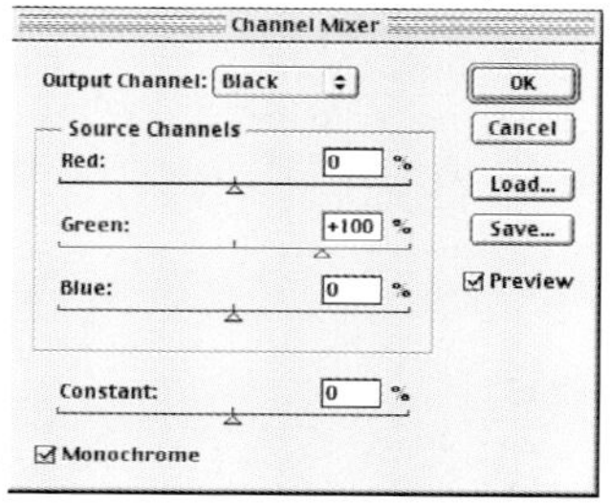

Channel Mixer Source

Channel Red    + 0
Channel Green  + 0
Channel Blue  +100

Monochrome checked on

### ADJUST HIGHLIGHTS AND SHADOWS

Remember, when converting color images with any of these methods to grayscale files, it is still necessary to adjust the white and black points and midtones, as described earlier, to achieve the desired halftone results.

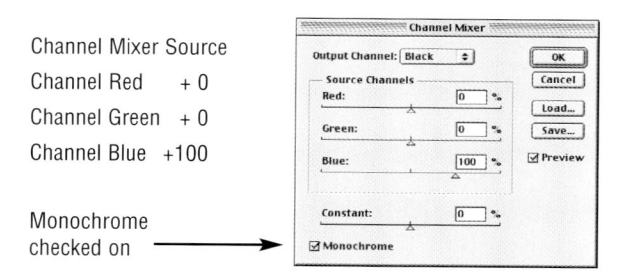

## GHOSTING METHODS

Photoshop offers more than one method to create the same results. Here are three of the easiest and different ways to Ghost an image.

1. **Use Levels** to reduce the shadow values of an image.
   - This is done with the shadow output Levels slider.
   - Move the triangle to the right until the desired amount of ghosting is achieved.

   **OUTPUT LEVELS SLIDER**

2. **Use Curves** to reduce the shadow values of an image.
   - This is accomplished by adjusting the shadow point of the Curve.
   - Reduce the shadow values until the desired amount of ghosting is achieved.

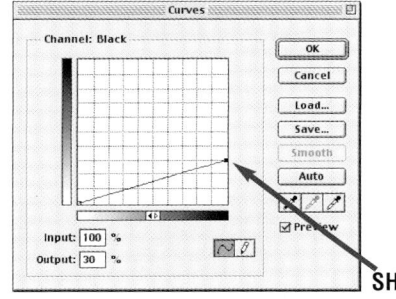

   **SHADOW ENDPOINT**

3. **Use *Edit>Fill*.**
   - Apply Select All. Use **Cmd/Cntrl** A.
   - Be sure the Foreground and Background colors are set to the Default position (Black and White).
   - Use the Fill menu with a percent of the Foreground or Background.
   - If the Background color is white, the higher the opacity value, the lighter the image becomes.

The example above used a white Background color with a 50 Fill.

The example to the right is altered so the Opacity value can be seen easily.

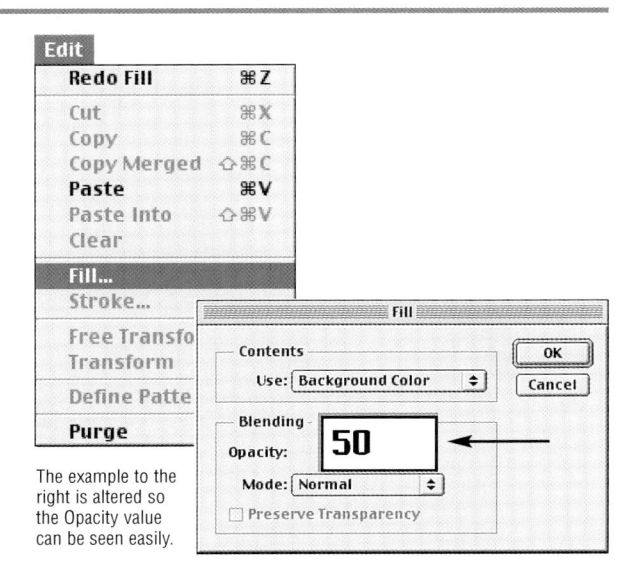

# PHOTOSHOP TIPS
## GHOSTING

**ALL OF THESE GHOSTING METHODS CREATE THE SAME OR ALMOST THE SAME END RESULTS.**

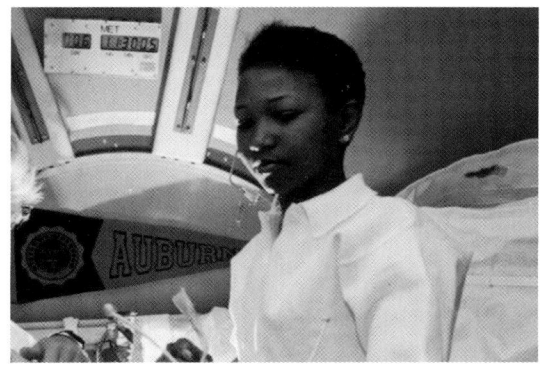

**ORIGINAL**

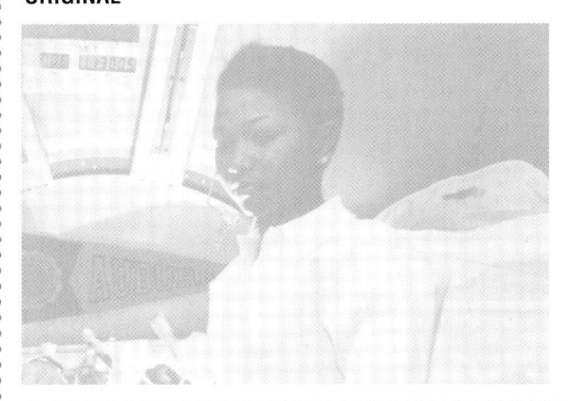

**GHOSTED WITH CURVES USING A 30% SHADOW POINT**

97

# PHOTOSHOP TIPS
## CREATING EXTRAORDINARY CONTRAST

### REFINED GRID IN CURVES

While in the curves dialog box, hold down the **Opt/Alt** key and click inside the grid areas to display the 10 x 10 grid.

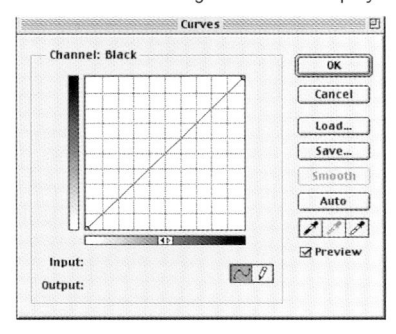

### ADDING ANCHORS

When adjusting an image using the Curves tool, if areas of the curve start to change in unwanted ways, anchor them in place by adding additional points along the curve.

### PLACE AND MOVE ANCHOR POINTS

While in the Curves dialog box, hold down the **Cmd/Cntrl** key and click inside the image. This will pick up the tones of the image you have clicked on and place an Anchor point on the Curve. Next use the up and down arrows keys to move the point in small increments.

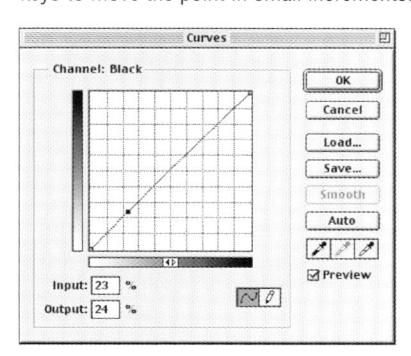

It is possible to use Photoshop's Curves tool to separate tones in specific areas of the image to create extraordinary contrast. You do this by identifying multiple points on the curve and then individually separating areas (moving each closer to a vertical axis) of tones to achieve super contrast. These additional changes are made after completing highlight and shadow adjustments and the basic or multi-point adjustments to the image as described earlier.

1. **Open the Curves tool and choose an area where you want more contrast.**

   Use the Eyedropper and hold down the mouse button over the point on the image to be adjusted; the Curves dialog box displays a small circle on the curve which corresponds to that specific area of the image.

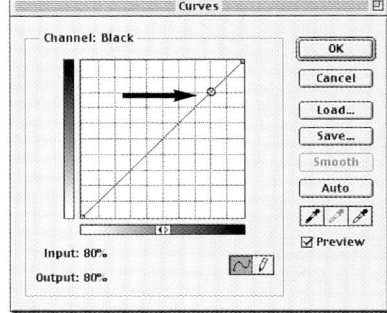

2. **Move the end points of the curve to your image's white and black points.**

   Anchor parts of the curve that should not change. Now place a point (1) on the curve slightly above the selected point and increase it by 2% or 3%.

3. **Next place a point (2) on the curve slightly below the selected spot and decrease it by 2% or 3%.**

   This will increase the contrast.

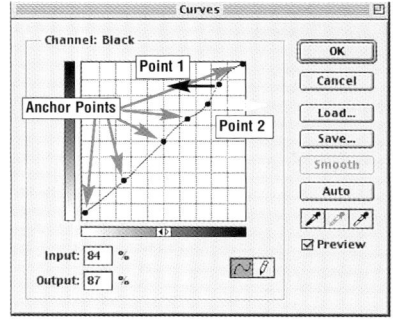

   If the points are not too close, this technique will separate the tones and create incredible contrast. Usually, a 2-3% change from the input to output reading is the maximum before posterization starts to show. Practice and testing will show you how far you can go without posterizing the image. As always, film and proofs must be produced and checked against the original image.

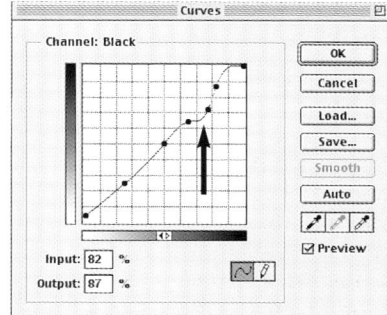

Finding the area you want to separate

Curve for "extraordinary contrast"

Taking contrast too far

98

Moirés are patterns or "artifacts" that come from rescanning already screened images. Visually a moiré causes noticeable unwanted patterns in the reproduction. Moirés are caused by the overlap of the dot pattern of the original image and the pattern imposed on the image when it is scanned. Moirés should be corrected before applying any sharpening effects. Some scanners have moiré correction as an option. For scanners that do not, try the techniques below.

## Base Scan tips

When trying to remove a moiré in an image that will be used at a reduced size i.e., 35%, you will achieve better results if you scan the already screened image at 100% of size, or at 2-3 times the usual resolution. Fix the moiré with one of the techniques below. Then, use Photoshop to resample the image down to the final size.

## Gaussian Blur

The Gaussian Blur filter can be applied to an image in varying degrees from 0.1-100 pixels in strength. A good starting value is 1 pixel. The filter can be applied to the entire image or a mask can be used to apply the effect to only the portion of the image that is most affected by the moiré. Because this effect blurs the image, USM should be used to bring back sharpness.

## Despeckle

This technique can be applied alone or in combination with Gaussian Blur. There are no settings for this filter and it does not always sharpen well. While checking the monitor is a good way to evaluate your success, remember to produce film and proofs to confirm your results.

# NO MORE MOIRÉS!

# PHOTOSHOP TIPS
## CROPPING

### CROPPING TOOL

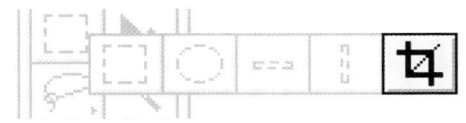

- In the Tool Palette, use the C key or the mouse to display the Crop Tool icon.
- Double click on the Cropping Tool to display the Crop Options Palette.

### HOW TO EXIT THE CROP TOOL

Use the **ESCAPE** key to exit or quit the Crop Marquee.

In some situations, the **Crop the image?** message will not be displayed. This always happens when the Crop Marquee is active and the Escape key is selected.

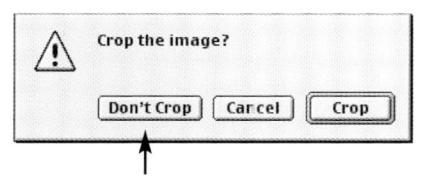

Use the **Don't Crop** to exit the Crop Marquee.

The above message is displayed when the Crop Marquee is active and the Crop Tool Icon is double clicked on.

---

One of the main tools for cropping images is the Cropping Tool. It is located in the Tool Palette. This tool has two options for random and exact cropping of images. Another way to crop an image is to use Selections, (see the next page).

### RANDOM CROPPING

1. **Select the Crop Tool.**

   To randomly crop an image, display the Crop Option Palette and make sure the Fixed Target Size is Unchecked.

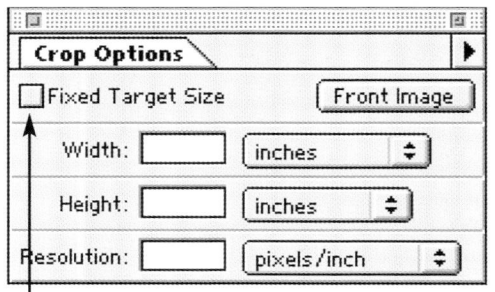

   Uncheck the Fixed Target Size for random Cropping.

2. **Scroll the Cropping Marquee over the image area.**

   Typically, begin cropping at the top left and move toward the bottom right of the image while holding the mouse down. The cropped area can be adjusted and fine-tuned by pointing to the corners of the Marquee with the cursor.

   1. Click and drag the corner points of the Cropping Marquee for scaling.
   2. To rotate the crop, move the mouse outside of the Cropping Marquee and click to OK the crop.

3. **Apply the Crop.**

   There are two options. Either double click inside the Cropping Marquee or depress the **Return/Enter** key.

---

### SCALING & ROTATING THE CROP TOOL

**Scaling.** To change the scale of a crop, move the corners and center points of the Cropping Marquee. Use the mouse and click on the corner or center points.

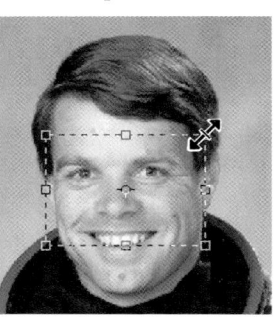

The above image on the left shows the points on a Cropping Marquee. The image on the right shows the effects of changing the Cropping Marquee.

**Rotation.** To change the rotation of a cropped area use the corners as a guide. Move the mouse outside of the corner areas, the double arrow icon will change to a hook-shaped arrow icon. Click on the hook-shaped arrow to manually rotate the Cropping Marquee.

The above image shows how a Cropping Marquee can be rotated.

100

## EXACT CROPPING

1. **Select the Crop Tool.**

   To crop images to an exact size and resolution display the Crop Option Palette and make sure the *Fixed Target Size* is checked.

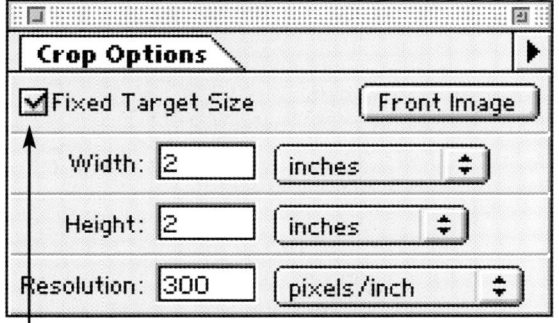

   • Check the Fixed Target Size for exact Cropping.

2. **Scroll the Cropping Marquee over the image area.**

   The cropped area can be adjusted and fine tuned by pointing the mouse over the corners of the Marquee. This will display a double arrow.

   1. Click and drag the corner points of the Cropping Marquee for scaling.
   2. To rotate the crop, move the mouse outside of the Cropping Marquee and click to OK the crop.

3. **Apply the Crop.**

   There are two options. Either double click inside the Cropping Marquee or depress the **Return/Enter** key.

## SELECTIONS AND EXACT CROPPING

1. Use the Rectangular Marque to make a Selection.

   The above example shows the Rectangular Marquee that was used to crop the image.

2. Go to the *Image>Crop* Menu option.

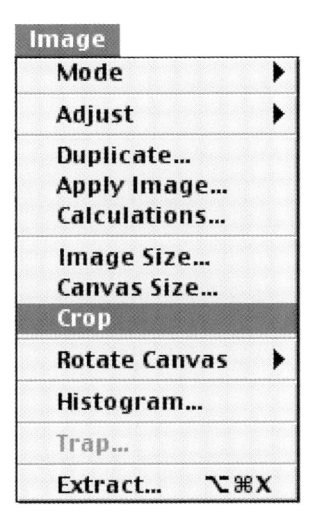

# PHOTOSHOP TIPS
## CROPPING

### BE CAREFUL TO APPLY THE CORRECT CROPPING

Using the Fixed Target Size to crop a small area on a image can cause the image to be come fuzzy.

This issue is about image resolution. If the cropping area on the image is too small and the image does not have enough resolution, Photoshop will try to create more image details. If there is not enough beginning resolution, Photoshop will create fuzzy results.

The solution to this problem is to rescan the image at a higher resolution. See Appendix A about resolution.

### FIXED CROP TIP

If the Fixed Crop option is new to you, it might be difficult to move the corner points vertically or horizontally. To overcome this problem, move the corner points on the diagonal.

101

# PHOTOSHOP TIPS
## SCALING

Using a known formula that produces predictable results is one of the keys to being successful with scaling. After you have learned the mechanics of the formula, you can then focus on measuring original images and creating the final layout.

Here is an example of how to use a calculator with this scaling method. To make it easier, do not work with fractions of an inch. Instead measure in decimal inches, millimeters, or point and picas.

Assume an area on a layout measures 11.54 mm (4.5 inches) and the same area on the original image measures 12 mm (4.7 inches). Ask yourself, is this an enlargement or a reduction? The answer to this scaling problem is that this is a reduction.

### EXAMPLE OF FORMULA FOR SCALING IMAGES

| Output size | / | Input size | = | Reduction Percent |
|---|---|---|---|---|
| 11.54 mm | / | 12 mm | = | 96.1% Reduction |

## SIZING AND SCALING IMAGES

One of the more difficult techniques for preparing scanned images is scaling them to the correct size. The purpose of sizing or scaling images is to accurately determine the final image size before it is scanned and placed in a page layout. Scaling images can be done with a variety of tools, including use of a scaling wheel, a calculator, or through Photoshop's Image Size Command. The most efficient and accurate method is to use a calculator before the scan is created.

### FORMULA FOR SCALING IMAGES UP

| Output size /Input size | = | Enlargement Percent |
|---|---|---|
| 2" / 1" | | (Example of 200%) |

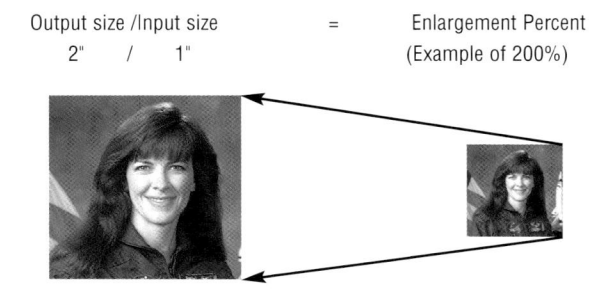

The example above illustrates a 200% enlargement. The images original size was 0.5 inches and was enlarged to 2.0 inches.

### FORMULA FOR SCALING IMAGES DOWN

| Output size/Input size | = | Reduction Percent |
|---|---|---|
| 1" / 2" | | (Example of 50%) |

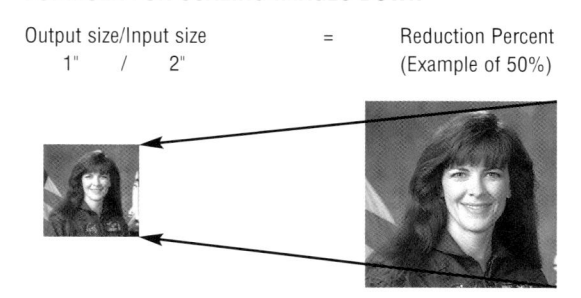

The example above illustrates a 50% reduction. The images original size was 2.0 inches and was reduced to 0.5 inches.

If you are new to this scaling method, use the formulas shown above to determine how to input values into your calculator. The values are measurements taken from distinct areas within the original image and the same distinct areas within the final layout.

## FINESSE THE SCALING

An important tip for achieving the best measuring accuracy is to use a ruler with fine increments such as points or millimeters. Inches will work, but it takes longer to convert fractions like 8th, 16th, or 32nds to decimals.

Another tip for sizing images is to recognize that cropping an image is more than measuring the original from side to side and comparing it to the layout window. Each scaling situation demands sizing from exact points within the original image to exact corresponding points on the layout.
This means it is necessary to measure two points within the image, such as the top of a head to the bottom of the feet and the same area within the layout. Usually end-users new to imaging find measuring and scaling images difficult to learn. Getting the image scaled right takes practice.

You might be thinking, *gee whiz this information is either too tedious or difficult to work with, so I will scan my image a little larger than I need, then do the cropping and scaling in Photoshop*. This is not a bad plan if only a few images are being used. In a high production operation where dozens or hundreds of images are to be scanned, then it becomes significant. Consider the consequences of supplying scaled images to the scanning department with miscalculated sizing instructions. The image(s) would have to be re-scanned or more costly work time would be required on the desktop. Therefore it is important to check and double check the scaling measurements so when a scan is created, it is at the correct size and resolution.

## SCALING, RESAMPLING, AND RESIZING

Photoshop has scaling options that are part of the Image Size dialog box. There are three Image Size dialog boxes in the next column. These dialog boxes show how the Constrain Proportions and Resample Image check boxes affect scaling images. When scanning images, it is often necessary to change the size of the image after it is scanned so that it fits correctly into your document layout. This involves simple scaling of an image. It often requires that you resample an image, either larger or smaller.

When a digital image is scaled (not resampled), no data is actually thrown away. The process either expands the image size by moving the pixels further apart (reducing the resolution), or it moves the pixels closer together (increasing the resolution). This can be done in Photoshop, but it is more often done in a page layout program. While this technique of scaling works, there are several risks associated with it.

The most obvious risk in scaling happens when scaling an image up to a larger size. You may reduce the resolution past the 2:1, 1.5:1, or 1:1 quality factor that you established in your original scan. The result is usually a pixilated image or an image that lacks the detail you expected.

A second, less serious, but not necessarily less costly effect is caused by sizing images down significantly in page layout programs. While the image quality is not adversely affected, the amount of time the image takes to output can be increased significantly. This happens because the RIP (Raster Image Processor) in the printer must calculate the original picture size, calculate the new image size, and then image the picture. (If you want to make it even worse, rotate the image in the picture box.) For one or two pictures, this usually isn't a big problem, but when you have many images, sizing down can add time to producing your project which can increase costs. The best solution is to go back to Photoshop and apply the proper cropping rotation and image resampling and then reimport the image.

In resampling, an image's data is either created or thrown away. Adobe Photoshop has an excellent built-in tool for just this function: Use Image Size. It is available under the Image menu.

---

These Image Size settings are commonly used for scaling an image symmetrically. They permit changing the image resolution without affecting the physical dimensions of the file.

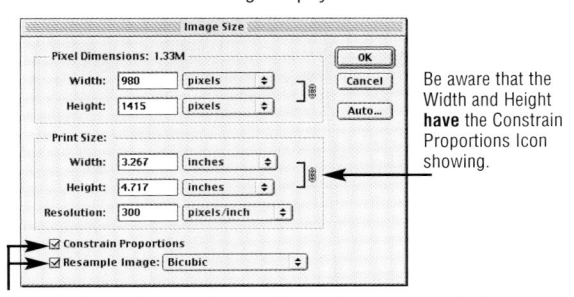

Be aware that the Width and Height **have** the Constrain Proportions Icon showing.

Note that Constrain Proportions and Resample Image is checked on. Interpolation is set to Bicubic.

This Image Size configuration adjusts the image resolution while the image is scaled symmetrically. The physical dimensions change, but the file maintains its original size in megabytes.

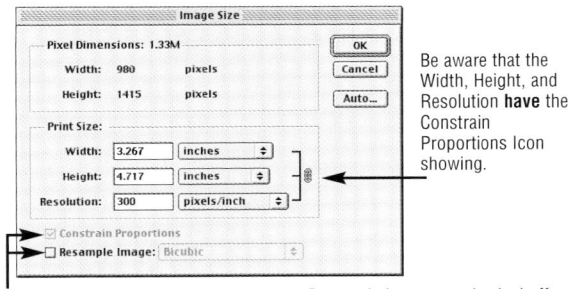

Be aware that the Width, Height, and Resolution **have** the Constrain Proportions Icon showing.

Note that Constrain Proportions and the Resample Image are checked off.

Using this Image Size configuration permits scaling an image amorphically (the vertical or horizontal direction can be altered independent of each other) and changing the image resolution without affecting the physical dimensions of the file.

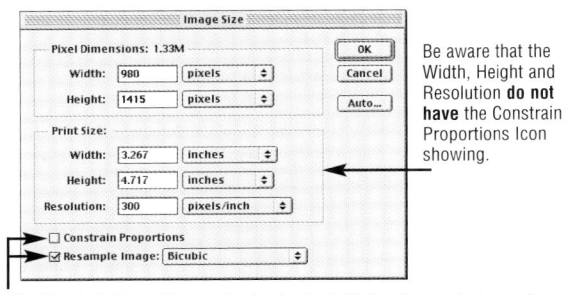

Be aware that the Width, Height and Resolution **do not have** the Constrain Proportions Icon showing.

The Constrain Proportions option is checked off. The Resample Image is checked on. Interpolation is set to Bicubic.

---

# PHOTOSHOP TIPS
## PHOTOSHOP SCALING

### INTERPOLATION

Each method of interpolation defines the specific calculation that is used to interpolate/create data where none exists. Bicubic is the slowest but produces the best quality. Nearest Neighbor is the fastest but may produce jaggies. Bilinear is between the other two in speed and quality.

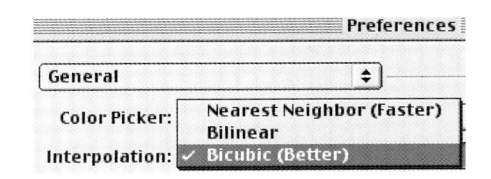

Resized-(scaling) No pixels are added. They just get bigger!

Resampled Up - Pixels added based on Bicubic interpolation. This can only be done in an image editing program.

# PHOTOSHOP TIPS
## ACTIONS BASICS

### ACTIONS PALETTE

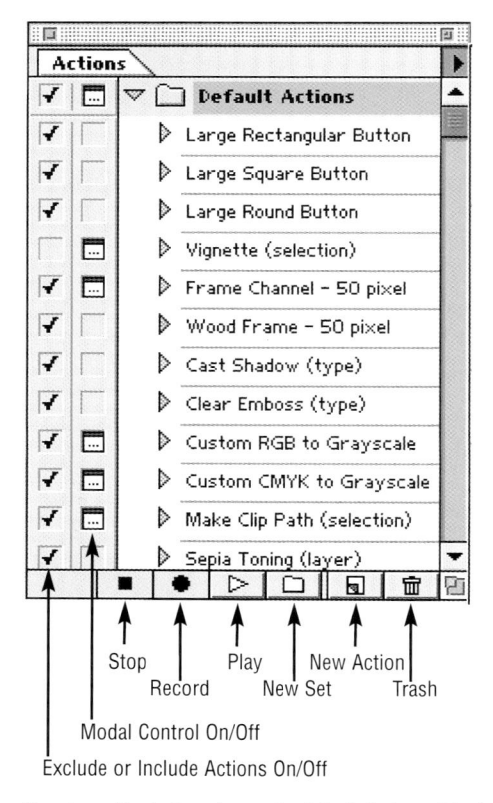

Stop
Record
Play
New Set
New Action
Trash
Modal Control On/Off
Exclude or Include Actions On/Off

The above illustration shows the default Actions (12 of them) that come with the Actions Palette. There are another 122 pre-made Actions in the Goodies Folder.

To turn Modal controls on or off for all the commands in an action or set, click the modal control icon to the left of the action name. For more about Modal controls see the sidebar on the next page.

### ACTIONS PALETTE SUCCESS TIPS

The Actions Palette is a feature of Photoshop 5.0.2 and 5.5 that allows programming of most Photoshop pull-down menu options. This feature is critical for repetitive operations in Photoshop. This programming tool is also called Scripting. It permits the end-user to easily click a button to (1) create a list of easy-to-access menu options, (2) create a string of menu commands, or (3) apply batch processing of a string of menu commands to groups of images. Unfortunately, the Action features do not work with the Palette Tools or with drawing options such as Selections or Paths.

### HOW TO CREATE (RECORD) A BASIC ACTION

- To create an Action, use the Pop-out menu and choose New Action.

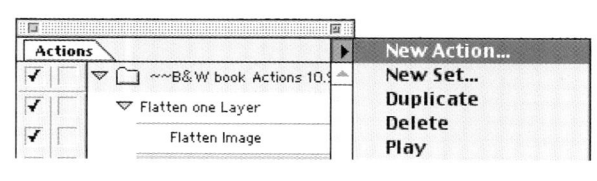

- Fill in the the New Action with a descriptive name. Click on the Record option. This starts recording most pull-down menu options.

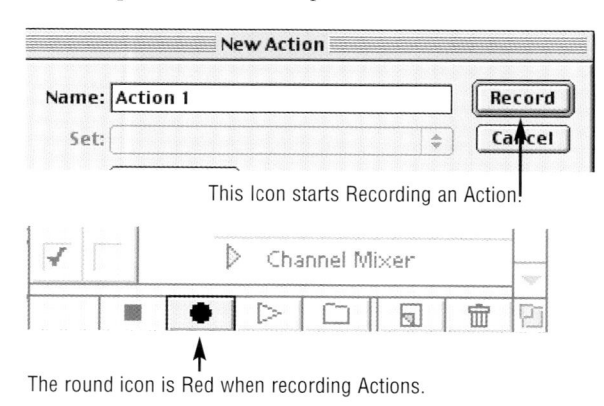

This Icon starts Recording an Action!

The round icon is Red when recording Actions.

### HOW TO STOP RECORDING AN ACTION

- Click on the square icon at the bottom left of the Actions Palette.

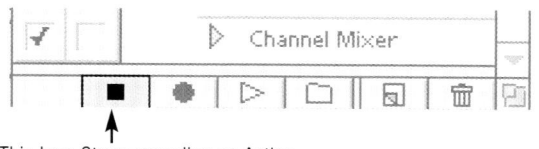

This Icon Stops recording an Action.

### HOW TO INSERT MENU ITEMS

- Create a New Action with the Actions Pop-out menu. Then Stop the Action.
- Use the Actions Pop-out menu to select the Insert Menu Item option.

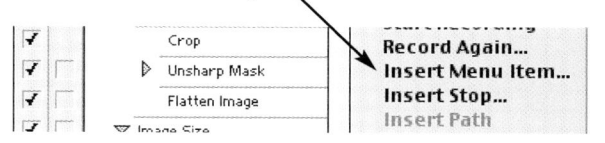

- Click on the Menu Item from the Photoshop pull-down menus you wish to record into the Actions list as a Menu Item and then OK it.

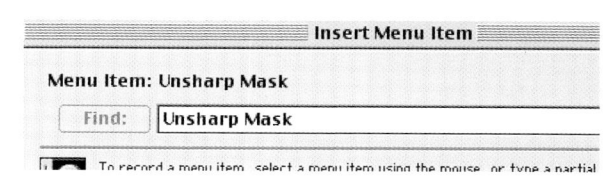

The example above shows the Insert Menu Item menu after a pull-down menu was activated. In this example Unsharp Mask was selected from the Filter Menu.

### HOW TO CREATE A STRING OF MENU COMMANDS

- Use Photoshops Pop-out menu and choose New Action. Fill in the the New Action dialog box with a descriptive name. Click on the Record option.
- Use the Pull-down menus to record the combination of menu options that are required for the Actions.
- To Stop, click on the square icon at the bottom left of the Actions Palette.

104

## HOW TO EDIT AND ACTION

Here are two methods of editing an Action.

**1. Use the drag-n-drop feature of the Action Palette.**

Drag-n-drop specific Actions from one set of Actions or to a new location in the Actions Palette.

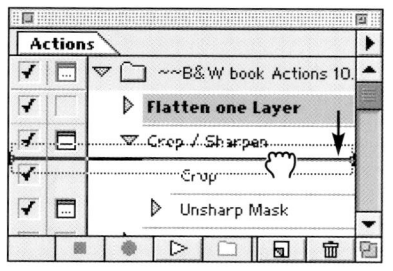

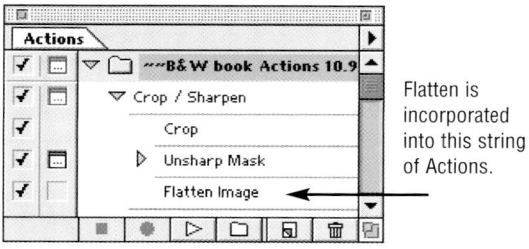

Flatten is incorporated into this string of Actions.

The two illustrations above show how Action commands can be moved to new locations in the Actions Palette. In this example, the Flatten Action was moved into a string of Actions, Crop and Unsharp Mask. The new string uses Crop, Unsharp Mask, and Flatten.

**2. Double click on a specific Action**

If the Action has a user-defined value associated within the Action, double click on that specific Action command. This will show the dialog box and its values of that particular Action. Change the value.

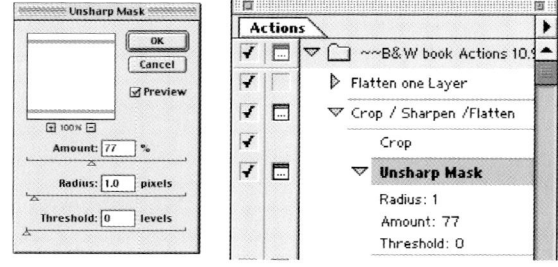

The example above shows the Modal controls of a user defined value in the Unsharp Masking dialog box of an Action.

## HOW TO PLAY AN ACTION

**1. Use the Actions Pop-out menu Play option.**

Use the mouse to select the Action in the list. Select Play from the Actions Pop-out menu.

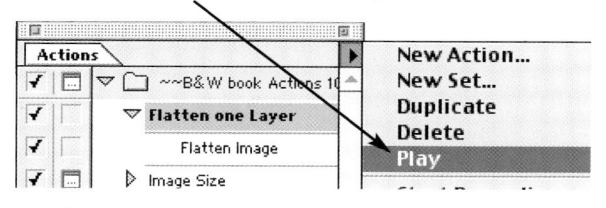

**2. Click on the triangular icon at the bottom of the Actions Palette.**

This Icon Plays an Action.

### VERIFY NEW ACTIONS

Run simple tests to verify each Set of Actions works before running them on a batch of images.

### HOW TO SAVE AND LOAD ACTION SETTINGS

- To Save an Action, use the Actions Pop-out menu.
- To Load Action settings, use the Actions Pop-out menu.

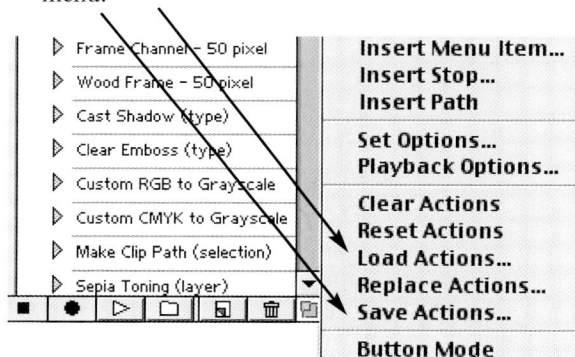

For cross-platform Actions, be sure to use the extension .atn.

# PHOTOSHOP TIPS
## ACTIONS BASICS

### GETTING STARTED TIP

When creating a single Action or a group of Actions clear the Actions Palette. This makes Actions easier to view and the Action creation process becomes less confusing.

### VERIFYING ACTIONS TIP

To test a new Action, set up a folder with only one or two images and then use **Automate>Batch** with the new Action.

### WHAT IS MODAL?

Modal controls are the commands in the Actions Palette that have user-defined values.

When Actions are first recorded, the modal controls run in Photoshop using the original specified values. The Modal control option lets you pause a command and display the information about the commands in its dialog box. Modal controls allow the Action to be altered so new values can be set and applied. When the Modal controls are altered, they require pressing Return/Enter to apply its effect.

105

# PHOTOSHOP TIPS

## ACTIONS - BATCH PROCESSING

### BATCH PROCESSING AT-A-GLANCE

1. Select the Set option.
2. Select the Action.
3. Select the Source.
4. Choose the Source Folder.
5. Choose the Destination.
6. Select the Destination Folder.

### NAMING TIPS

- Name folders with sensible and descriptive names. This can make a new process such as setting up batch processing more understandable.
- Name folders with characters that will place the folders on the computer system in an easy-to-find location.

  For example use AAA (triple A) followed by a descriptive title. Be sure your operating system is setup so you are viewing folders and files alphabetically. This places the folder with the AAA at the top of the list making it easier to find. After you are done using Actions, rename it by removing the AAA. Be careful on Windows computer systems when using this method, Windows does not accept certain characters at the beginning and end of a name.

### HOW TO APPLY BATCH PROCESSING

Actions can be used with batch processing features. To start use the *File>Automate>Batch*.

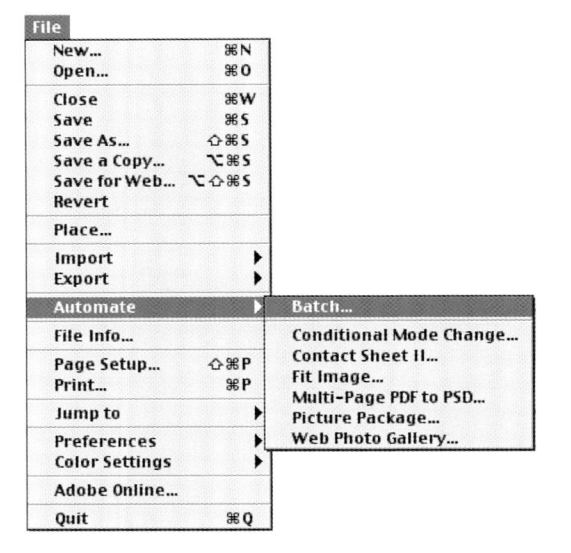

### SETTING UP BATCH PROCESSING

The Batch dialog box has six fundamental options for batch processing.

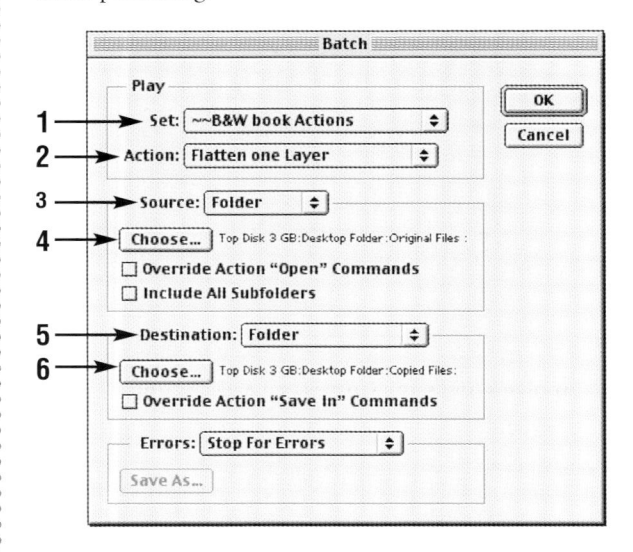

### BATCH PROCESSING STEP BY STEP

1. **Select the Set option.**

   This defines the set of Actions that will be available for the batch processing.

2. **Select the Action.**

   The Action is made available in this menu option.

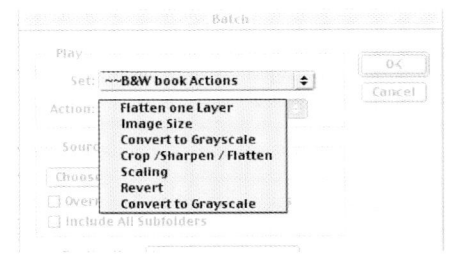

3. **Select the Source.**

   This has two options: Import and Folder. In this example we chose Folder.

4. **Choose the Source Folder.**

   This option identifies the folder where the images reside that are to be processed.

- Navigate through your computer system to the folder with the files that are going to be processed with this Action. Once the source folder is identified, click on the **Select** option.

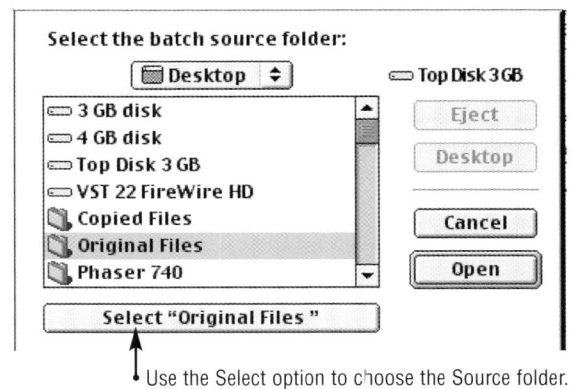

  Use the Select option to choose the Source folder.

**Tip:** If possible, place the original files in an easy-to-choose place on your computer system. Typically, we suggest dragging the folder and the files to a logical place such as your desktop.

106

5. **Choose the Destination.**

   This has three options: None, Save and Close, and Folder.

   - *None.* There is no destination setup.
   - *Save and Close.* This allows applying the Action then re-saving the file.
   - *Folder.* This allows a folder to be used to place processed files. In this example, we chose Folder.

6. **Select the Destination Folder.**

   This is where the processed file will be placed.

   - Navigate through your computer system to the folder where you want to place the files. Once the source folder is identified, click on the **Select** option.

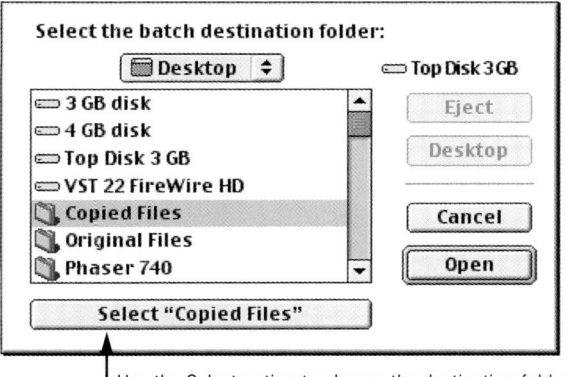

Use the Select option to choose the destination folder.

**Tip:** If possible, place the original files in an easy-to-find place on your computer system. Typically, we suggest dragging the folder and the files to a logical place such as your desktop.

## SCENARIOS FOR ACTIONS

### SCENARIO 1
Use the Actions *Insert Menu Items* to make commonly used pull down menus such as Curves, Levels, and Filters easier to access. This is the easiest way to start working with Actions. The *Insert Menu Items* can create an easy-to-use working environment.

### SCENARIO 2
Use Actions to create a string of Menu commands. A good strategy for automating your workflow is to create a number of short Actions (a string of 2 to 5 pull down menu commands) and then apply at the appropriate moment in your working session.

For example, during the production of this book, we had to create grayscale images of screen shots. A third-party screen shot application was used that placed the screen shot in the clipboard. The screen shot was pasted into a Quark page that was turned into an EPS file. The EPS was opened in Photoshop, converted to grayscale, cropped, had Unsharp Masking (USM) applied, and was Flattened. This set of Actions necessary to just prepare the screen shot for page layout.

An Action was created to crop an image using a Selection. Then the image was scaled to a desired resolution, USM was applied, and then the image was Flattened. This helped automate the process of converting screen shots to cropped, sharpened images that were ready for page assembly. This particular Action can be seen in the Actions Palette example on the right.

### SCENARIO 3
Use Actions to apply a string of menu commands to a a batch of images with the click of a button. There numerous situations where this can save time. Here are a few suggestions:

1. Scaling high resolution files to low resolution.
2. Applying the same Curves or Levels settings.
3. Sharpening images.
4. Converting color images to grayscale.
5. Ghosting images.
6. Flattening images.

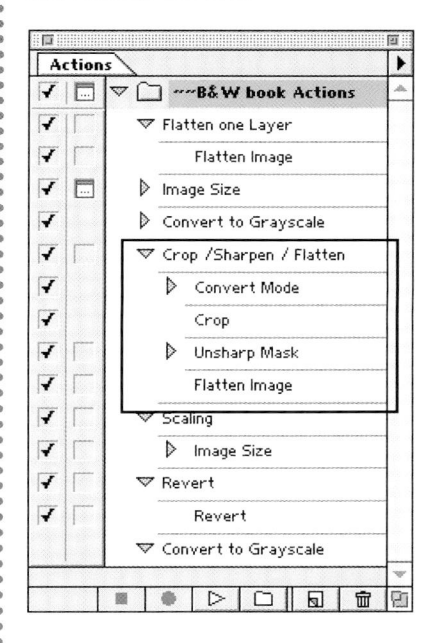

# PHOTOSHOP TIPS
## ACTIONS - BATCH PROCESSING

### CUSTOMIZED ACTIONS

**107**

# PHOTOSHOP TIP
## CREATING A MIRROR IMAGE

**ORIGINAL IMAGE**
The image is 4.0" x 5.5" at 300 dpi.

We chose to the Copy and Paste method in this exercise to place the image into the new Canvas area. We know there are other methods that would work but we think this was the easiest technique for this exercise.

Changing the Canvas Size is common way to add more image area that will extend an image's background. Access to Canvas Size in Photoshop is through the *Image>Canvas Size* option. We know there is more than one way to extend a background in Photoshop. The examples on the next four pages illustrate how to use the Canvas Size feature. On pages 108 and 109, the examples show how to create a mirror image. This technique will double the size of the image area.

1. **Once the image is open, apply Select All Cmd/Cntrl** A and then use Copy (**Cmd/Cntrl** C).

   This copies the Selected area to the clipboard. The copy of the image will stay in the clipboard until the computer is shut down.

2. **Go to** *Image>Canvas Size*.

   In this example, the image's width is 4 inches. Change the Canvas Size width from 4 inches to 8 inches. Be sure to change Anchor Area in the Canvas Size dialog box. Anchor the image on the left side of the Canvas.

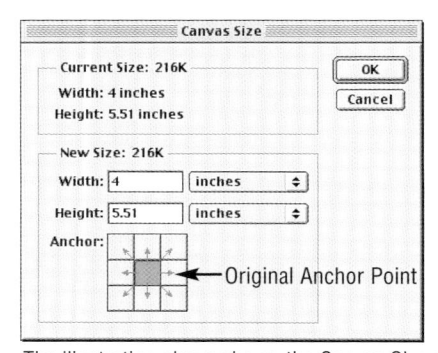

The illustration above shows the Canvas Size dialog box.

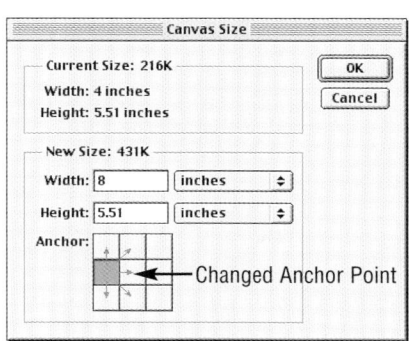

The illustration above shows the Canvas Size dialog box with a new Canvas Size of 8 inches. Note the Anchor point. Changing it places the image on the left side of the new Canvas.

This area represents the new Canvas.

The image above shows the new Canvas Size on the right side of the image.

3. **Paste the image from the clipboard.**

   This will create a Layer. Double click on the new Layer and give it the name **Right Side** Layer.

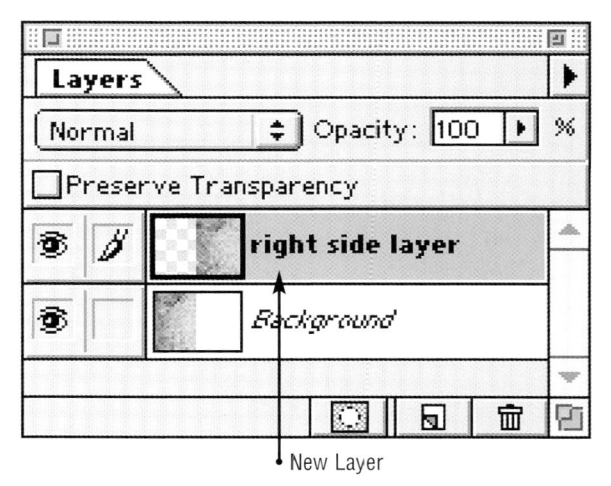

New Layer

108

4. Flip the image horizontally.

Apply *Edit>Transform>Flip Horizontal* to the right side of the image.

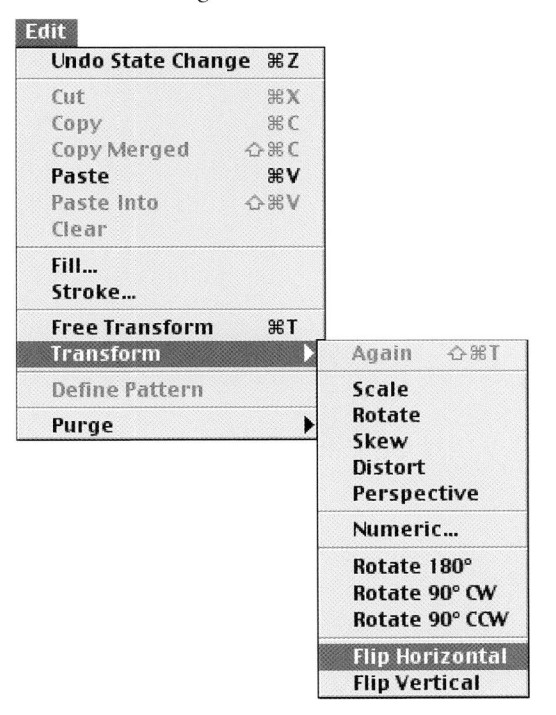

6. Flatten the image.

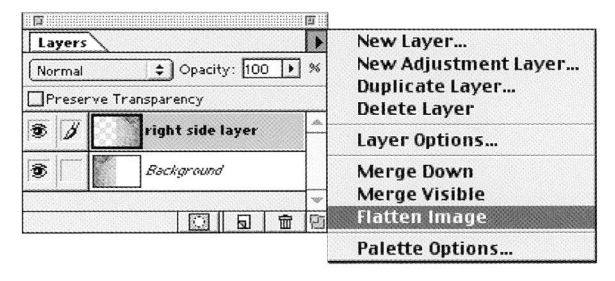

7. If necessary, use the Rubber Stamp Tool to clone any unusual shapes from the center of the new image.

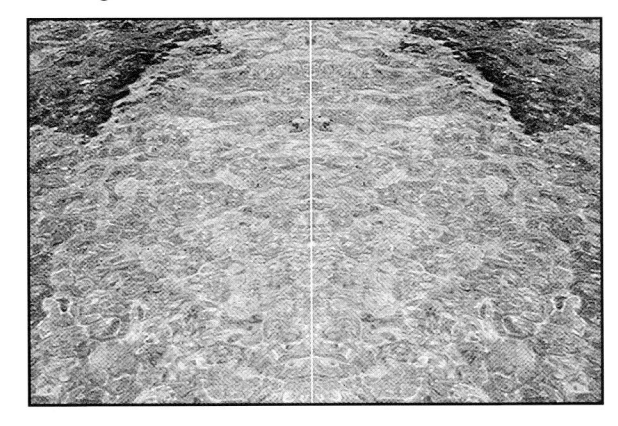

5. Use the Move Tool to position the image.

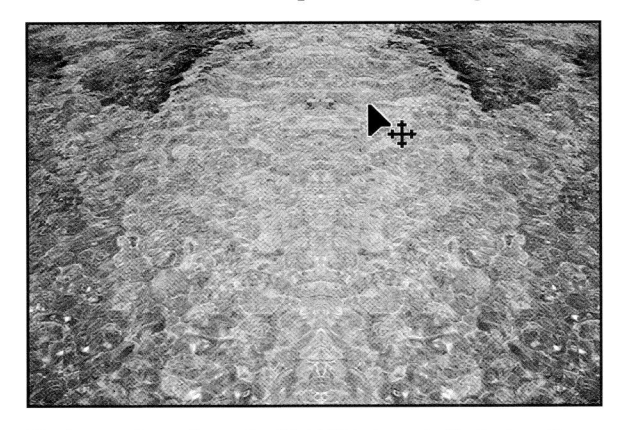

The image above shows the Right Side Layer in its final position.

The image above shows an exaggerated line in the center of the image. Sometimes when creating a mirror image all image details do not fit visually. Before applying any retouching methods try using the arrow keys to move the image into a better position.

If that does not work then it might be necessary to clone out the problem area. See page 79 about cloning.

# PHOTOSHOP TIP

## CREATING A MIRROR IMAGE

### MIRROR IMAGE AT-A-GLANCE

1. Once the image is open apply Select All **Cmd/Cntrl A** and then use Copy **Cmd/Cntrl C**.
2. Go to *Image>Canvas* Size.
3. Paste the image from the clipboard.
4. Flip the image horizontally.
   Apply *Edit>Transform>Flip Horizontal* the right side image.
5. Use the Move Tool to position the image.
6. Flatten the image.
7. Option.Use the Rubber Stamp Tool for cloning.

109

# PHOTOSHOP TIP

## EXTENDING BACKGROUNDS

**ORIGINAL IMAGE**
The image is 3.0" x 2.013" at 300 dpi.

**HOW TO EXIT TRANSFORM TOOLS**
Use the **ESCAPE** key to exit the Transform Marquee.

Another variation to extend the background of an image involves increasing the Canvas area and then using Transform to scale part of the image. In this example, only a small portion of the image area needs to be extended to make it fit into the layout.

1. **Extend the Canvas area for the image.**

   The new Canvas Size will become 3.5".
   Be sure to change the Anchor Area in the Canvas Size dialog box. Anchor the image on the left side of the Canvas.

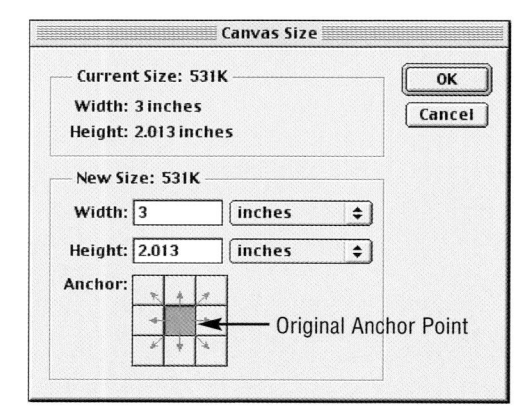

   The illustration above shows the Canvas Size dialog box.

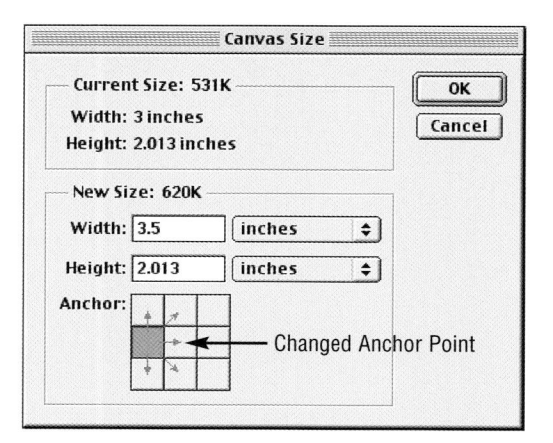

   The above illustration shows the Canvas Size dialog box with the new Canvas Size of 3.5 inches and the Anchor point changed.

The new Canvas area

2. **Create a Selection over the water on the right side of the image.**

   Be careful to Select the water only and not the raft.

The illustration above shows a Selection of the water area.

110

3. Go to *Edit>Transform>Scale*.

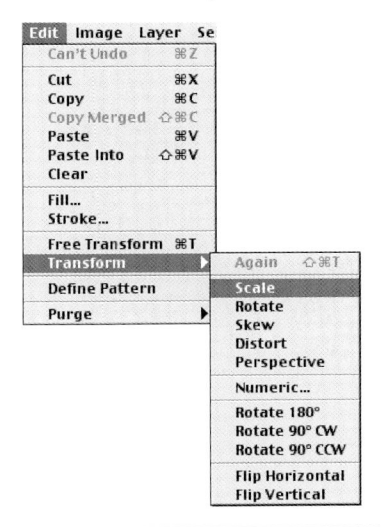

4. **Drag the round icon from the right side center of the Transform Marquee to the far right side of the image.**

   Be careful to Select the water area and not the raft.

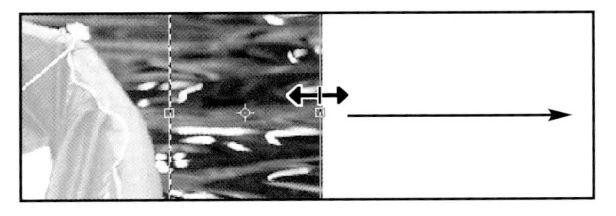

5. **Apply Transform.**

   There are two options to apply the Transform option.
   - Double click inside the Transform Marquee.
   - Apply the Return/Enter key.

The illustration above shows the final results of using the *Transform>Scale* option to extend the water area.

The illustration above shows the Transform Marquee over the water area. Notice the round icons on the corners and in the center of each side of the Transform Marquee.

# PHOTOSHOP TIP

## EXTENDING BACKGROUNDS

### EXTENDING A BACKGROUND AT-A-GLANCE

1. Create new Canvas Size.
2. Create a Selection over the correct image area.
3. Use ***Edit>Transform>Scale*** on the Selection.
4. Drag the right side center round icon to the right.
5. Apply the Transform.

**BE AWARE:** Not all images will work as easily as the two imaging situations we choose on pages 108-111. These two imaging situations were clear cut and easy to work with. Our purpose in using easy examples was to be sure it was understood how to use Canvas Size and Transform.

In some imaging situations, changing the Canvas and using Transform to extend a background can cause time-consuming Photoshop cloning and retouching.

In the final example below, we tried to extend the left side of the image using Canvas and Transform. This was problematic because the lower left side of the image does not have the best details to work with. This made the project more complex and time-consuming because image data had to be created.

To create refined and natural looking details in the lower left side of the image, the raft details have to be copied or pasted and then cloned to make the raft look natural. This project took just over one hour of retouching time using copy and paste with different image areas, Transform, Rubber Stamp, Snapshot, and Curves.

**111**

# PHOTOSHOP TIPS
## DUST BUSTING

### SNAPSHOT VS THE RUBBER STAMP (CLONING)

The image example could have been repaired using the Rubber Stamp Tool, but we chose to use a Snapshot with Dust and Scratches. Here is our reasoning.

While the Dust & Scratches filter destroys the image details by smoothing image grain and noise, the images source pixels stay in the same X and Y position. The Rubber Stamp Tool does not do this. The Rubber Stamp Tool works by moving the image data from a source to a new destination. It is therefore possible to get higher quality with the Rubber Stamp Tool, but it takes more time.

Using the Dust and Scratches with the Snapshot has a better chance of lining up and matching surrounding tones because they are in the same X and Y coordinate positions. This gives the end-user a better chance of matching surrounding tones when painting out imperfections with fuzzy image data from the Snapshot. This is why we believe it is easier to paint from a Snapshot.

We know the Rubber Stamp can create the same or, in some cases, better results as the Snapshot by moving image tones from a source to a new destination to eliminate dirt, etc. We find in many situations, it takes more time and skill. This why we find it easier in this situation to paint with the Snapshot.

**Note:** We did this image editing both ways with the Rubber Stamp Tool and using a Snapshot with Dust and Scratches applied. If it took under three minutes to use the Snapshot, it took at least 6 minutes (twice as long) to use the Rubber Stamp. The final results were the same.

For more about how to create a Snapshot see page 22.

## DUST & SCRATCHES

Dust & Scratches is a Filter menu option; *Filter>Noise>Dust & Scratches*. It is a great tool for removing minor imperfections quickly. This filter works well with the use of Selections in areas that have blemishes and with Snapshots before the filter is applied.

### USE DUST & SCRATCHES WITH A SNAPSHOT

Use the History brush to paint out dirt in the image. Set the values in the Dust & Scratches dialog box until the scratch or largest particle of dust is barely removed.

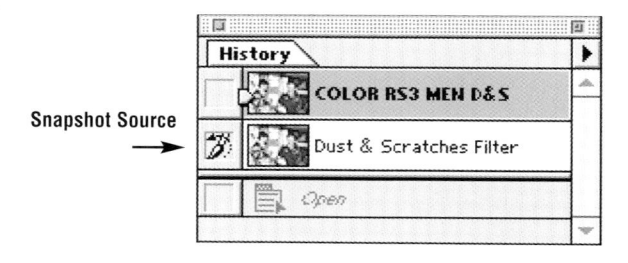

Snapshot Source →

### REMOVING DUST FROM AN IMAGE.

1. Apply either Gaussian Blur or Dust & Scratches filters to degrade an image so that the largest dust area is barely removed.
2. Use the History Palette to Take a Snapshot of the degraded image.
3. Use Undo after the Snapshot to revert to the original image.
4. In the History Palette, select the source of the new snapshot.
5. Next, select the History brush from the Tool Palette. Be sure the correct size brush and opacity are set.
6. Paint out the dirt in the image.

The above image is full of imperfections.

### USE DUST & SCRATCHES WITH A SELECTION

Create a Selection over the image area with imperfections. Experiment with the values in the Dust & Scratches dialog box until the scratch or largest particle of dirt is removed. This will be a trade-off between removing imperfections and degrading image detail.

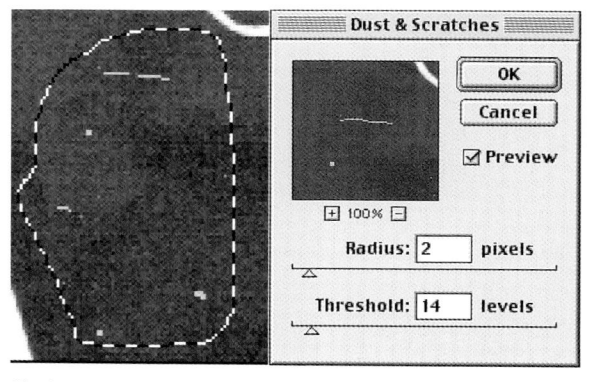

The image above is a close-up of the Selection that was used to apply Dust and Scratches to imperfections.

The illustration above shows values that were used to remove the imperfections within the Selection and for the Snapshot.

The image above is the final results of using Dust and Scratches with a Selection and a Snapshot.

112

The best method for working with line images is to start with it as a grayscale image. This allows maintaining all the original image tones that will be adjusted when creating high-quality line images. Once the grayscale image is captured, use tools like: Curves, Levels, Threshold, Brightness and Contrast, Posterize, and the 50% Threshold option. Any of these tool can be used to make the image high contrast. We prefer the Threshold Tool. Use it to bring out the correct details in the line image. After using Threshold, convert the grayscale file to a Bitmap file.

# PHOTOSHOP TIPS

## LINE IMAGES

1. **Scan the image as grayscale at a resolution between 800 dpi and 1200 dpi.**
   - This might sound like too much resolution, but to achieve high quality, these amounts are required.

2. **Use Threshold to create a high contrast image.**
   - Notice how the raw scan picked up details in the paper. Threshold reduces those areas, so the background details are changed to paper white.

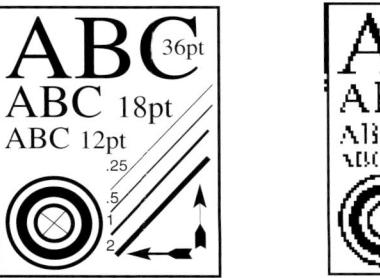

### HANDLING LINE IMAGES AT-A-GLANCE

1. Scan the image in the grayscale mode and adjust resolution between 800 dpi to 1200 dpi.
2. Use Threshold to create a high contrast image.
3. Convert the grayscale Mode to the Bitmap Mode.
4. Save As.

Original Text and Line work in Quark

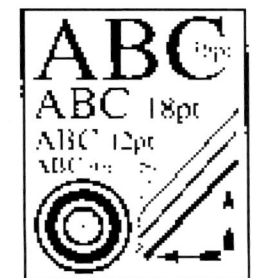

72 dpi scanned text

These two images are the raw grayscale scans before Threshold adjustments. Each image was scanned with different settings, so each image required a different Threshold value.

300 dpi scanned text

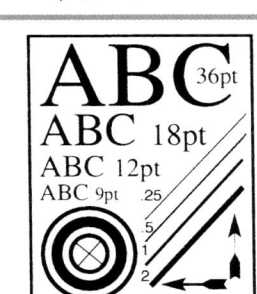

600 dpi scanned text

150 Threshold setting

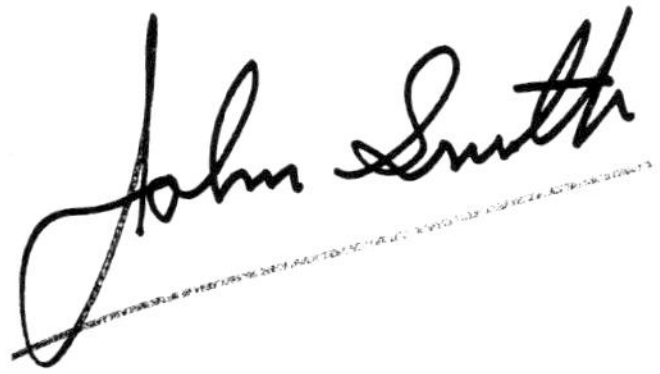

128 Threshold setting

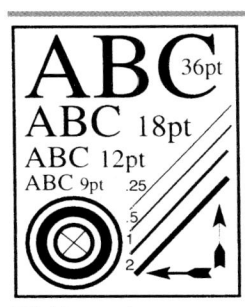

800 dpi scanned text

1200 dpi scanned text

200 Threshold setting

175 Threshold setting

In the six examples above, different resolution values show the effect on scanned text images with a 50 Threshold.

In our examples above, we used 1200 dpi images with different Threshold values to show its effect on text and handwriting.

Scanned continuous tone and line images are both considered raster images. The difference is that Line images usually get reproduced as one-bit-per-pixel images with only two tones which are black and white. Continuous tone images typically have eight-bits-per-pixel with up to 256 shades of gray.

In terms of resolution, the difference between a line image and a continuous tone image is that line image requires more image resolution than continuous tone images. The reason that line images require more resolution is to reduce jagged edges or aliasing on curved or diagonal lines.

It is common for line images to have 3 to 6 times more image resolution. This means, for example, if a continuous tone images resolution is 300 ppi, then a line image might be 1200 ppi.

The implications are that when you first scan the line image as a grayscale file, it will take up more disk space because it is an eight-bit image.

For more about image resolution, see appendix A.

**113**

# APPENDIX A:
## RESOLUTION

If an image does not have enough information to resolve the finer details of the original, it will appear fuzzy. Here are three examples of image resolution.

**RESOLUTION 300 DPI**

**RESOLUTION 150 DPI**

**RESOLUTION 50 DPI**

## INPUT RESOLUTION (BASICS)

Image resolution or pixel data is usually created with a scanner or digital camera and is referred to and measured by the rate at which a scanner or camera samples image details. Resolution is described by a variety of terms like spots, pixels, line pairs, and dots. These terms are used in conjunction with different metrics such as inches or millimeters. This section will refer to image resolution as Pixels Per Inch (ppi) and Dots Per Inch (dpi).

When continuous tone images are rasterized into bit-mapped images, a series of rectangular grids define the image. The grid of pixels can be seen in the example of the enlarged image below.

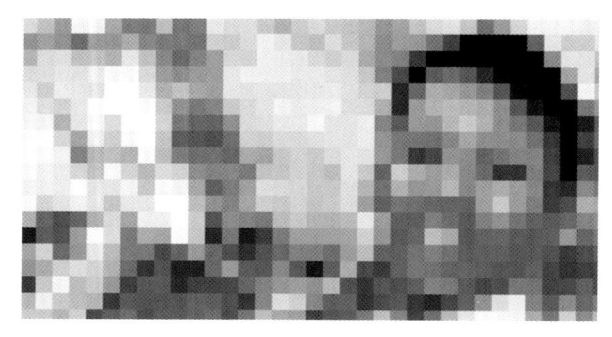

The number of pixels per inch describe an image file. If image resolution is new to you, the example below illustrates how to think about image resolution for a 4"x 5" image at 300 ppi.

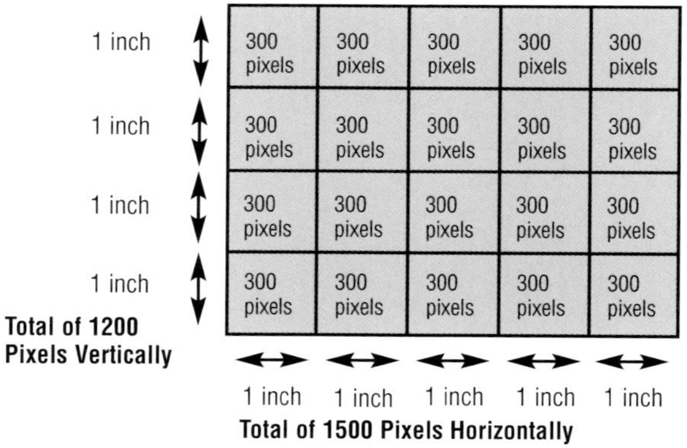

| | | | | | |
|---|---|---|---|---|---|
| 1 inch | 300 pixels | 300 pixels | 300 pixels | 300 pixels | 300 pixels |
| 1 inch | 300 pixels | 300 pixels | 300 pixels | 300 pixels | 300 pixels |
| 1 inch | 300 pixels | 300 pixels | 300 pixels | 300 pixels | 300 pixels |
| 1 inch | 300 pixels | 300 pixels | 300 pixels | 300 pixels | 300 pixels |

**Total of 1200 Pixels Vertically**

1 inch  1 inch  1 inch  1 inch  1 inch
**Total of 1500 Pixels Horizontally**

Pixels Per Inch and Dots Per Inch are different terms for the same measure of image resolution. The above example could be discussed as a 4"x 5" image at 300 ppi or at 300 dpi.

## RESOLUTION FUNDAMENTALS

Three key factors identify image resolution; they are:

1. Physical dimensions of an image, such as inches vertically and horizontally.
2. The number or pixels per inch.
3. File Size usually in megabytes.

These factors can be seen in Photoshop's Image Size dialog box.

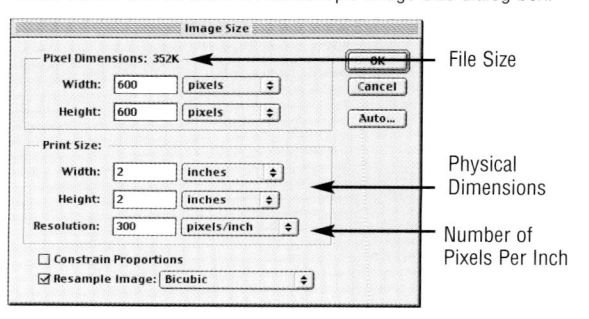

- File Size
- Physical Dimensions
- Number of Pixels Per Inch

| Physical Dimensions | Pixels Per Inch | File Size Megabytes |
|---|---|---|
| 4 X 5 | 300 ppi = | 1.72 mb |
| 2 X 10 | 300 ppi = | 1.72 mb |
| 1 X 20 | 300 ppi = | 1.72 mb |

Image resolution can be described and expressed in a number of ways. Above are three examples of files with the same pixel resolution and file size in megabytes, but which have different physical dimensions.

Note in the above example that the physical dimensions are all equal to 20 square inches.

114

## USE BITS AND BYTES BASICS TO DETERMINE FILE SIZE

Digital computers use the binary counting system to keep track of data by using a series of zeros and ones that map a certain position or bit location in the computer.

Bits are the smallest unit of information recorded in a computer. Bits are defined by one of two switch conditions (on or off).

### Counting terms for bytes (rounded off):
- 8 bits = 1 byte
- 1000 bytes =1 Kilobytes
- 1,000,000 Bytes = 1 Megabyte

Disk space and RAM are defined by kilobytes and megabytes. Kilobytes represents a thousand characters of information (10 to the third). Megabytes represents a million characters of information (10 to the sixth). While megabytes are rounded off (this makes the math easier), one megabyte actually equals 1,048,576 bytes.

By knowing how images are digitized (scanned) into bits and pixels, you can understand how file size is determined.

There are many methods to calculate file size. One is to use known values such as:

(1) A bit is the smallest unit of information recorded in a computer and (2) there are 8 bits in a byte.

A critical concept to understand is that 8 bits of computer information, or one byte, has the same exact relationship to an 8-bit image. Instead of computer bits creating bytes of data, the scanner's sensor system creates 8 bits of scanned image information in one pixel. The relationship is that one byte is equal to one pixel.

When the relationship of bits and bytes to a pixel is understood, it becomes easy to determine image file size.

### BIT DEPTH AND DISPLAYABLE SHADES/COLORS

| | | | |
|---|---|---|---|
| 1 bit | $2^1$ | = 2 shades black and white | - Line work |
| 4 bit | $2^4$ | = 64 shades/colors | |
| 8 bit | $2^8$ | = 256 shades/colors | - Grayscale |
| 24 bit | $2^{24}$ | = 256 shades/colors per channel 1.68 million colors | - Color |

## FACTOR PIXELS TO MEGABYTES FOR GRAYSCALE

- Convert one square inch of pixel data at 300 ppi into bytes. (300 x 300 or 300 squared). That would be equal to 90,000 bytes.
- Divide 90,000 by 1,048,576 and the dividend would equal 0.085 megabytes per one square inch at 300 ppi.
- One square inch of pixel data divided by megabytes equals 0.085 mb per square inch:

  Equation to factor 300 ppi images to megabytes:

  90,000 / 1,048,576 = 0.085mb per square inch.

- The next part is easy, determine how many square inches are in the final scanned image area. The 4"x 5" example equals an area of 20 square inches.
- Multiply 20 square inches by 0.085 mb.
- It equals 1.7 mb in 20 square inches.

In some cases, this method introduces slight rounding errors and is not exact, but it is close and provides an easy-to-use method in determining image resolution and file size. (The rounding error is introduced by using 1,048,576 and rounding off the answer to 0.085 instead of 0.08583068848 to calculate the common denominator of bytes for file sizes).

## FACTOR PIXELS TO MEGABYTES FOR RGB IMAGES

Multiply 3 by 0.085 mb to equal 0.255 mb.

This becomes the common factor for one square inch of RGB data at 300 ppi.

## FACTOR PIXELS TO MEGABYTES FOR CMYK IMAGES

Multiply 4 by 0.085 mb to equal 0.34 mb.

This becomes the common factor for one square inch of CMYK data at 300 ppi.

# APPENDIX A:
## RESOLUTION

### OTHER RESOLUTION TERMS

In some imaging applications, resolution is identified by thousands of pixels in the file. Terms such as 1K by 1K, 2K by 2K, 4K by 4K are used. This measurement defines the maximum resolution in pixels that was created in an image file.

For example, if a scanner's sensor is capable of capturing 1024 pixels; 1024 pixels is the maximum number of pixels in each direction vertically (v) and horizontally (h).

2K means 2048 pixels is the maximum number of pixels in each direction in the file and 4K means 4096 pixels is the maximum number of pixels in each direction in the file.

When describing images by the total number of pixels in thousands, it is important to remember three factors to completely understand image resolution. They are: (1) the physical dimensions of the image, (2) the number of pixels per inch, and (3) the file size.

Below is an examples of how image resolution can be described by the maximum number of pixels in each direction, megabytes, image area, and pixels per inch.

### Example:

A black and white 2K by 2K image file has 2048 v by 2048 h pixels.

This file can also be described as a 4.1 mb black and white image file with dimensions of 6.8 inches square at 300 ppi. The image file has a total of 2048 pixels vertically and horizontally over a 6.8 inch image area.

115

# APPENDIX A:
## RESOLUTION

### DETERMINING CORRECT SCANNING RESOLUTION

The formula for determining input resolution is:
Input Resolution = (Quality Factor) X (Line Screen) X (% Enlargement or Reduction)

The chart below shows the results of this calculation for images scanned at 100% of actual size.

| Input Resolution | | Line Screen | | | | | |
|---|---|---|---|---|---|---|---|
| | | 65ls | 85ls | 100ls | 133ls | 150ls | 200ls |
| Q U A L I T Y  F A C T O R | 1:1 | 65 ppi | 85 ppi | 100 ppi | 133 ppi | 150 ppi | 200 ppi |
| | 1.5:1 | 97.5 ppi | 127.5 ppi | 150 ppi | 199.5 ppi | 225 ppi | 300 ppi |
| | 1.7:1 | 110.5 ppi | 144.5 ppi | 170 ppi | 116.1 ppi | 255 ppi | 340 ppi |
| | 2:1 | 130 ppi | 170 ppi | 200 ppi | 266 ppi | 300 ppi | 400 ppi |

2:1 Best Quality – 1:1 May produce acceptable results. Test first.

### HOW MUCH CAN I ENLARGE AN IMAGE ON MY SCANNER?

This chart shows how much a scanner at specific resolutions can enlarge an image and what the resulting dpi will be.

| | | Maximum Scanner Resolution | | |
|---|---|---|---|---|
| S C A L I N G | 100% | 300 ppi | 600 ppi | 1200 ppi |
| | 200% | 150 ppi | 300 ppi | 600 ppi |
| | 300% | 100 ppi | 200 ppi | 400 ppi |
| | 400% | 75 ppi | 150 ppi | 300 ppi |

If you want to be able to make 400% enlargements of an image and still maintain the best DPI:LS ratio for an image that will be reproduced with a 150 line screen, then this chart shows that you will need a 1,200 dpi scanner.

### DETERMINE THE CORRECT INPUT RESOLUTION

To determine input scan resolution, it is necessary to plan for the ultimate use of the image. This entails working backwards from the intended output. The question to consider is: will the final image be used: for print, photo finishing, design, Web, or multi-media applications?

In the printing process, continuous tone images are reproduced with a halftone screen that creates the image's tones and details. Halftone dots are a scheme to fool the eye into believing it is seeing continuous tones and shades of gray. The halftone screen ruling defines the number of halftone dots in one inch. Screen ruling or halftone resolution offer a guide to image quality.

### DETERMINING SCANNER RESOLUTION FOR PRINT

Here are guidelines for input resolution and its relationship to the line screen of the halftone output.

- Input resolution (scanner or camera resolution) is determined and measured by the number of pixels (ppi/ppm) or dots (DPI/DPM) in an inch or millimeter.
- Halftones are determined by the number of lines per inch in the screen used to produce them. In preparing an image for printing to an imagesetter, the number of pixels necessary to achieve a quality reproduction is established based on the halftone line screen. Calculations used to convert pixels into halftone dots show that the best image detail reproduction is achieved when the file contains a 2:1 pixel to line screen ratio.

These rules of thumb for input image resolution are based on the NyQuis Theorem. These guidelines suggest that if an image is to be printed at 150 line screen that twice as many input pixels (2:1) are created for the final output size. While this 2:1 rule of thumb is a good starting point to determine image resolution, some imaging professionals have experimented with reducing input resolution and have found that it is possible to achieve good results with as low as 1.5:1 input image resolution for halftone printing. To determine input resolution, the best method is to run several tests at different resolutions and choose the best results.

**Below are three examples of a formula to calculate input image resolution.**

| Input Resolution | = | Halftone Screen Lines Per Inch | X | Magnification | X | 2 | |
|---|---|---|---|---|---|---|---|
| [ 300 PPI ] | = | [ 150 LPI ] | X | [ 100%] | X | [ 2 ] | SAME SIZE IMAGE |
| [ 600 PPI ] | = | [ 150 LPI ] | X | [ 200%] | X | [ 2 ] | 200% ENLARGEMENT |
| [ 150 PPI ] | = | [ 150 LPI ] | X | [ 50%] | X | [ 2 ] | 50% REDUCTION |

An example of how the 2 to 1 rule is used is to examine an image scanned at 300 pixels per inch (ppi). This image is suitable for screening at up to 150 LPI while still maintaining the best quality. To ensure the best reproduction quality, the file needs to contain two pixels for each line screen line. Generally, 1.5 to 1 times the line screen can produce acceptable results depending on your specific project, the printing process, and the type of stock on which you are planning to print. This is especially true if the image is sampled down in Photoshop.

### DETERMINING SCANNER RESOLUTION FOR THE WEB

72 dpi is commonly used as a guideline for input resolution for images going to the web. This is based on the resolution of the computer's monitor.

## OUTPUT RESOLUTION BASICS

Output resolution relates to the capabilities of digital imaging devices such as imagesetters and digital printers.

Three factors determine halftone output resolution:

1. Number of shades of gray to be reproduced.
2. Resolution of the output device.
3. Halftone line screen ruling desired.

To determine the optimum resolution for the imaging process, it is necessary to identify the number of shades of gray the output device is capable of producing. Imagesetter and printer resolution is determined by each manufacturers hardware and software specifications of the particular output device. The quality of the printing device will determine halftone screen rulings that are based on the printing presses and quality capabilities.

The following formula provides a method to determine and adjust the number of shades of gray. By learning this simple formula, it is easy to see the cause and effect of changing any of the three variables:

1. **Shades of gray.**
2. **Imagesetter resolution.**
3. **Halftone line screen.**

This formula shows how changing either the imagesetter dpi or the halftone line screen will alter the number shades of gray.

A simple formula used to determine the maximum shades of gray available is as follows:

### FORMULA TO DETERMINE THE NUMBER OF SHADES OF GRAY

| Number of Shades of Gray | = | (Imagesetter Output DPI | / | Halftone Screen) Frequency LPI | Squared | + | 1 |
|---|---|---|---|---|---|---|---|
| *Examples* | | | | | | | |
| 257.0 | = | (2400 DPI | / | 150 LPI) | 2 | + | 1 |
| 189.0 | = | (2400 DPI | / | 175 LPI) | 2 | + | 1 |
| 65.0 | = | (1200 DPI | / | 150 LPI) | 2 | + | 1 |
| 145.0 | = | (1200 DPI | / | 100 LPI) | 2 | + | 1 |
| 37.0 | = | (0600 DPI | / | 100 LPI) | 2 | + | 1 |
| 10.0 | = | (0300 DPI | / | 100 LPI) | 2 | + | 1 |

Choose the imagesetter resolution and line screen combination that produce 256 levels (shades) of gray

An imagesetter can place a certain number of tiny dots in a square inch area. The number of dots it can place defines its resolution. Imagesetters provide a range of resolutions from 300 to over 3000 DPI.

In traditional pre-press work, a range of line screens for halftone reproduction has been established. Typical values are 65, 100, 133, 150, and 200 line screens. The line screen selection will vary based on factors including the paper choice and the type of press. Your print shop can help you choose the correct line screen to meet your projects reproduction needs.

The combination of these two factors, imagesetter resolution, and the halftone line screen, limit the number of possible shades of gray available at a specific imagesetter resolution and line screen value. This relationship is best defined by the use of the following formula at the bottom of this page. If you try different values in this equation, you will discover that lowering the line screen or increasing the imagesetter resolution increases the number of shades of gray.

# APPENDIX A:
## RESOLUTION

### HERE ARE TWO EXAMPLES OF ADJUSTING DIFFERENT FACTORS IN THIS FORMULA

**Example One:**

256 shades of gray can be produced with a 2400 dpi imagesetter at a 150 line screen.

257 shades of gray = (2400/150) squared +1

**Example Two:**

189.0 shades of gray can be produced with a 2400 dpi imagesetter at a 175 line screen.

189.0 shades of gray = (2400/ 175) squared +1

These examples also illustrate, that there is no benefit in exceeding imagesetter resolution because the data will not be used.

# APPENDIX A:
## RESOLUTION

Photoshop also has an Auto Resolution feature that will determine the correct resolution based on a specified line screen ruling and a quality factor.

The Draft quality always produces a 72 DPI resolution.

The Good quality uses a 1.5:1 pixel to line screen ratio.

The Best uses a 2:1 ratio.

Note that the Screen value is used only for the calculation, you still need to select the correct line screen in the Page Setup dialog box or in your page layout program.

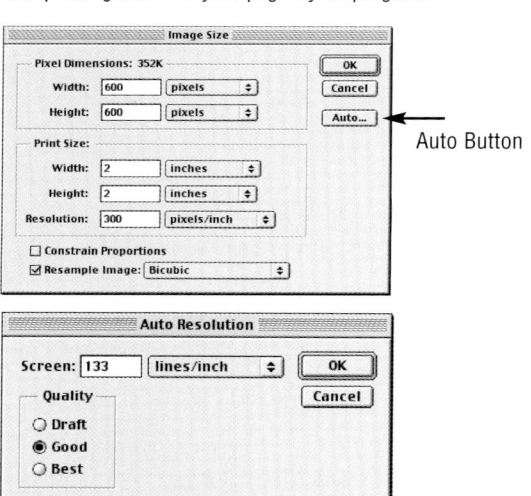

Auto Button

## INPUT & OUTPUT RESOLUTION FOR PRINT COMMON DENOMINATORS

Both types of resolution (input and output) are related to the halftone printing process. An image's input resolution is determined by the halftone screens frequency. This makes halftone screen rulings the common connection between determining input and output resolution factors for continuous tone images.

To determine and select any halftone screen ruling depends on key factors in the printing process. These factors are (1) the type of printing press (web-fed or sheet-fed) and (2) quality characteristics required for the reproduction. Better quality reproductions requires higher screen rulings and inversely lower quality demands lesser screen frequencies.

Testing by the printer determines the images halftone screen ruling. When the printing parameters are defined for the printing press or digital printer and for the quality factors (screen ruling), it is possible to establish the input scanning resolution.

In a fundamental sense, input pixels of images provide a basis to create halftone dots. To understand input and output resolution relationships, a rule of thumb suggests that two pixels are used to create one halftone dot. This guideline establishes input scanning and resolution.

For example, a high quality sheet-fed press permits using a halftone screen ruling of 200 lpi. Using this 2:1 rule of thumb, the input image would be scanned at 400 pixels per inch. Inversely, a web-fed newspaper printing press might only allow 100 lpi halftone screen ruling to be used. Using the 2:1 rule of thumb, the input image would be scanned at 200 pixels per inch.

## RESOLUTION TIPS FOR NON-PRINT APPLICATIONS

The majority of scanning applications are for print-related businesses. Other applications, like photo finishing, require higher amounts of image resolution to reproduce continuous tone images. Multi-media and on-line work requires using low resolution images.

In photo finishing applications, input image resolution is based on the resolution capabilities of the output device such as a transparency film recorder. Guidelines for input resolution vary depending on desired quality. To get the highest quality results, use the same amount of image resolution for the input scan as the output printer. For example, to achieve high quality results from a 1200 dpi imagesetter, the suggested input resolution is 1200 ppi. If less quality is required, then using less resolution such as 600 to 1200 ppi might work. In this situation, acceptable results can be achieved making it possible to save disk space and time in the imaging process. Of course, experimentation is essential for both producing input resolution that meets your needs and teaching you about the performance of your imaging equipment.

Scanner resolution is measured by the number of pixels or dots used with different units of measurement, such as inches or millimeters. For example, 300 pixels per inch (ppi), 300 dots per inch (DPI), 12 pixels per millimeter (ppm) refer to the the same resolution. On high-end systems, "Res" numbers are often used. The value Res 12 is equivalent to 304.8 ppi. For an image to be reproduced at a specific quality level, it is necessary to have the correct resolution (or pixels per inch). If not, the image's reproduction will not have enough information to resolve the finer detail of the original.

**Make your own calibration tools.** Here are two quick and inexpensive tools to determine if your service provider or digital printer is producing consistent and calibrated results.

## OPTION 1 - MAKE YOUR OWN CALIBRATION RAMPS

- Create a new file, 8" wide x 1" high.
- Select Grayscale and 72 DPI.
- Then with the foreground color set to the default 100% black and the background color set to the default white, use the Gradient Tool in the tool box to create a ramp like the one you see to the left.
- Then select Image>Adjust>Posterize from the menu and posterize it with 11 levels. The result will be in even 10% increments; use 21 levels if you want 5% increments. Now you have a ramp you can send to an output device to check calibration. The value requested in Photoshop should be the value read by a densitometer.
- Use the Text Tool to identify each step with the particular value.

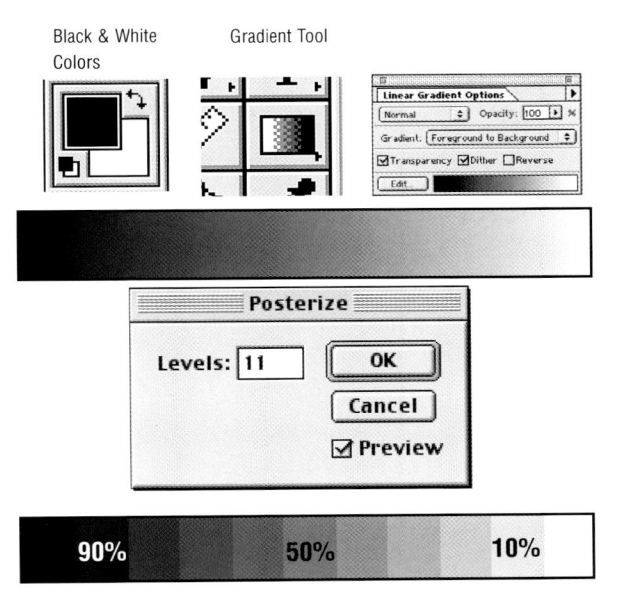

## OPTION 2 - MAKE CALIBRATION RAMPS WITH 5 STEPS

This method allows you to use your eye and a 10x magnifying glass (a loop), and, of course, a densitometer if you own one, to examine this self-made control target. It allows you to determine if your imaging process is consistent and calibrated. This technique uses an extreme highlight of 2%, a shadow of 98%, and a 50% midtone value with square dots. These values become easy to identify at different stages of the imaging process, because the 2% and 98% are almost white or black. The 50% midtone has equal amounts of white and black dots.

- Make a new file, 5" wide x 1" high.
- Select Grayscale and 72 DPI.
- Set the Rectangular Marquee to Fixed Size, 72 pixels wide and 72 height.
- Use the Color Picker in the Grayscale mode. Adjust the Color Picker to the correct dot values 2%, 5%, 50%, 95%, and 98%. Change the Foreground color to those values.
- Create Marquees in the new image area. Use *Edit>Fill* command to fill of them with 2%, 5%, 50%, 95%, and 98% dot values.
- Use the Text Tool to identify each step with the particular value.

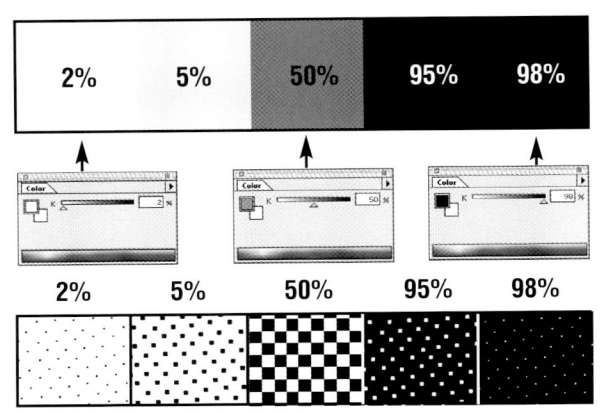

The above illustration provides an example of how 2%, 5%, 50%, 95% & 98% dots would appear while viewing them with a 10x loop.

# APPENDIX B:
## CALIBRATION TIPS

Option 2 is a calibration tool that enables you to determine if your imaging process has changed by using your eye and a 10x magnifying glass.

- This technique is a comparison method. You compare a previously created guide to the most current guide that was created. This guide could be film or proofs from a service provider, output from a digital printer or film from a imagesetter.
- If the values look different, this indicates a change in your imaging process. Then some type of corrective action has to take place.

  For example, if you are working with a service provider and and these values have changed from the proofs and film they have previously sold you, they should be contacted.
- If your imaging process does not or can not use the extreme highlight and shadow values, then change them to values that are representative of your specific process.

119

# APPENDIX B:
## CALIBRATION TIPS

### CALIBRATION RESPONSIBILITY

Because calibration must occur at all stages along the reproduction process, the responsibility for specific calibration adjustments falls to the person or company in charge of a specific aspect of the reproduction. Due to the altered workflow encountered in the world of desktop publishing, the printer is no longer solely responsible for this issue. If you choose to handle a specific area of the process, you are responsible for the calibration of that area.

### CALIBRATE OR BUST?

A properly calibrated system is by far the best environment to work with digital images. However, we live in a world where most people do not have imagesetters or controlled lighting conditions in their working environment. Because of this, it is especially important to learn to "work by the numbers" even if your system is using a color management approach.

The operator must learn to use the digital densitometer provided in Photoshop with the Info palette and they must learn to communicate with their service bureaus, so that when they ask for a 5% dot on film they get a 5% dot consistently. In addition, proofing and evaluating is an absolute necessity. Don't take shortcuts. Having an un-calibrated system often means that what you see on screen is not what you get on output.

## OVERVIEW

Calibration is a complex issue and in the scope of this book can only be addressed in a cursory manner. Specifically, we will comment on the calibration of input scanners and dot gain.

### Calibration

When a reproduction system is calibrated, all the components in the chain should agree at every stage of the process. Calibration is accomplished by measuring values at various stages of the process. A calibrated system will permit a specific dot value, captured by a scanner, to be measured and adjusted on the workstation, and be output to the imagesetter so the final film will have that exact value. For example, a 50% dot is captured during scanning, confirmed on the workstation, and output to film. The 50% dot value is confirmed by measuring at each stage of the process with digital measuring devices such as a densitometer or Photoshop's Info palette. When each stage numerically agrees, the reproduction system is calibrated.

### KEY AREAS TO CALIBRATE

- Scanner or Digital camera
- Monitor
- Image processing
- Digital printer
- Imagesetter
- Film chemistry
- Platemaking
- Printing press

### Optimization and Predictability

Calibration is the basis for optimization. After a system is in calibration, it is then possible to adjust, control, and optimize the image values to achieve good reproduction with Photoshop.

For example, a 5% dot value is used to produce a good reproduction of highlight areas. After measuring, it is determined that the original scan was digitized with a 15% highlight dot value. By knowing the system is calibrated, adjustments can be consistently made to reduce the 15% dot to a 5% dot.

The results on the final output film would be the optimum value of a 5% highlight dot. If the system was out of calibration, it would be impossible to achieve predictable and optimized results.

### System Setup

Establishing any type of image reproduction system is not a quick process. Some businesses expect instant results because they have a lot of money and time invested. To establish a black-and-white image reproduction system, equipment needs to be installed and calibrated, bugs need to be worked out, personnel need to be trained, a work-flow system needs to be established, ancillary systems like proofing must be established, customer requirements must be defined, then the product has to be produced. This process typically takes from one to six months.

### Scanner setup

Scanner setup can be a difficult and technical process. A lot of time and frustration can be saved if you utilize vendor support or seek out a qualified pre-press professional. If the critical areas of the reproduction are not correct after scanning, they need to be adjusted either through the scanner software or through Photoshop.

The most productive strategy is to establish average setup parameters that allow the scanner to provide the best data with minimal adjustments through Photoshop. However, depending on the scanner interface, this is not always possible.

## Test the system

To calibrate a system, testing is necessary to determine what adjustments need to be made. A good starting point is to acquire a grayscale step wedge from the scanner vendor, a graphic arts dealer or from a photographic supply house. With this method, you scan a grayscale into the desktop workstation. Use the eyedropper and the Info palette in Photoshop to measure the the whitest and darkest step on the grayscale.

For example, when setting up your system, if the scan of the grayscale measures a 10% dot in the area of the scale that you have determined should contain no dot, then adjustments need to be made to cause the correct value to appear where you expect to see it. The specific input scan correction will depend on the software for each desktop scanner.

Start by adjusting scanner controls to determine if they can change the highlight or shadow point of the scan without degrading the overall results. If the correct highlight is achieved, but the rest of the image is too light, then it might not be possible to use the scanner's controls to normalize the image, and you will need to use Photoshop to do the job. If this is the case, the goal in scanning is to find the settings that capture the best image detail and balance of tones. Then use Photoshop to finish the process.

After the scanner controls are adjusted so the grayscale has the best data the scanner can capture, use Photoshop to measure and adjust the highlight and shadow areas to the target values. The goal is to establish the setting of the scanner and Photoshop to closely match the grayscale. Making proofs is critical to determining your success in this process.

## Run multiple tests

This process will take a number of iteration of film and proofs. After the grayscale or standard guide looks acceptable, several average images will be reproduced with the average setup data. If this testing is done in Photoshop, only the highlight and shadow should require adjustment, because Photoshop is designed to correctly establish the midtone on an average image without additional user intervention. After a number of average originals are scanned, adjusted, proofed, and evaluated, a trend will emerge to illustrate the good and bad characteristics of the average setup. Once these trends are identified, corrective action is necessary to correct for any negative results of the initial average setup data. This is done until the program is fine tuned, making it possible to produce average images without major problems. Testing and proofing should also be done with several light and dark images. This will establish the correct midtone adjustment ranges for these images.

# APPENDIX B:
## CALIBRATION TIPS

### VISUAL RESULTS

After the proofed results begin to look like the original, it is necessary to draw relationships of the original and proofs to the monitor. The goal is to make the monitor look like the original, the proofs, and the final output.

### DAY-TO-DAY TIPS

- Consistency is required to establish the average setup.
- When a change is required, make one adjustment at a time.
- When a change is done, the results need to be examined and compared to the original.
- Record the adjustments.
- Use Save and Load.
- Sometimes it's best to keep track of the adjustments on paper.

# APPENDIX B:
## CALIBRATION & DOT GAIN TIPS

### PHOTOSHOP AND DOT GAIN

In theory, you would expect to use Photoshop's controls to compensate for dot gain in an image in addition to any Gamma adjustments that you make to compensate for light or dark images. For example, If your printer tells you that they have a 20% dot gain on a particular press, you might want to reduce the midtones an additional 20% over the amount you already adjusted it to normalize it for tone compression. Well, DON'T DO IT!

While this seems like a good idea, in theory, most of the dot gain has already been controlled by setting the proper white and black targets for the specific reproduction process. Photoshop's adjustment features for Gamma and the choice of a proper line screen ruling for the paper and press further aid in this process. Instead, the question to ask your printer is, "Do you shoot your halftones with any extra reduction in midtones to ensure they print well on your system?" They may even have a specific Photoshop Gamma reduction they recommend. Find out what that is and use it.

### DOT GAIN FACTOR RELATIONSHIPS TO HALFTONE TARGET VALUES

| Printing Press | Paper Stock | Line Screen Ruling | Highlight Dot | Shadow Dot | Dot * Shape |
|---|---|---|---|---|---|
| Sheet-fed | Newsprint | 85-120 | 3-5 | 85-90 | Round |
| | Uncoated | 100-150 | 3-7 | 90-95 | Round |
| | Coated | 133-200+ | 3-7 | 90-98 | Round |
| Web | Newsprint | 65-120 | 1-3 | 75-90 | Round |
| | Uncoated | 100-133 | 3-7 | 85-95 | Round |
| | Coated | 133-200+ | 3-7 | 90-98 | Round |

Round dots have proven to display the least amount of dot gain. Square dots provide sharper results. Elliptical dots create smoother flesh tones and less banding.

---

Dot gain is an increase in size of halftone dots from the value that was expected to a larger size. Dot gain in the printing process causes halftone dots to enlarge when printed. In general, most printing processes cause dot gain. The factors that contribute to dot gain include screen ruling, dot shape, printing plates, press blankets, paper, ink, and printing presses. Dot gain will degrade a reproduction especially if the image was not setup to allow for dot gain. The image will usually look too dark.

### Build in dot gain

The best way to avoid dot gain problems with the reproduction is to prepare the reproduction with dot gain built in. The customer, the film supplier, and printer must communicate and run tests to establish guidelines for each party in the project. Conceptually, the testing involves printing a test form made up of targets and black-and-white reproductions that easily identify the input dot values and the printed dot values. During the test, each stage of the reproduction process is checked and evaluated for the degree of dot gain: digital files, imagesetter film, plating, and the printed dot values. When the amount of dot gain is determined, the black-and-white reproduction can be produced with that amount of gain built in (most printers will know what values you should build in for their presses).

### Dot gain and curves

Dot gain is measured by a percent dot value and is measured in the midtone regions of the reproduction.

For example, if the reproduction system has a 20% dot gain, the 50% dots will print at 70% value. This does not mean all the dot values grow 20%, it means the midtone values gain by 20%. In printing processes, dot gain is thought of in term of curves, with the 50% dot area showing the most gain.

Dot gain can be generated from a variety of sources. The list seems endless. Dot gain can come from variables in the darkroom like fluctuating temperatures of the chemicals in the film processor or film fog, improper pre-press techniques for exposing printing plates, different absorption properties of the papers that are used in printing, or even from the way the printing surfaces of the press are prepared. After dot gain is identified and compensated for in a particular area of the reproduction system that area can be considered calibrated.

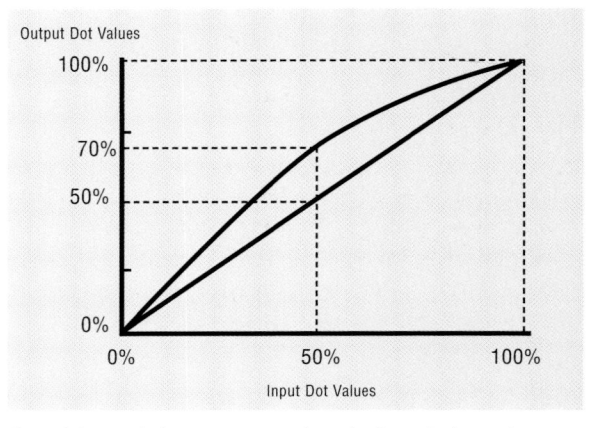

A graph is a typical way to express dot gain. A graph shows the largest amount of dot gain takes place in the 50% midtone areas. In this example, the 50% dot value prints at 70% for a 20% dot gain. Other image areas such as the highlight and shadow areas are affected by dot gain but not as dramatically.

The image to the left has been adjusted for a 20% dot gain and printed on a press with 20% dot gain. It prints correctly.

The image to the right simulates the effects of printing an image that has 20% dot gain image built-in on a press with 35% dot gain. It prints too dark.

## Control dot gain

Once you understand in what area of the process dot gain is occurring, you then need to develop a strategy to control it. You can compensate for dot gain in different places. In the digital world there are no standards established for where in the process to correct for dot gain. Communication with your service bureau/printer is key to achieving the best quality results. Here are some additional guidelines to help you through the process.

1. Some service bureaus/printers routinely adjust customer supplied halftones, some don't. Discuss your project before producing halftones so that you do not double compensate for dot gain.

2. Make sure the imagesetter that you're using for output is calibrated to produce a requested dot value ± 1%.

3. Talk to your printer about the type of press and paper that is being used for printing. Ask the printer to provide you with the amount of dot gain they get on that printing press from film to finished piece.

4. Learn about the relationship of line screen ruling to printing stock and press and how it controls dot gain. See the side bar on page 122 for guidelines.

There are a variety of options to compensate for dot gain. Each image reproduction process should develop consistent guidelines for compensation for the dot gain.

The most often used option is to adjust the scanned original to produce what you believe to be good highlight, shadow and midtone values based on the printers dot gain specifications. If you use this method, it is important to have proofs produced that accurately show how the image will print with the dot gain added back in. When the correct information is provided, this method should provide good results for a given paper and press condition at the specified amount of dot gain. As a guideline, you can produce the image so that it looks good on a non-compensated proof, and then reduce the midtone curve of the image to compensate for the printer's specified dot gain.

## More about dot gain

Typically, highlight dots appear to gain very little, if at all, in a sheet-fed printing process. In web printing, especially on newsprint, highlight dots can gain over 5%.

Imagine a printing process that was determined to have a 30% dot gain overall. To reproduce the image correctly, it would be necessary to identify the amount of dot gain from each area of the reproduction process then compensate for this gain during the image processing stage. i.e., make the proper adjustments in Photoshop for highlight, midtone, and shadow placement. Typically in a process where the highlight gains 3%, a 2% target dot value would be compensated for in the halftone film. So when printed, it would reproduce as a 5% dot.

Conversely, if the shadow areas gained 10%, the shadow dots would be created with an 85% target dot value. So when printed it would reproduce as a 95% dot. This example illustrates that by anticipating dot gain in the printing process, it is possible to compensate in the highlights, shadows, and midtones of an image to achieve a good reproduction.

# APPENDIX B:
## CALIBRATION & DOT GAIN TIPS

### DOT GAIN IN SCREEN TINTS

A note to the prepress savvy: You should also compensate for dot gain in the flat tint screen values you request inside the desktop layout program you use. Most of the dot gain is at the 50% dot and above. Printers usually compensate for this by using pre-compensated screens. Talk to your printer before you select your final screen values so that you agree on how to compensate for dot gain in flat tints.

# APPENDIX C:
## SCANNING TIPS

### SCANNER TIP

Ensure enough image data has been captured during scanning. It is necessary to experiment with the scanner controls so the complete range of the original's details from the highlight to the shadow are gathered. After these tests you should be able to preset the scanner controls to capture just enough of each original's important details before scanning. The rule of thumb for scanning is to have a little more image information in the highlight and shadow than is necessary, and throw it away after the set white and black sequence in Photoshop. If that does not happen then trying to artificially manufacture image details becomes an impossible and time-consuming task.

### SCANNING TIP # 1

*Learn the capabilities and mechanics of the scanner.*

- Read the instructions and how the scanner's controls are used.
- Learn how the scanner controls really work through experimentation. This not only includes image processing tools for highlight, midtone, and shadow adjustments, but calibration methods, USM (UnSharp Masking) techniques, cropping, sizing, and resolution capabilities.

### SCANNING TIP # 2

*Each vendor has his or her own system to identify the scanner controls.*

For Example: What one vendor calls a midtone adjustment another one might call a Gamma control.

### SCANNING TIP # 3

*Organize input materials to be productive.*

- Establish essential paperwork, but use simple and thorough methods to identify critical information for images to be scanned.
- Use standard input sheets that identify job parameters: the kind of originals, enlargement and reduction factors, final resolution, special image adjustments, guide lines for target values, and when the job is due.
- Keep the job manageable using a batch approach.
- Establish a system for returning originals to their original sleeves or paper mounts.

### SCANNING TIP # 4

*Use the correct scanning mode.*

- Most scanners have multiple modes for scanning such as: halftone, continuous tone, and line modes.
- Continuous tone is used for grayscale images.
- Line mode for line work.
- The halftone mode is not useful for capturing continuous tone and line images for image reproduction. It is used for layout and design work.

### SCANNING TIP # 5

*Use Standard Target Images.*

- Periodically use known images to check for consistent results. These are tools like gray scales or vendor supplied images. These images should have standard image areas for highlight, shadow, and midtone values that make it easy check the imaging process.

### SCANNING TIP # 6

*Capture enough image resolution - but not too much.*

- The rule of thumb for halftone imaging is 2:1 for input resolution based on the final output image size.
- Use 72 dpi resolution for Web images.
- Not enough resolution will make the imaging process go faster, but will make the image reproduction look fuzzy.
- Too much resolution will slow down the imaging process and provide more image resolution than is necessary.
- Get close to the right amount of resolution for each original to optimize the imaging process and achieve good results.

### SCANNING TIP # 7

*Always capture enough image details.*

- Identify the scanner controls to measure and adjust highlight and shadows in critical areas.
- Highlight areas should read around a 240 digital value.
- Shadow areas should read around a 10 digital value.

### SCANNING TIP # 8

*Identify the limits of your scanner.*

- Learn how the sensor's size and resolution capabilities react. All scanners have different capabilities. Read the instructions to identify the scanner's specifications and capabilities.
- Experiment with problem images such as full range images that have important light and dark areas.
- Running tests will illustrate the limits of the scanner, how to adjust the controls to achieve certain results and its trade-offs.

# APPENDIX C:
## SCANNING TIPS

**SCANNING TIP # 9**

*Get the scan right up front.*

Do as much image processing as possible during scanning, such as adjustments to highlight, shadow areas, contrast adjustments, and USM (UnSharp Masking).

- Each scanner has its own particular characteristics for image processing.
- Identify each of the image processing tools in the scanner. Then learn how to apply them. This saves time later on the desktop.

**SCANNING TIP # 10**

*Be Patient.*

- Scanning and reproducing images is a skill that is not learned overnight. It takes time and experience to relate to the main concepts, methods and techniques that achieve certain visual results.

**TYPICAL STEPS FOR DESKTOP SCANNING (B&W OR COLOR) FOR MOST BLACK AND WHITE AND COLOR SCANNERS**

1. **Open Photoshop and place the image on the scanner bed.** Choose the correct scanner plug-in from the File>Import>Menu.
2. **Preview and crop the image.**
3. **Once the scanner's software is active, choose the appropriate image processing settings.**

   This will include settings such as:

   Size>Mode (grayscale or color)>Resolution>Scaling>Tone>Sharpness, Descreen>and other important features.
4. **Scan the image.**
5. **Save the image in Photoshop to your hard disk.**
6. **Recrop and scale the image in Photoshop if necessary.**
7. **Apply any image processing with Photoshop.**

   This includes adjusting highlights, midtones, shadows, or sharpness.
8. **Save the final image.**

Here are two strategies for scanning images.

**Option #1.**

Learn the controls of the scanner before working in Photoshop. Use the scanner's imaging processing controls to adjust the image data before scanning. After the scan is created, work in Photoshop to fine tune the image.

**Option # 2.**

Leave the scanner's settings at a common setting (such as the default values) for most all scans. Then begin working in Photoshop to adjust highlights, midtones, and shadows. Apply USM to fine-tune the image.

# APPENDIX D:
## SCANNER CALIBRATION

The purpose of these instructions is to offer tips and techniques for calibrating a desktop scanner with Photoshop. This will make the scanning process more productive. These instructions are not meant to be a substitute for experience, but rather one of many methods about how to use Photoshop with a scanner to get good results.

Technically, this method adjusts image contrast by changing the tone reproduction characteristic when scanning.

### LIMITATIONS OF SCANNERS

1. If you are trying this technique on an older desktop scanner, the scanner might have a technical limitation that may prevent you from achieving the suggested target values. The main limitation is usually in the scanner's sensor system. Scanners with sensors that are not refined will not be capable of detecting darker tones of the target image. In technical terms, the scanner has poor dynamic range. This will cause the darker shadow tones to potentially have the same measurements in the target image steps #16 (3/4 tone) and #22 (the shadow). This will make it difficult, if not impossible, to achieve good shadow details.

2. Measuring Images is important: Photoshop allows you to measure halftone density (percent dot values) for this calibration method. To refine this technique, optical density of reflection or transparent originals can be measured with a densitometer.

- Read the previous sections in this book.
- Have basic knowledge of Photoshop and, specifically, the black and white imaging tools.
- Be familiar with most aspects of the Curves tool.
- Know the mechanics of your scanner's hardware and software.
- Have an IT8, Q60, or grayscale target. These quality control target images are used for scanning and imaging work. They are available in transparent and reflection versions depending on the type of scanner.

### Ordinary Grayscales Will Work But...

The techniques outlined in this book will work with transparent and reflection gray scales that you might already own or that you can buy from a graphic arts supplier.

The difference between an ordinary grayscale and the IT8 target are the number of steps and the density values in each of the steps. The steps on a non IT8 grayscale are usually different than the ones outlined in this book. In case you're not going to use the IT8 target, the density values have been supplied for transparent and reflection grayscales. Be aware that using another target image besides an IT8 increases the number of variables. Therefore, risk of failure increases.

Using an alternative grayscale would entail measuring the grayscale target with a densitometer until the target densities are found. In many instances, finding the same exact densities is not possible. What happens in this situation is the end-user begins to estimate as close as possible to the target densities. This is a satisfactory method for experienced professionals, but if you are just getting started with scanning and Photoshop you will probably get confused. Hence, using a grayscale will work, but we suggest getting an IT8 target. The IT8 is a good quality-control tool that imaging professionals should own.

Reflection IT8 Target

Transparent IT8 Target

### PLACES TO PURCHASE IT8 TARGETS

- **Eastman Kodak Company**
  Phone: 800-234-0426
  Item Q60E1 Q60 Color Target - 4" x 5" Ektachrome - Catalog # 8294738
  Item Q60 R1 Color Target - 5"x 7" Ektacolor Paper - Catalog # 1907914
- **AGFA Dealers**
- **Fuji Dealers**

## IT8 Reflection Target Areas & Values:

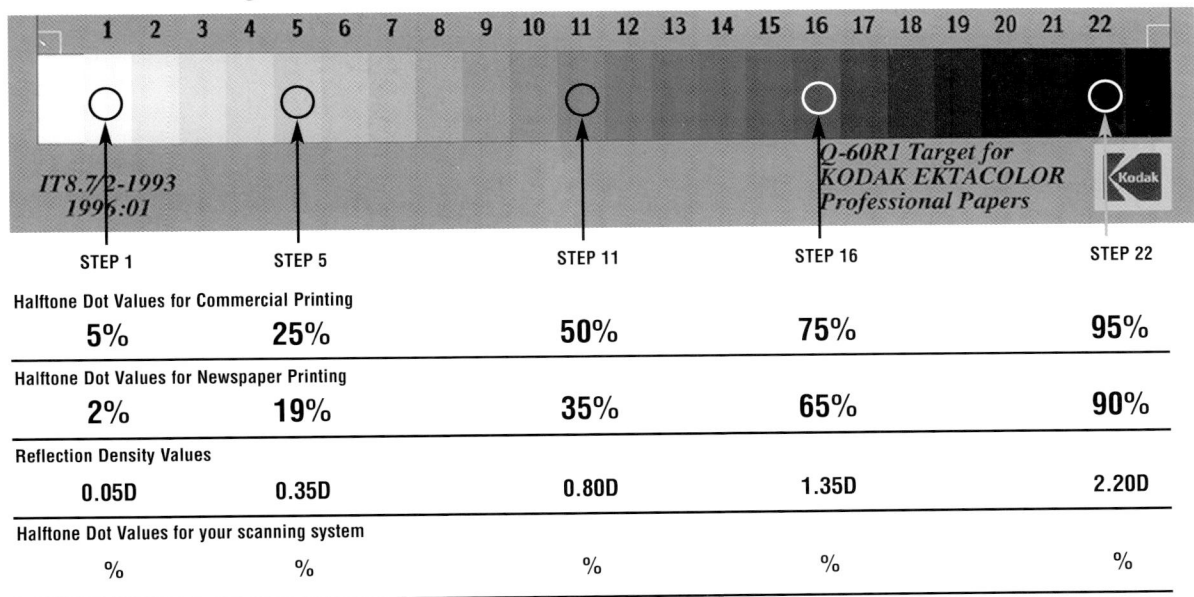

|  | STEP 1 | STEP 5 | STEP 11 | STEP 16 | STEP 22 |
|---|---|---|---|---|---|
| Halftone Dot Values for Commercial Printing | 5% | 25% | 50% | 75% | 95% |
| Halftone Dot Values for Newspaper Printing | 2% | 19% | 35% | 65% | 90% |
| Reflection Density Values | 0.05D | 0.35D | 0.80D | 1.35D | 2.20D |
| Halftone Dot Values for your scanning system | % | % | % | % | % |

## IT8 Transparency Target Areas & Values:

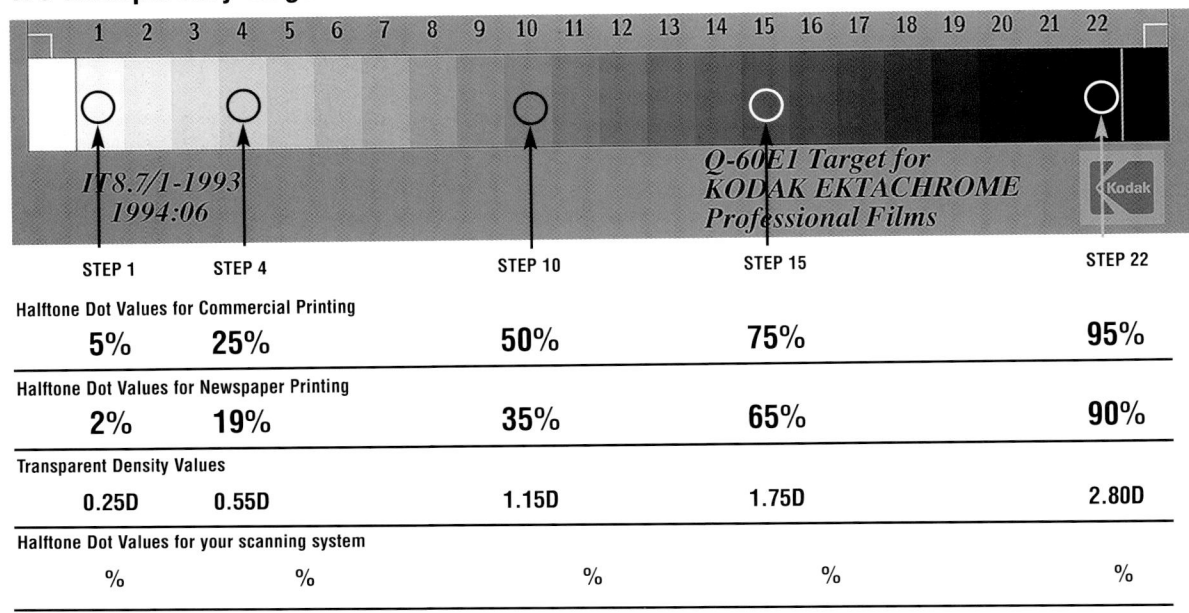

|  | STEP 1 | STEP 4 | STEP 10 | STEP 15 | STEP 22 |
|---|---|---|---|---|---|
| Halftone Dot Values for Commercial Printing | 5% | 25% | 50% | 75% | 95% |
| Halftone Dot Values for Newspaper Printing | 2% | 19% | 35% | 65% | 90% |
| Transparent Density Values | 0.25D | 0.55D | 1.15D | 1.75D | 2.80D |
| Halftone Dot Values for your scanning system | % | % | % | % | % |

# APPENDIX D:
## SCANNER CALIBRATION

**COPY THIS PAGE**

After you copy this page, record the Scanner Calibration Halftone Values of your scanner in the blank areas of the chart we have provided.

**USE THE SAMPLER POINTS IN THE FIRST FOUR STEPS.**

To make measuring these target points easier, use the Sampler points. Typically we place them on the first four points and use the Eyedropper to measure the fifth point.

**THESE VALUES ARE NOT ABSOLUTE:**

1. We use a systems approach to scanner and system calibration. The halftone target values are guidelines for optimizing a scanner. They have proven to be a good beginning point for both commercial and newspaper printing. These supplied values will change and most likely need refinement for different types of imaging conditions such as different Photoshop Preference parameters, changes in dot gain characteristics, halftone resolution, papers, printing press types (web or sheet-fed), and customer requirements.

2. The density values that have been described will vary depending on the manufacturer of the target image and the calibration of your densitometer.

# APPENDIX D:
## SCANNER CALIBRATION

### WHEN ADJUSTING CURVES, BE AWARE!

- Do not bend the final Curve too dramatically.
- Multiple points are usually required to adjust the Curve (between 2 and 5 points are typical).
- Poorly adjusted Curves will introduce posterization.(Posterization will degrade the image reproduction.)
- Each scanner will have its own characteristics at the default settings.
- Each Curve adjustment will be different for each scanner.

### SAVE ALL OF THE CALIBRATION FILES

Create a folder and make a back up of all the files that are created in this process. Title the folder Calibration Images/Files and place it in the Photoshop Goodies folder.

In the Calibration Images/Files folder are the default scans of Reflection and Transparent IT8 Targets and the Curve parameter files that were created. Use numbers and descriptive name titles to make the Curve parameters become available at the top a list. It makes them easy to find. Here is an example:

1- Ref B&W Average Curve
2- Trans B&W Average Curve
3 - Ref B&W Low Key Curve
4- Trans B&W Average Curve
5 - Ref B&W High Key Curve
6 - Trans B&W High Curve

### EXAMPLE OF A PROPERLY ADJUSTED CURVE:

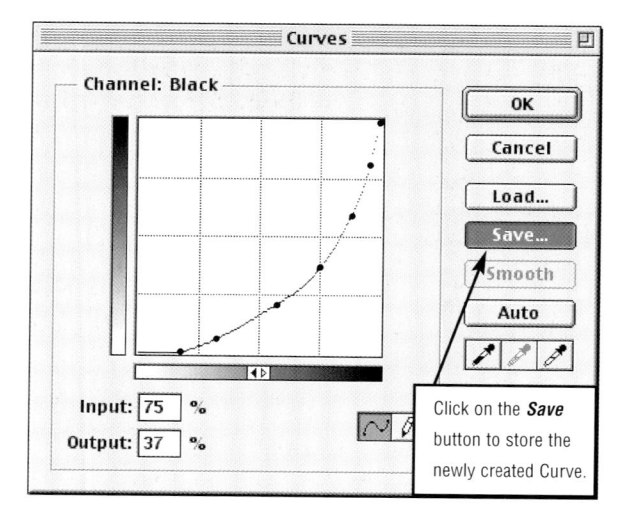

*Click on the **Save** button to store the newly created Curve.*

This curve produces smooth transitions between tones when applied to an image.

---

1. **Scan the image into Photoshop using the scanner's default settings.**

   - To save time during this process, use a low resolution setting. Work on the low resolution file and then apply the final Curve to a high resolution scan. Remember to save the image that was scanned at the default settings before doing any image processing.

2. **Use Photoshop Curves to adjust key areas on the target image.**

   - There are five areas on the target image to adjust. Use Curves in Photoshop (Cmd/Cntrl M). Adjust the Curve until the target values are achieved on the image that was scanned at the default settings.

   This adjustment is usually done by first setting the white and black points with Curves and then dragging the midtone points on the Curve.

   The Info Palette is used with the Sampler Points to verify the target values during these adjustments.

### EXAMPLE OF A POORLY ADJUSTED CURVE:

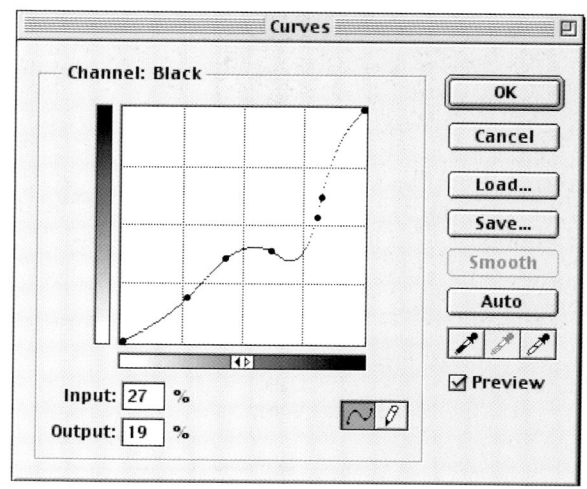

This type of curve might produce the correct values on the IT8 Target, but transitions between tones are not smooth. The results of applying this kind of curve to an image will make it have a posterized or banded effect.

**To fix the bumps in the curve, add points, and place the points so the curve has smooth transitions between the tones.**

---

3. **Save the parameter file of the new Curve in Photoshop.**

   After the Curve is adjusted to the target values at all five points, save it as a parameter file in Photoshop. Use the Save button in the Curves dialog.

4. **Load the saved Curve into the scanner.**

   Load the saved Curve through the scanner's software. In some scanners, an import command is used.

# APPENDIX D:
## SCANNER CALIBRATION

The example above shows the results of scanning without any type of calibration. This image was scanned at the scanner's default values.

The example above shows the effects of a properly prepared curve that produces smooth transitions between an image's tones and creates visually good results.

The example above shows the effects of a poorly prepared curve that produces bad transitions between an image's tones. The effect is called Posterization or banding.

**STEPS FOR OPTIMIZING A SCANNER WITH PHOTOSHOP CURVES:**

1. Scan the IT8 image into Photoshop using the scanner's default settings.
2. Use Photoshop Curves to adjust 5 key points on the target image.
3. Save the parameter file of the new Curve in Photoshop.
4. Load the saved Curve through the scanner's software.
5. Verify the Curve works by scanning the target.
6. Fine tune the images contrast.
7. Scan a few average images with the new Curve.
8. Option: Use the existing scanner controls to optimize scans.
9. Finesse or enhance the final image in Photoshop.

5. **Verify that the Curve works, rescanning the target.**
- Scan the target image with the imported Curve to verify that the newly scanned image file will create the listed values in the five steps.

6. **Fine tune images with this technique.**
- Refining this technique requires making a few test Curves and outputting the scanned image to a proofing system. The proof can be digital or pre-press proof or even conventional film and printing.

7. **Scan a few average images with the newly established Curve.**
- Use the newly established Curve to scan average-looking images. Most likely, the images will come out not quite perfect but, probably better than at the default setting of the scanner.
- A practical approach to test the Curve is to scan a few images that represent your typical scanning needs. You will find the Curve does not work 100% in all situations because each image's lightness and darkness is different. To handle this you will have to create a few Curves, perhaps 3 to 8, that covers most of the scanning situations. Identify these Curves with easy to understand names.
- This means the halftone target values recommended in this book will have to be altered to handle different types of images.

8. **Option: Use the existing scanner controls to optimize scans.**
- If your scanner doesn't have features to load pre-established Photoshop Curves, there are two an alternative methods.
- One is to use the scanner controls. The techniques are the same except you have to use the scanner's specific image processing features with the target image.
- The second method is to set the scanner's controls to a standard adjustment, like the defaults settings, and create a scan of the IT8 target. Then create and save the Photoshop Curve that achieves the target values. Apply the newly saved Curve(s) to each scanned image.

9. **Finesse or enhance the final image in Photoshop.**
- Once the image is scanned and optimized by the customized Curve, begin work, setting and fine tuning the highlight, midtones, and shadow points on each image.

# APPENDIX E:
## AT-A-GLANCE INDEX

This section will **help** guide the reader who might be lost, overwhelmed, confused, or just tired of too many Photoshop details and needs just the bare facts about a particular topic of interest. The page numbers for where to find more information is provided to help you navigate to the topic.

### NEUTRAL GRAY BACKGROUNDS - see page 9

1. In Photoshop, create a new file.
2. Adjust the background color of the Tool Palette.
3. Select All of the new image file.
4. Fill the Selection with the Background Color.
5. Copy the Selection to the computer's clipboard.
6. Paste the neutral gray image into the Appearance dialog box. Select the neutral gray pattern and set the Desktop.

### USING ADOBE GAMMA - see page 11

1. Go to the Help Menu and open the Color Management Assistant.
2. Choose the step-by-step wizard.
3. Select the starting point profile.
4. Set the monitor's brightness and contrast.
5. Select the phosphors for your monitor.
6. Set the Gamma.
7. Set the White Point values of your monitor.
8. Save the profile.

### SNAPSHOT - see page 22

1. Correct or alter the image overall.
2. Take a Snapshot. Undo (Optional).
3. Select the Source of the new Snapshot.
4. Click on the Top Snapshot on the right side area.
5. Select the History Brush from the Tools Palette and correct the image.

### SELECTIONS BASICS TO PRACTICE - see page 28

1. Creating a basic Selection.
2. Adding and subtracting from Selections.
3. Inversing a Selection's active and non-active areas.
4. Saving Selections as Channels.
5. Loading Selections onto an image.

### CREATING SOFT-EDGED VIGNETTES - see page 34

1. Use the Rectangular Marquee to create a Selection.
2. Apply Feathering to the Rectangular Marquee Selection.
3. Inverse the Selection.
4. Fill the Inversed Selection with white from the Background color.

### CONVERTING PATHS TO SELECTIONS - see page 40

1. Create a Path and save it.
2. Convert the Path. Use the Path Palette Pop-out menu to convert the Path into a Selection on the image.
   a. Create a hard-edged Selection.
   b. Create a soft-edged Selection.
      Use the Feather Option.

### HOW TO CREATE A CLIPPING PATH - See page 41

1. Use the Path Tool to draw a Path around the part of the picture you want to silhouette.
2. Choose Save Path from the Path Palette Pop-up menu.
3. Choose Clipping Path from the Paths palette menu.
4. Save the image as an EPS file with the Clipping Path.

### REPRODUCING GRAYSCALE IMAGES - see page 58

1. Examine the original.
2. Capture image data - scanner or camera.
3. Identify the image category and tones.
4. Measure and adjust highlights.
5. Measure and adjust shadows.
6. Measure and adjust midtones.
7. Apply Unsharp Mask.
8. Save file for output or export.
9. Review image for rescanning or corrections.

### RETOUCHING STRATEGIES - see page 76

1. Use Snapshots.
2. Use Selections with Curves.
3. Use Dodge and Burn.
4. Use the Rubber Stamp for cloning.

### CREATE A SNAPSHOT FOR RETOUCHING - see page 77

1. Correct or alter the image overall.
2. Use the Pop-out menu on the History Palette to take a Snapshot. Undo (Optional).
3. Select the Source of the newly created Snapshot.
4. Click on the Top Snapshot on the right side area.
5. Select the History Brush from the Tools Palette and correct the image.

### CLONING - see page 79

1. Choose the Rubber Stamp Tool with an appropriate size brush.
2. Set the Source for Cloning. Depress the Opt/Alt key and click with the mouse.
3. Move the brush to the Destination. Depress the mouse button to paint from the Source to the Destination.
4. Paint with the Rubber Stamp Tool.

### FOUR WAYS TO CREATE LAYERS - see page 83

1. Drag-n-drop one image onto another image.
2. Use Copy and Paste.
3. Use the Duplicate Layer feature or Layers Palette Icon.
4. Click on the Duplicate Layer icon.

### DROP SHADOWS - see page 91

1. Create a new Layer with Transparency.
2. Load the Channel as a Selection and use *Edit>Clear*.
3. Duplicate the Layer.
4. Name the Shadow Layer.
5. Place the Shadow Layer at the bottom of the Layers Palette.
6. Create the Drop Shadow.
7. Move the Shadow Layer at the right and down.
8. Use Gaussian Blur to soften the shadow.
9. Change the opacity of the Shadow Layer.
10. Flatten the Image.

### BATCH PROCESSING - see page 106

1. Select the Set option.
2. Select the Action.
3. Select the Source.
4. Choose the Source Folder.
5. Choose the Destination.
6. Select the Destination Folder.

### MIRROR IMAGE - see page 109

1. Once the image is open, apply Select All **Cmd/Cntrl A** and then use Copy **Cmd/Cntrl C**.
2. Go to *Image>Canvas* Size.
3. Paste the image from the clipboard.
4. Flip the image horizontally.
   Apply *Edit>Transform>Flip Horizontal* the right side image.
5. Use the Move Tool to position the image.
6. Flatten the image.
7. Option. Use the Rubber Stamp Tool for cloning.

### EXTENDING A BACKGROUND - see page 111

1. Create new Canvas Size.
2. Create a Selection over the correct image area.
3. Use *Edit>Transform>Scale* on the Selection.
4. Drag the right side center round icon to the right.
5. Apply the Transform.

### REMOVING DUST FROM AN IMAGE - see page 112

1. Apply either Gaussian Blur or Dust & Scratches filters to degrade an image so that the largest dust area is barley removed.
2. Use the History Palette to Take a Snapshot of the degraded image.
3. Use Undo after the Snapshot to revert to the original image.
4. In the History Palette, select the source of the new snapshot.
5. Next, Select the History brush from the Tool Palette. Be sure the correct size brush and opacity are set.
6. Paint out the dirt in the image.

# APPENDIX E:
## AT-A-GLANCE INDEX

### HANDLING LINE IMAGES - see page 113

1. Scan the image in the grayscale mode and adjust the resolution between 800 dpi to 1200 dpi.
2. Use Threshold to create a high contrast image.
3. Convert from the grayscale Mode to the Bitmap Mode.
4. Save As.

### OPTIMIZING SCANNERS WITH CURVES - see page 129

1. Scan the IT8 image into Photoshop using the scanner's default settings.
2. Use Photoshop Curves to adjust 5 key points on the target image.
3. Save the parameter file of the new Curve in Photoshop.
4. Load the saved Curve through the scanner's software.
5. Verify the Curve works by scanning the target.
6. Fine tune the images contrast.
7. Scan a few average images with the new Curve.
8. Option: Use the existing scanner controls to optimize scans.
9. Finesse or enhance the final image in Photoshop.

# GLOSSARY

**Analog** — Description of the continuous wave or signal (such as the human voice) using an electrical voltage variation. Used for voice, visual, and computer data communication. The digital or pulse output of a computer or terminal must be converted to an analog signal before it can be transmitted over analog-grade lines.

**Anamorphic Sizing** — Unequal scale change in the horizontal and vertical direction of a scanner. This enables the scanner to adjust the ratio in the horizontal and vertical direction.

**Artifact** — A visible anomaly, that is a defect in an image caused by limitations in the reproduction process.

**ASCII** — (American Standard Code for Information Interchange) Standard by which many computers assign code numbers to letters, numbers, and symbols. Used for text exchange between computer platforms.

**Banding** — A visible stair-stepping of shades in a gradient.

**Binary** — A numbering system having only two values, 0 and 1. Base 2 numbering scheme.

**Bit** — The smallest unit of information recorded in a computer. It can define, by itself, one of two conditions (on or off). Bits are denoted as the numbers 1 (on) or 0 (off).

**Bit-Map** — An image formed by a rectangular grid of picture elements (pixels). The computer assigns a value to each pixel, from one bit of information (to indicate black or white), to 24 bits per pixel for full-color computer displays, to as much as 64 bits per pixel for some types of full-color images.

**Brightness** — The intensity of a color or tone regardless of its hue or saturation.

**Byte** - A unit of measure equal to eight bits of digital information. The standard unit measure of file size, e.g., kilobytes, megabytes, or gigabytes.

*1000 Bytes of computer information = 1 Kilobyte*

Kilobytes represents a thousand characters of information.

*1,000,000 Bytes of computer information = 1 Megabyte*

Megabytes represents a million characters of information.

Actually one megabyte = 1,048,576 bytes.

*100,000,000 Bytes of computer information = 1 Gigabyte*

Gigabytes represents a 100 million characters of information.

**Calibration** — Setting equipment to a standard measure to produce reliable results.

**Cartesian Co-ordinates** — The Cartesian coordinate system uses geometric coordinates in an **x** and **y** grid system to locate points on a plane, such as a bed of a scanner or in software applications like Photoshop and QuarkXpress.

**CCD** — (Charge Coupled Device) A light receptive senor device that detects light as electrical voltage and converts the electricity into direct current.

**Centimeters** — Measurements based on the metric system 2.54 cm are in one inch.

**Channel** — Photoshop uses the term Channels to describe black and white and color image data. In Photoshop, one channel is typically defined as having up to eight bits of grayscale image information. Continuous tone images created with a scanner use Channels as a way to describe the black and white and color image data. A black and white grayscale image has one channel. An RGB color image has three channels. A CMYK color image has four channels. It is possible to have up to 24 channels in Photoshop.

**Chromalin™** — An off-press color proofing system developed by DuPont. The proofs are single laminated sheets produced from film separations.

**CIE - Commission Internationale del'Eclairage**.- This is an international group that has developed a set of color definition standards.The CIE system defines a color model that provides a standardized mathematical approach. It includes viewing and lighting schemes that attempt to describe color the way the human eye perceives it without any color vision defects. The CIE system uses three values, such as XYZ, RGB, or LAB to numerically identify and map out color gamuts of devices or images. The CIE system is universal and is capable of representing many different types of color spaces. It is being used more in scanning, color separation programs, PostScript imaging environments, and color management systems.

**Colorimeter** — A precision instrument used to accurately measure tri-stimulus values of a color in the way the human response system sees color. Typically colorimeters are used to measure the Red, Green, and Blue light of a monitor.

**Color Management System (CMS)** - A CMS is an open system architecture that supports specialized imaging software that characterizes each system component such as a scanner, monitor, or printer. The purpose of a CMS is to automatically ensure that all the system components will interrelate and agree numerically and visually. After each system component is profiled, the color managed system keeps track of color information and peripheral device characteristics to create a calibrated and optimized imaging system.

**Color Space** — Three-dimensional model (or representation of a 3D model) used to organize colors to show progressions of hue, lightness, and saturation. Device-independent color spaces are based on international standards (CIE).

**ColorSync™** — Apple Computer's (the computer manufacturer) system-level color management solution for working with ICC profiles.

**Continuous-Tone Copy** — Image that has a complete range of tones from black to white: negative or positive photographs, paintings, and drawings. Continuous tone originals do not have screened dots patterns.

**Copy Dot Scanning** - Copy Dot scanning is a method that converts conventional black and white line and halftone film that represent black and white or four-color printing into digital data that is used in a completely electronic workflow. The films to be Copy Dot scanned are placed in register on a scanner that uses hardware and software designed for this process. The scanner creates a high-resolution file for each color plate and a low-resolution color view file, for-position-only (FPO), that represents a four color image. The resulting digital files are high quality one-bit-per-pixel images, that are moiré pattern free, that reproduce exactly as the supplied films.

**CT** (Continuous tone). — A file format used for exchanging high-level scanned information.

**Data Compression** — "Squeezing" of data for the purpose of transmission throughput or storage efficiency. Portions of the data are removed using an algorithm that will restore the data when needed.

**Default** — Command or parameter that takes effect if no other option is specified.

**Delta E** — Delta E is a value used to identify the differences between two colors. It is measured in CIELAB color space. Lower Delta E values are preferred when creating profiles or comparing and matching colors.

**Densitometer** — A method of measuring tonal value based on the light absorbing properties of grays or colorants. Densitometers are used to measure the transmission of reflection of samples through selected blue, green, red, and visual filters.

**Density** — The ability of a material to absorb light. Measure of the light-transmission of a transparent or translucent object or the light-absorbency of a reflective surface. In photography, measurement of the opacity of a transparent or translucent object. On a film negative, the greater the density area, the more black or more developed it is. Density is measured from 0 to 4.0. It is calculated by measuring the reflectance or transmittance of light and calculating theoretical light absorption.

**Density Range** — A density range is a comparison between light and dark shades of an original image. It is expressed in density measurements. Specifically, it is the mathematical difference from the lightest (Dmin) to the darkest area (Dmax) of an original.

*Density Range Examples:*
Transparency original 3.00 Dmax— 0.30Dmin = 2.70 Density Range
Reflection original 1.80 Dmax — 0.05 Dmin = 1.75 Density Range

**Descreening** — An image reproduction method that removes pre-existing halftone screens from scanned color proofs or black and white halftone films. The result of the descreening process is a moiré pattern free, eight-bit black or white or color image that can be resized or retouched.

**Digital** — Method of data storage and/or transmission wherein each element of information is given a unique combination of numerical values (bits). Each bit indicates either the presence or absence of a condition (such as on-off, yes-no, true-false, open-closed). Modems convert the pulsating digital signals into analog waves for transmission over conventional telephone lines.

**Digital Image Values** — Digital image values represent black and white, grayscale, and color images. Typically, digital images have values that range from 255 to 0. This describes an eight-bit black or white or color image. Eight-bit-per-pixel images offer 256 shades or tones that are suitable for black and white and color continuous-tone imaging. All types of eight-bit images use the value of 255 for the brightest pixel or white image area and the value of 0 for the darkest pixel or black image area.

**Digital-to-Analog Conversion** (D/A or DAC) — Conversion of digital information into a state of fluctuating voltage levels.

**Direct-Digital Color Proof** — A proof made from a stored data file onto a substrate without producing intermediate separation film.

**Display** — Temporary visual representation of computer output on a CRT or other electronic device.

**Dmax** — The highest level of density of a film positive or negative.

**Dmin** — The lightest level of density of a film positive or negative. For example a Dmin of a color transparency might read 0.20 density. The Dmin of a halftone negative might read 0.03 density.

**Dot** — Smallest visible point that can be displayed on a display surface.

**Dot Gain** — Dot gain is usually described as the increase in halftone dot values that occur during the printing production process. Total dot gain is measured as the difference in apparent dot size between the final printed product and the original film. Dot gain occurs as the result of both mechanical and optical influences on the original dot size. Dot Loss is also referred to as Dot Gain.

**Dots, Halftone** — Minute, symmetrical individual subdivisions of the printing surface formed by a half-tone screen. Halftone screens are a scheme to fool the eye into believing it is seeing continuous tones shades of gray or color when an image is reproduced.

# GLOSSARY

**DPI (Dots-Per-Inch)** — A method of denoting the resolution of a scanned image, a digitized image in a file, or an image as rendered by an output device. Also, used interchangeably with pixels per inch (PPI).

**Drum Scanner** — An optical input device that mounts reflective or transparent input media on a revolving cylinder for digitizing.

**Dynamic Range** - Dynamic range describes the ability of a scanner's sensor systems to measure the number of shades or tones of an original image from white to pure hue or black. It is one of the most important measurements of a scanner. Dynamic range is measured and described in density units and bits per pixel.

**EPS** — Encapsulated PostScript, this format carries a pict preview. In bitmapped mode, it also supports transparent whites.

**Export** — To output data in a form that another program can read.

**File** — A named collection of information stored as a unit on a secondary storage medium such as a disk drive.

**Film** — Photosensitive material, generally on a transparent base which will receive character images and may be chemically processed to expose those images. In imagesetting, any photosensitive material, transparent or not, may be called film.

**Flat-bed Scanner** — An optical input device that mounts the image on a flat plane rather than a revolving cylinder.

**Gamma** — The measure of compression or expansion of the shades of colors in an image. Gamma correction compresses or expands the range of tones in each hue.

**Gamut** — The range of hues that can be reproduced from a given technology, process, and set of colorants in all combinations.

**Gigabyte** — A unit of measure of stored data corresponding to one billion bytes of information.

**Gradation** (contrast) — A relationship of the distribution of tone values in the reproduction to the original.

**Graphics** — Term used to refer to any presentation or generation of information in visual form.

**Grayscale** — (1) An orderly variable progression in definite steps of gray densities ranging from minimum zero (white) to maximum density (black). (2) A strip of standard gray tones placed at the side of the original copy during photography or scanning to measure tonal range obtained. Used in processing film or materials such as photographic paper and plates.

**Grayscale Image** — The representation of an original scene that has a range of gray tones between black and white.

**Halftone** — an image created with a pattern of data for different sizes used to simulate a continuous-tone photograph, either in color or black and white. The halftone screen converts continuous-tone copy to line copy (discrete dots of varying sizes and shapes) for printing on a press.

**Hard Disk** — Non-flexible media that can hold much more data than a floppy disk. Hard disk storage is measured in megabytes and gigabytes. It is more expensive than a diskette, but is capable of storing much more data.

**High Contrast** — Reproduction technique in photography with high gamma in which the difference in darkness (density) between neighboring areas is greater than in the original.

**High Key** — A very light original image (possibly overexposed) that contains important detail in the highlight area.

**Highlight** — The lightest or whitest part of an image with discernible detail. A highlight is represented in a halftone image by the smallest dot patterns. A specular highlight is whiter and lighter, but has no detail.

**Histogram** — A graphic representation of the number of pixels with given color values, showing the breakdown or distribution of color values in a picture.

**ICC** — The International Color Consortium (ICC) is a group that sets up standards for creating ICC profiles.

**ICC Profiles** — An ICC profile is a digital file with embedded information that corrects color and grayscale information due to the deficiencies of a device in a digital workflow such as a scanner, digital camera, monitor, digital printer, or printing press.

**Imagesetter** — Device that sets type, graphics and half-tone imagery using digital lasers outputting at high resolution to photosensitive material or plain paper.

**Input** — Raw data, text, graphics, imagery, or commands inserted into a computer.

**Input/Output** (I/O) — Term for the equipment used to communicate with a computer system. Examples of I/O devices are: a keyboard, a mouse, a floppy disc drive, or a printer.

**IT8** — A type of transparent or reflective image that is used as a calibration guide or target used to set up a scanner or imaging system. In the past, this has been referred to as a Q60 guide.

**JPEG** — (Joint Photographic Expert Group) An image compression/decompression standard that divides the image area into cells to condense information based on content analysis.

**K** — (1) Abbreviation for the color black. K is used so that it is not confused with an abbreviation for the color blue. (2) Represents "kilobytes" of information which is comprised of 1024 bits. The K is upper-case to distinguish it from lower-case k, which is a standard international unit for "kilo," meaning 1,000.

**LAB** — A color space used to describe CIE-based color coordinates. L = luminance, a + b = two color components.

**Laser Printer** — Computer output device that uses a laser to generate the character image. It uses some of the same methods to produce the final image as a copier.

**Levels of Gray** - Levels of Gray are used to identify characteristics of images. Line art only requires 2 levels of Gray: black and white. B&W or Color Continuous tone images require a minimum of 256 levels of gray or color tones.

**Line Image** — Line images are different from continuous-tone images, they reproduce without halftone screens patterns in the printing process and have only two tonal values, black and white.

**Lockdown Curve** — A Lockdown Curve is a Photoshop Curve that has pre-established points anchored or fixed. It is created by anchoring key points manually. Typically five point Curves are used to manually adjust the highlight, 1/4 tone, midtone, 3/4 tone, and shadow points of an image.

**Lossless** — Data compression algorithms that store data in a more efficient format that does not cause any data loss in the compression process. Typically this type of compression has a ratio of up to 8:1.

**Lossy** — Data compression algorithms that assumes some of the data in an image file is unnecessary and can be eliminated without affecting the perceived image quality. Typically this type of compression has ratios between 10:1 and 100:1.

**Low Key** — A dark image (possibly underexposed) that contains important detail in the shadow area.

**LPI** (Lines Per Inch) — A measure of the frequency of a halftone screen.

**LUT** (Look Up Table) — A method of converting from one color space (color representation) into another, either to compress the source color gamut or to map specified colors into the available gamut of an output device such as a display, printer, or film recorder. Also, the table of colors that a computer can display at a given time.

**Mask** — A mask is used to block out part of an image. In Photoshop, selections are part of a masking system to work on specific parts of an image. Photoshop channel masks are used to create selections. Each Photoshop channel is defined as an eight-bit grayscale images. High contrast black and white masks can be created in a Channel or continuous tone *gradient masks*.

**Megabyte (Mbytes)** — A unit of measure of stored data corresponding to a million bytes of information. (Actually 1,048,576 bytes of computer storage.)

**Memory** — A device into which data can be entered, in which it can be held, and from which it can be retrieved at a later time. Data is stored in digitally encoded bits, and manipulated as needed during calculation processes. The amount of memory a computer has directly affects its ability to perform complex functions.

**Midtones** — Tonal values located between highlights and shadows. Midtone placement controls contrast of the reproduction by determining the separation of tones in an image.

**Moiré** — Undesirable screen pattern in color process printing caused by incorrect screen angles of halftones.

**Monitor** — Electronic display unit that uses a cathode ray tube to generate text, graphics, and imagery. It looks like a normal TV set, however, the monitor has a much higher degree of resolution.

**Monitor Calibration** — The process of optimizing the color settings of a monitor to match selected colors of a printed output.

**Monotone or Monochrome** — Artwork reproduced in one color only. Also black-and-white copy.

**Off-Press Proof** — A color or black and white proof generated prior to the production press run and prior to, or in lieu of, a press proof.

**Offset Lithography** — Commercial form of lithographic printing. Offset lithography is a planographic printing method; it is the only major printing method in which the image area and the non-image area of the printing plate are on the same plane. They are separated by chemical means, on the principle that grease (ink) and water (the etch in the fountain solution) do not mix. The ink is transferred from the plate onto a rubber blanket and then to the paper.

**Opacity** — Relates to the degree of transparency that an image exhibits. An Opacity feature is usually, but not always, associated with the Photoshop painting tools. In Photoshop, an image with 100 % Opacity does not let image data from other images that are underneath it show through.

**Output** — Process of sending computer results to a computer's monitor or printer.

# GLOSSARY

**Photomultiplier Tube** (PMT) — A light sensitive tube that can detect very low light levels by amplifying the signals applied to it. Usually associated with drum scanners.

**PICT Preview** — A preview that is available with PICT files. PICT files are a Macintosh file format.

**Pixel** — An acronym for Picture element; minimum raster display element, represented as a point with a specified color or intensity level. A two-dimensional array of dots that define the form and color of an image. Measurement is indicated as PPI (pixels per inch).

**Pixel Per Millimeter (PPM)** — A term that expresses a number of pixels in one millimeter. The factor to convert pixels per inch to pixels per millimeter is to divide the number of pixels in one inch by 25.4.

*For example, 304 ppi divided by 25.4 = 12 ppm. (304/25.4=12)*

In Europe and other parts of the world, this metric resolution value is referred to as Res 12. (Be careful to get the decimal place correct when determining pixels per millimeter).

**Posterize** — The accidental or intentional effect of reducing the number of shades in an image between the lightest and darkest shades.

**PostScript™** — The standard device-independent language developed by Adobe Systems that describes the appearance of pages in documents. PostScript describes a page in its final form, ready for imaging on an output device. Encapsulated PostScript describes a graphic, image or complete page in a final form in a way that can be exchanged between application programs so that one PostScript described item can be included in another layout.

**PPI** (Pixels Per Inch) — A measure of the amount of scanned information. The finer the optics of the scanner, the higher the scan resolution. PPI is equivalent to DPI.

**Prepress Proof** — Proof made before the final press run by exposing the film negatives or positives to pigmented or dyed light sensitive materials. When assembled, it will be similar in appearance to the finished printed product.

**Prescan** — A preliminary or preview scan of an original to determine the correct setup and cropping prior to full scanning.

**Printing Plate** — Surface, usually made of metal, that has been treated to carry an image. The plate is inked and the ink is transferred to the paper or other surfaces by a printing press. Printing plates are also made of rubber, synthetic rubber, and plastics.

**Proof** — Working copy of some material used for review and approval. A reasonably accurate sample of how a finished piece is intended to look.

**RAM** (Random Access Memory) — Volatile memory that can be written to or read from by a program, and in which the memory locations can be accessed in a random sequence. RAM may be expanded by adding memory chips or memory boards.

**Random Proof** — A proof consisting of many images ganged on one substrate and positioned with no regard to final page imposition.

**Raster** — The series of lines of information such as the parallel horizontal scan lines that form a television or video display image.

**Raster Image** — This is also known as a bitmapped image. It has a series of lines of information that form a grid of image data. The image data is usually referred to as pixels.

**Raster Image Processor (RIP)** — Part of an output device that rasterizes, or converts mathematical and digital information into a series of dots, so they can be rendered and imaged onto a screen, film, paper, or other media.

**Reflective Art** — Items that are reproduced using light reflected from their surface.

**Resolution** — The measure of image details. The smallest discernible detail in visual rendering. Resolution may be stated in terms of spot diameter, line width, pixel matrix dimension, raster lines, or dots/inch.

**RES** — Unit of measure of resolution in number of lines per millimeter, such as RES8 or RES100. To convert RES to DPI, multiply the RES value by the number of millimeters in an inch, 25.4 (for example, RES12 = 300 DPI).

**Retouching** — Art of making digital, chemical, or dye corrections by adding or removing density or color, on continuous-tone film, on color transparency materials or on reflection prints. Digital retouching makes changes to pixel values to enhance image appearance.

**RGB** (Red, Green, and Blue) — A color space that represents colors as an additive mixture of red, green, and blue light.

**RIP** — See Raster Image Processor above.

**Scale** — To change the proportion of an image by increasing or decreasing its size.

**Scan** — To examine or capture an image by means of a moving light beam or "flying spot." Scanning technology is used in imaging, optical character recognition as well as in other areas.

**Scanner** — Electronic input device that converts art or continuous-tone images into digital form. Digital scanners convert line art (black-and-white), monochrome images (gray levels), and full-color images into pixel arrays. Some scanners are also color separation machines that use circuits to color correct, compress the tones, and enhance detail.

**Screen** — To break up continuous-tone copy into dots for reproduction as a halftone. Line screens are designated by the number of ruled lines they contain: from 50 lines per inch to 500 lines per inch. The greater the number of lines per inch, the sharper and finer the printed half-tone. The selection of the screen is dictated by the paper, press, and the nature of the copy.

**Screen Ruling or Frequency** — The number of lines per inch in the halftone screen. The lower the number, the larger and more widely spaced the dots. Higher screen rulings allow reproduction of fine detail.

**Selection** — A feature in Photoshop that permits the end-user to highlight an image area and create a mask. When a selection is saved, it becomes a channel.

**Service Bureau** — A business that specializes in outputting computer files on laser imagesetters, film recorders, large-format plotters and other types of output devices.

**Shades of Gray** - Shades of gray is a term used to describe the number of black or white or color continuous tones of an image. One of the more frequent uses of the term shades of gray is to describe hardware characteristics of an input scanner or an imagesetter.

**Shadow** — The darkest part of an image with discernible details, represented in halftone images by the largest dot patterns.

**Sharpen** — Electronic photo-retouching function for enhancing image detail and contrast either globally or in selected regions of the picture.

**Sheet-Fed** — Press configuration where the paper is fed into the press as sheets rather than a roll of paper. This is known as a *web fed*.

**Sneakernet** — A manual method of carrying or transfer files on a disk from one computer to another. When using the sneaker net method make sure your sneakers are tied tight so you don't trip and drop your disk as *you walk the disk* files from one machine to another.

**Spectrophotometer** — An instrument used to measure wavelengths of light. The readings from a Spectrophotometer are used to generate spectral reflectance curves as a way to define and describe color information.

**Specular Highlight** — Small reflection or detail highlight in a photograph that is reproduced in halftone form with a 0% dot value.

**Spot** — Smallest region of an input or output image whose tone can be controlled independently from all other regions. A digitally generated halftone dot is constructed using a matrix of spots.

**TIFF** (Tagged Image File Format) — A file format developed by Aldus Corporation for exchanging bitmapped, monochrome, and full-color images between applications.

**Tolerance** — In Photoshop Tolerance describes a certain distance between adjacent pixels. Tolerance is used with the Wand Tool for making selections and the Paintbucket Tool for painting. The Tolerance values can be adjusted for these tools. For example, when the Wand Tool is set to a Tolerance of one, only a small selection will be created because the distance between the selected pixel value and adjacent pixels is only one.

**Tone Compression** — A reduction in the range of the hues and values in an original.

**Transparency Original** — A positive photograph on transparent film such as Agfachrome™, Kodachrome™, or Ektachrome™ film, usable as copy for color separation and viewed by transmitted light. A positive color image of the original drawing, painting, or scene on a colored photographic film is also referred to as a chrome.

**Transparency (Photoshop)** — Transparency is a characteristic of a file used in Photoshop that allows (1) the image to have different opacity levels, (2) working with Layers.

**Transparency Scanner** — An optical input system for digitizing images from small format positive or negative transparency film.

**USM** (Unsharp Masking) — The term comes from a conventional color separation camera technique that uses a unsharp photographic mask to increase contrast between light and dark areas of the reproduction and gives the illusion of sharpness.

**WYSIWYG** — An acronym for What You See Is What You Get. WYSIWYG relates to having a computer monitor appear like the final printed results.

# BIBLIOGRAPHY

Adams, Richard and Joshua Weisberg
*The GATF Practical Guide to Color Management*
Sewickley, PA
1998

Adobe Systems Incorporated
*Adobe Photoshop User Guide Version 5 for Macintosh,*
San Jose, CA
1999

Blatner, David and Bruce Fraser
*Realworld Photoshop*
Peachpit Press
1998

Beale, Stephen and Cavuoto, James
*The Scanner Book*
Micro Press
Torrance, CA
1989

Bruno, Michael H.
*Principles of Color Proofing,*
Gamma Communications
Salem, NH
1986

Campbell, Alastair
*The Mac Designer's Handbook*
Running Press
Philadelphia, PA
1992

Hannaford, Steve
*An Introduction to Digital Prepress*
AGFA Corporation
Wilmington, MA
1990

Lawler, Brian P.
*What Makes a Good Halftone?*
Self Published (805) 544-8814
San Luis Obispo, CA
1992

Deke McClellan
*Photoshop 5 Bible*
IDG Books Worldwide Inc.
Foster City, CA
1998

Molla, R. K.
*Electronic Color Separation*
R.K. Printing & Publishing Company
Montgomery, WV
1988

Murry, James D. and William vanRyper
*Graphic File Formats*
O'Reilly & Associates, Inc.
Sebastopol, CA
1994

Romano, Frank and Richard Romano
*The GATF Encyclopedia of Graphic Communications*
Sewickley, PA
1998

Rich, Jim
*Photoshop, B&W Scanners, & Curves*
Rich & Associates
Chevy Chase, MD
1995

Sakhuja, Sanjay
*Digital Color Prepress Volume Two*
AGFA Corporation
Wilmington, MA
1990

Southworth, Miles
*Pocket Guide to Color Reproduction*
Graphic Arts Publishing Co
Livonia, NY
1979

Tapscott, Diane, Lisa Jeans, Pat Soberanis, Rita Amladi, Jim Ryan
*Production Essentials*
Adobe Press
Mountain View, CA

Weinmann Elaine and Lourekas Peter
*Photoshop 5 for Windows &Macintosh: Visual QuickStart Guide*
Peachpit Press
Berkley, CA
1998

### Other Titles to Consider Reading

*Photoshop 5 Artistry*
Barry Haynes and Wendy Crumpler
New Riders Publishing
1998

*Photoshop 5 for Windows &Macintosh Visual QuickStart Guide*
Elaine Weinmann and Peter Lourekas
Peachpit Press
1998

*Photoshop 5/5.5 Wow Book*
Linnea Dayton and Jack Davis
Peachpit Press
1998

*Photoshop 5 Bible*
Deke McClellan
IDG Books Worldwide Inc.
1998

*Real World Photoshop*
David Blatner and Bruce Fraser
Peachpit Press
1998

# INDEX

## A

Adjusting
- Curves, 128
- Curves endpoints, 50
- dot gain, 12
- images for reproduction, 58
- Input Levels, 49
- Line images, 56
- midtones with one point, 64
- Output Level, 49
- resolution, 117
- Scanner controls, 121
- States, 21
- white point for monitor calibration, 11

Actions Basics, 104
Actions Palette Success Tips, 104
Add and Subtract from Selections, 28
Adding Anchors to Curves, 98
Adjust midtones, 64
Adjusting Dot Gain for grayscale images, 12
Adjustment Layer, 88
Adobe RGB (1998), 8
Anti-aliasing, 26
Arbitrary Map, 51
At-A-Glance Index, 130
Auto Range Options, 51
Average Image, 69

## B

Background color, 2
- Default, 2
- Switch, 2
- Fill clear, 90
- Fill Ghost, 97

Background Layer, 82
Batch Processing step-by-step, 106
Bitmap type 89,
Blur 55,
Brightness & Contrast, 57
Brightness/Contrast, 51
Brush Size Option, 5
Build in dot gain, 122

## C

Calculate input image resolution, 116
Calculations, 95
Calibration, 45, 120
- goals, 120
- hardware and software, 45
- key areas for, 120
- monitor, 9,10,11
- optimization and, 120
- responsibility, 120
- system testing and, 121
- gray ramp, 48, 119
- when to perform, 120
- *See also* Dot gain

Calibration ramps with 5 steps, 119
Channel Mixer, 96
Cloning, 79
Colors
- background, 2,14,18,29,36,48,119
- Channels, 94

Color Channels in Color, 5, 94
Color Palette, 47
Color Sampler Tool, 46, 78
Color Settings, 12
- CMYK Setup, 12
- Grayscale Setup, 12
- Profile Setup, 13
- RGB Setup, 8

Color Picker, 4, 48
- Select Black Target, 48
- Select White Target, 48

Color Settings and Photoshop Calibration, 8
Color to Grayscale, 94, 95, 96
ColorMatch RGB, 8
ColorSync2, 8
Continuous-tone images, 44
Creating a Mirror Image, 108
Creating a neutral gray background, 9
Cropping, 100
Curves tool, 50
- anchors and, 51
- Auto button/Auto Range options and, 51
- midtone adjustment, 59
- moving endpoints, 50
- point adjustments, 98
- point removal, 98
- tool display, 51
- *See also* Levels tool

## D

Dark images, 68
Degrading Filters, 55
Deleting Layers, 85
Densitometer, 46, 52, 59, 63, 119, 120, 126
Density, 59
Deselect a Selection, 26
Desktop scanners, 124, 125
- controls, 124
- bit depth, resolution, 58, 115, 126, 128
- instructions, 125
- mechanics of, 124
- *See also* Scanners

Despeckle, 99
Determine the Correct Input Resolution, 116
Determine the Number of shades of gray, 117
Determining Dot Gain values, 12
Determining Scanner Resolution for Print, 116
Determining Scanner Resolution for the Web, 116
Dial-in Value Boxes, 49
Different Counting Scales, 59
Digital Data, 44
Display & Cursors, 5
- Color Channels in Color, 5
- Painting Cursors, 5
- Use Dither, 5
- Use System Palette, 5
- Video LUT Animation, 5

Displaying a Channel, 31
Dodge & Burn, 78
Dot Gain, 12, 16, 44, 45, 62, 122
- build in, 122
- control, 123
- curves and, 12, 122
- defined, 45
- example of, 122
- halftone target values and, 122
- in real world, 122
- in screen tints, 123
- *See also* Calibration

# INDEX

Drag-n-Drop, 83
Drop Shadow, 91
Dust & Scratches 55, 112
 with Selection, 112
 with Snapshot, 112

## E

Edit menu, 19
 Undo, 19
 Fill clear, 90
Eight-bit-per-pixel line images, 56
Embedding Profiles, 14
EPS file format, 66
Evaluating an image, 60
Evaluating Originals, 71
Exact Cropping, 101
Expanding Selections, 27
Extending backgrounds, 110
Extraordinary Contrast, 98
Eyedropper, 46
Eyedropper and Color Sampler Tool, 46

## F

Factor Pixels to Megabytes, 115
Feathering, 34
File Format Extensions for Windows, 66
File menu,
 Page Setup option, 11
 Preferences option, 4
File Size, 83
Filter menu, 12
 Blur, 55
 Gaussian Blur, 55
 Sharpen option, 12

Flatten, 82
Flattening Layers, 85

## G

Gaussian Blur, 55, 91
General Computer Shortcuts, 3
Get Organized, 70
Ghosting methods, 97

go-by-the-numbers method, 8
Gradation Bar, 51, 64
Gray levels, 51

## H

Halftones, 45
 troubleshooting, 70, 72
 line screens, 45, 53, 117
Halftone Dot, 45
Halftone Screen data, 53
Hard Edged Selections, 34
High Key, 63
Highlights, 61
 adjusting, 58, 60, 61, 62
 dark, 45, 48, 49, 50, 52, 58, 59, 61, 62, 63, 68
 establishing, 61
 importance of, 61
 lack of detail in, 61, 63
 locating, 61
 setting, 61
 Thresholding, 62
 Troubleshooting, 70, 72
 *See also* Shadows
Histogram, 52
 in levels control, 48
 scan view with, 52
History Behavior, 18
History Eraser Tool, 18
History Palette, 19
History Source, 21
How to apply Batch Processing, 106
How to Create a Selection, 28
How to Inverse Selections, 29
How to Load a Selection, 30
How to Reproduce Grayscale images, 44
How to save Selections, 29

## I

ICC profiles, 8
ICC vs ICM Profiles, 8
Image menu, 60
 Adjust option, 46, 48, 60
 Histogram option, 52
Images, 61
 average, 61, 69

 category identification of, 61
 characteristics of, 60, 61
 continuous-tone, 44, 45, 51, 58, 59, 60, 68
 dark, 61, 64, 68
 detailed control for, 98
 evaluation of, 60, 61
 light, 61, 68
 line work, 56, 113
 saving, 66, 67
 sharpening, 54, 65
Imagesetter,
 mis-calibration, 53
 resolution, 45, 117
Info Palette, 46
Input Resolution (Basics), 114
International Color Consortium (ICC, ) 8
Interpolation, 103
Interpolation to Bicubic, 4, 103
Invert and Inverse, 33
Invert Channels, 33
IT8, 126
Item Locator, 2

## J

JPEG, 41, 66, 83

## L

Lab Color L Channel to Grayscale, 95
Lasso Tool, 26
 Free-form Lasso, 26
 Magnetic Lasso, 26
 Polygon Lasso, 26
Last State in the History List, 20
Layer Effects, 91
Layer Mask 86, 87
Layer vs Layer Mask, 86
Layers, 83
Layers Basics, 82
Layers with Transparency, 82
Levels Tool, 48-49
 Auto button/Auto Range option and, 51
 Histogram and, 52
 for midtone adjustment, 52
 *See also* Curves tool

**137**

# INDEX

Legacy Files, 14
Line art, 56
Line Image Tools, 56
Line images 56, 113
Line shots, 56, 113
Line work, 56, 113
Linear and Non-Linear States, 19
Linear States, 19
Low Key, 63
Line screens, 45
Lines per inch (LPI), 45, 116
Light images, 45, 48, 49, 50, 52, 58, 59, 61, 62, 63, 68
Limitations of Scanners, 126

## M

Mac vs Windows, 2
Magic Wand, 27
Main Selection Tools, 26
Make your own ramps, 49
Marching Ants, 28
Maximum Number of Channels, 29
Measuring Tools, 47
Merging Down Layers, 85
Merging Visible Layers, 85
Midtone adjustment,
    control guidelines, 23
    dark, 21
    dark images and, 22
    light images and, 22
    with one control point, 18
    process, 18
Mis-calibration, 53
    *See also* Calibration
Missing Profile, 15
Modal, 105
Mode Change, 94
Moiré, 99
Monitor calibration, 9, 10, 11
Monitor Profile, 10
Move Tool, 82
Multiple Undos, 19
Multi-point method, 64, 69, 98

## N

Noise, 55
Non-Linear States, 19

## O

One-bit-per-pixel line images, 56
Opening the first image, 15
Optimizing A Scanner, 129
Output Levels, 49, 97
Outline type, 89
Output Resolution Basics, 117
Oval Marquee, 26

## P

Page Setup, 53
    Halftone Screen Data, 53
    Transfer Function, 53
Paths and Selections, 40
Paths and Silhouettes, 41
Pen Tools 38
    Add a Point to the Path Pen Tool, 39
    Convert-Anchor-Points Tool, 39
    Direct-Selection Tool, 39
    Free form Pen Tool, 39
    Magnetic Pen Tool, 38
    Subtract a Point from the Path Pen Tool, 39
Photoshop and dot gain, 122
Photoshop ColorPicker, 4
Photoshop file format, 67
Pick a color Channel, 94
PICT format, 67
Pixels Per Inch and Dots Per Inch, 114
Place and move Anchor Points, 98
Plug-ins & Scratch Disks, 7
    Plug-Ins, 7
    Scratch Disk, 7
Positioning Layers 84,
Positive benefits for using ICC profiles, 8
Posterize, 57
Posterization, 72, 98, 128
Preferences General, 4

Anti-alias PostScript, 4
Auto-update open documents, 4
Beep When Done, 4
Dynamic Color Sliders, 4
Export Clipboard, 4
Save Palette Locations, 4
Short Pantone Names, 4
Show Tool Tips, 4
Proofs, 44
Palettes,
    Actions, 104
    Channels, 26
    Colors, 47
    History, 18
    Info, 46, 47
    Layers, 82
    Pen, 38
PostScript, 45,58, 66, 67, 89
    encapsulated, 66
Printing, 44, 45

## Q

Quick Mask Basics, 37
Quick Mask Success Tips, 36

## R

Random Access Memory, 7
Random Cropping, 100
Recovering From Imaging Mistakes, 18
Rectangle Marquee, 26
Reflective, 44
Removing a Layer Mask, 87
Reproduction process, 44, 45
    system establishment, 44, 45
Resampling, 103
Reset, 3
Resetting Dialog Box, 3
Resizing, 103
Resolution, 114, 116
    determining correct, 116
    halftone line screen and, 116
    imagesetter, 117
    input, 114, 116

# INDEX

scaling and, 103
*See also* Auto Resolution feature
Retouching Strategies, 76
Revert, 18
Review Process, 45
RGB Levels, 44, 46, 50, 52, 57
RIP (Raster Image Processor), 45
Rubber Stamp Tool, 79

## S

Save, 66
    formats, 66
    options, 66
    settings, 48, 53, 70
Scaling, 102
Scan
    correct mode and, 118, 120
    Saving, Scaling, Resampling, and Resizing, 103
Scanner Calibration, 126
Scanning Tips, 124
Scratch Disk is Full, 7
Set Highlights and Shadows, 62
Set White/Black, 48
Settings, 48, 58
Shadows
    adjusting, 58, 60, 61, 62
    dark, 45, 48, 49, 50, 52, 58, 59, 61, 62, 63, 68
    establishing, 61
    importance of, 61
    lack of detail in, 61, 63
    locating, 61
    setting, 61
    Thresholding, 62
    Troubleshooting, 70, 72
    *See also* Highlights
Shadows on Images, 90
Sharpen, 54, 65, 73
    rules of thumb, 54
Sharpening, 54
Sharpness, 72
    excess, 72
    lack of, 72
    *See also* Unsharpen Mask (USM)
Sizing and Scaling Images, 102

Snapshots, 20, 77
Snapshot, 23
    There is no original, 23
Snapshots verses Selections, 77
soft edge with Quick Mask, 36
Soft-edged Selection, 34
SRGB, 8
step-by-step Wizard, 10

## T

Targeting Layers, 84
Target Value, 58, 59, 61, 62
    dot, 58, 59
    guidelines, 58, 59
The reproduction process, 58
Third-party viewing applications, 11
Threshold 56, 113
Thresholding & Video Support, 62
TIFF format, 66
Tips for Success, 2
Tolerance, 27
Tone Compression, 45
Toning Tools, 78
Tool Palette at a Glance, 2
Transfer Functions, 53
Transparency, 82, 90
Transparent Originals, 44
Transparent Whites, 66
Type Layer, 89
Type Tool, 89
Types of Layers, 82
Tone compression, 45
Troubleshooting, 70, 71, 72, 73

## U

Undo/Redo, 18
Universal way to load Selections, 30
Unsharpen Mask (USM), 54, 65, 73
    adjustment range, 54
    increasing, 54, 65, 73
    *See also* Sharpen; Sharpness
Unsharp Masking, 54, 65, 73
Using Snapshots, 22

USM Threshold, 73

## V

Video LUT Animation, 5
View a Layer Mask, 87
Viewing channels in black and white, 94
Viewing in Quick Mask, 32
Viewing Layers, 84

## W

Why Recovering Methods Fail, 23
Window Menu
    Actions, 104
    Channels, 26
    Colors, 47
    History, 18
    Info, 46, 47
    Layers, 82
    Pen, 38
Working Space, 8
workflow, 8, 11, 14, 15, 30, 107, 120
Working Space for Grayscale images, 14
Working Space Guidelines, 16

# ABOUT THE AUTHOR

Jim Rich – has been president of Rich & Associates since 1990. This Washington, D.C. area consulting firm specializes in publishing, industry pre-press, and computer training. He brings a perspective of over twenty five years of research, consulting and training experience with black and white and color reproduction methods in the graphic arts and the desktop imaging markets.

Jim works with both end-users and vendors, including companies such as the Adobe Systems Inc., Bozek Desktop Inc., the Bureau of Engraving and Printing, Crosfield Electronics, Electronics for Imaging, the Graphic Arts Technical Foundation, the U.S. Government Printing Office, the National Geographic Society, the National Newspaper Association, R.R. Donnelley & Sons, the Washington Post, various trade shops, service bureaus, newspapers, photography and design businesses. His responsibilities have included selecting and installing black and white and color scanners, page layout systems, pre-flighting methods, color management systems, hands on production, research and development, and production management.

Jim enjoys teaching and has developed a variety of training programs that teach the basic-through-advanced fundamentals of black and white and color reproduction methods. His expertise and extensive color experience permits him to teach black and white and color image reproduction, calibration techniques, and electronic page layout methods for most any imaging workflow.

Jim holds a Masters degree from the Rochester Institute of Technology in Printing Technology.